Toying with God

TOYING WITH GOD

The World of Religious Games and Dolls

Nikki Bado-Fralick and Rebecca Sachs Norris

BAYLOR UNIVERSITY PRESS

Book Design by Diane Smith
Cover Design by Nicole Weaver, Zeal Design
Cover photographs courtesy of Kevin Salemme, Charles B. Fralick,
and Courtney Cutler. Interior photographs courtesy of Courtney
Cutler.

4-12-22

Library of Congress Cataloging-in-Publication Data

Bado-Fralick, Nikki.
  Toying with God : the world of religious games and dolls / Nikki
Bado-Fralick and Rebecca Sachs Norris.
    p. cm.
  Includes bibliographical references and index.
  ISBN 978-1-60258-181-4 (pbk. : alk. paper)
  1. Play--Religious aspects. 2. Games--Religious aspects. 3. Dolls
--Religious aspects. I. Norris, Rebecca Sachs. II. Title.
  BL65.P6B33 2009
  790.1'3--dc22
                                2009027659

CONTENTS

ACKNOWLEDGMENTS

M any people have helped and supported us along the way. We would particularly like to thank family, friends, and colleagues who have provided valuable input and support, especially Harry Norris, Karen Sacks, Charles Lindholm, Eric Waite, and Karla Moore.

We also wish to acknowledge the following institutional grants that have supported our work in the area of religious games and toys: a Collaborative Grant from the American Academy of Religion; grants from the Liberal Arts and Sciences College and the Miller Faculty Fellowship of Iowa State University; Davis Experiential Learning Grants administered through Merrimack College; and Merrimack College Faculty Development Grants.

PREFACE

Advance to the shrine of San Giovanni Rotondo. If not owned you may buy it. If owned pay owner 5 times the rent.

(*Catholicopoly* Faith card)

In the journey of researching and writing this book we have wandered through a fascinating and often humorous land filled with cuddly Jesus dolls and dolls with *hijabs*, resurrection eggs, Passover plague toys, karma points, celestial weapons, and Jesus bandages. We *love* these games and toys. Sometimes we find them perplexing or offensive, other times amusing or educational, but we love the idea of religious games and toys. They evoke the magic of childhood combined with the mystery of religion, all through the mundane media of plastic, cardboard, and paper. They reference heaven, cesspools of sin, and enlightenment. yet are available online at numerous sites, including eBay and religious specialty stores. They are palpable evidence of global commerce, pluralism, and shifts in social engagement—signifiers of twenty-first-century meaning-making.

We entered the magical wonderland of religious games and toys through similar experiences. Nikki's adventure began with the Latter Day Saints' board game *Mormonopoly*, which she initially thought was a joke but decided would be a great activity for her religious studies students. Since then her collection of board games has increased such that it can occupy a large world religions class, and her office is filled with both humorous and serious religious tchotchkes.

Rebecca found a Christian action figure of Job online, complete with boils, and bought it, thinking, as Nikki had of *Mormonopoly*, that it was a joke. Who would let their child play with a toy that had nasty sores all over it? Then someone showed Rebecca the Armor of God play set—which outfits a child to look like a young crusader. Next she found the *Missionary Conquest* game . . . and she was hooked. Her collection has likewise grown to fill her office.

Since those early days, we have journeyed with Apostle Paul, raced to the Kabah, redeemed cities of bondage, defended Solomon's temple, earned Blessing Points, worn the Breastplate of Righteousness (literally, during conference presentations), wielded the sword of the spirit, trekked from Mecca to Medina through *Kosherland* and *Bibleland*, spun around the *BuddhaWheel*, and played our karma cards successfully to become pope.

Our offices have become local centers of attraction for students and faculty alike. Religious games—both commercial and those created by our students as class projects—abound. From one shelf, Jesus' eyes follow you everywhere; on another, Jesus and Moses action figures battle with Freud; and on yet another, a plush Buddha sits in meditation while nun finger puppets look on. Talking religious dolls chatter or pray in every corner, while a coven of Witch Barbies circles overhead. We have Krishna, Śiva and Hanuman, and Kali lunch boxes, and a wide assortment of mints—After the Last Supper mints, Testamints, Enlightenmints, and After the Rapture mints—that wait to freshen our breath. We can touch up our makeup with the Looking Good for Jesus compact and get ready for a long afternoon of board-game salvation and enlightenment. Evening brings a long soak in Wash Your Sins Away bubble bath or Zen soap as we retire with a choice of soft and cuddly Jesus, Esther, Buddha, Kali, or Ganesh stuffed dolls.

The transition from bemusement and bafflement to academic investigation, however, was not so simple. As we wondered what these toys were about and why they had become so widespread, we began to realize that we were on the trail of an enigmatic phe-

Hindu lunch boxes with Śiva and Krishna

nomenon. The fantasy and joy of play that attracted us to these toys seemed to disappear as we moved closer and saw them as educational pastimes or commercial ventures. The dance of religion and play drew us in until we saw that it opened the door to a world of changing relationships and shifting boundaries among religion, play, commerce, politics, ritual, and gender.

Deeper questions began to form. Why has so much of the study of religion been confined to text? And why do many of us have a sense of discomfort or unease about the association of religion with play, commerce, or other worldly activities? Is it that we are trying to keep religion holy by maintaining a safe distance between it and our day-to-day lives? Or perhaps that we are trying to hold it sacred against the encroaching forces of routine existence, which are—if not sinful—at least ordinary?

But such demarcations are not real; the sacred is not a separate realm. It is the ground of the universe and is immanent, participating in everything and found in the everyday. And religion, severed from other cultural expressions as a convenient analytical device, is not and has never been separate from other human endeavors and experiences. Embodied religion is not constrained; religion enters all aspects and dimensions of life.

What comes to mind when you think of religion? For some it is a sense of deep joy, a feeling of connection with a sacred reality, one that may be reached only after long discipline and dark nights of the soul. For others religion evokes hard pews and dry sermons, restless children and scratchy clothes. Religion is televangelists working feverishly to enlarge their flocks and people swaying together in song. It sets moral codes and cultural mores, telling us how to live with each other. Religion is the highest level of mindfulness and consciousness as well as utter self-loss in trance and swooning in the Lord. It encompasses vastly different experiences and expressions in different cultures and at different times in history.

Religion also surges out past artificial boundaries, its rituals flowing freely in time and space and including activities of the everyday. In many cultures religion is not relegated to a specific hour of Friday, Saturday, or Sunday worship in a building that is set apart. For some, religion is found under a full moon in a grove of trees, in the wind blowing across the plains, or through snow falling on water. It asserts itself in colorful shrines set in unexpected niches between buildings tucked away just off the street. Religion is Thank You St. Jude notices in the paper and Go Away Evil incense in the living room. It thrives in the colors, sounds, smells, and tastes of the world.

When we started to research this book, we were told by many that play has no place in religion, that toys are not proper religious artifacts, and that the study of religious games and dolls was not proper scholarship. But a look at the history of religion from ancient times shows us how deeply games and play were intertwined with religious practice—in card games, the relation of dice to ancient divination practices, and the place of mythology in ancient sports. In fact, today's apparent barriers between religion and other experiences became increasingly fluid or illusory the more deeply we looked at religious toys. And the study of how people live and practice their religious lives every day seems to us, and to a growing number of scholars, proper scholarship indeed.

The historical connection between games and religions has set the stage for the variety of religious board games on the market today, but past practices have a very different character than their modern counterparts. One source of dissimilarity is that the contemporary American approach to religion is largely dualistic, separating it from other aspects of life. For many, linking religion with games or play is contradictory or even sacrilegious. Religion, considered to be a serious obligation, addresses the most significant human concerns, and games are, well, only games. Games and toys are regarded as trivial, often considered merely children's playthings and not items that should be associated with religious practice or the highest forms of thought and inspiration. But the idea of childhood as we know it is very recent; in earlier times, children did not have games separate from those of adults. The production and promotion of games and toys just for children, and the increasing specialization of educational and now religious games and toys, are a result of changing cultural forms as well as global commerce and Internet marketing.

In like manner, in the historical and sometimes troublesome connections between dolls and religions, dolls were not simply playthings. Although many Americans associate dolls with playing mommy, or with Raggedy Ann and Cabbage Patch dolls, the world of religious dolls can be far removed from images of innocent play. Long associated with magical powers, dolls have held an important role in ancient religions and today still maintain a central role in ritual practices within religions such as Hinduism, Buddhism, and Shinto. Within the Abrahamic religions, dolls sometimes pose a problem for those who interpret the prohibition against graven images strictly, such as the Amish, Orthodox Jews, and some Muslims. But there are ways of getting around the prohibition, and the world of religious dolls today is a lively and thriving business, as well as a source of political and religious controversy.

Just as the idea of religious games and dolls seems irreverent to many, the involvement of religion with money and business is often construed as problematic. Yet religion has always been affiliated with money, and this relationship is absolutely necessary in a country with separation of church and state. Religious institutions compete for customers, buildings require upkeep, and organists must be paid. This practical dimension of religion as an institution is reflected over and over in contemporary religious games: *Episcopopoly* even has a fund-raising square. It is a common worry that money is, if not contaminating religion, at least distracting people from it. Perhaps money itself is not really the issue, though. For many people, innumerable religious objects and commodities are evidence that consumerism has overtaken religious morals and values in importance. Rather than commerce serving religion, religion appears to be serving commerce.

Religious objects of all kinds are subject to the same market forces as other commodities, and the impulse in the culture at large is to buy, buy, buy. But unlike ordinary commodities, religious toys are not simply manufactured to make money; their makers claim that their raison d'être is to transmit religious ideals and ethics, especially to children. Parents and religious institutions are ever looking for newer ways of interesting children in religion, children who have been exposed to the latest toys and the newest game technologies and are firmly situated in the very American cultural imperative of fun.

In order to compete, and because children will not play with toys unless they are attracted to them, marketing for religious games takes its cues from tried-and-true marketing strategies, promoting them as fun and easy. "No Bible Knowledge Required!" is an oft-repeated mantra on game boxes and in online sales pitches. But the connection of religion and fun produces areas of deep discomfort and unease. If religion addresses some of the deepest concerns of humanity, it may be hard to see how fun and play can be reconciled with the serious business of saving souls or reaching enlightenment without mocking religion. Is it okay for religion to be fun? After all, everything can be marketed as fun, even—or especially—Satan! Is playing with these religious games kosher? Are we toying with God when we create or play religious games?

The paradoxes inherent in the worlds of fun and play, Western discomfort with the association of religion with fun or play, and the ubiquitous presence of fun as a *necessity* in American culture reflect a deep ambivalence in the way we live and the way the media portray how we should live. Not only do ads taunt us with images of other people having incredible fun at whatever they're doing (having their taxes done, serving breakfast, getting windshields repaired), but in addition fun is integrated into corporate life as a means of building community and increasing productivity.

Some fun. The boundaries between work and fun dissolve or at least shift under corporate efforts to formalize fun, and a similar process is at work with religious toys and games that are meant to educate children about religious values. Is play really *play* anymore when it takes on an educational or utilitarian purpose?

One of the most direct connections between play and religion is found in ritual. While ritual elements are sometimes fairly easy to spot in play, especially the formalized play of sports or competitive games, it is often harder to see the playful aspects of ritual. Sometimes this has more to do with knowing where and how to look; traditional Western scholarship often places play and ritual at opposite ends of a spectrum that ignores the playful side of religious ritual. Yet the threads of fun, play, playfulness, ritual, and ritualizing weave together in the kinesthetic and embodied world of practice.

Calling on these aspects of religiosity, companies sometimes suggest how children should play with their games and dolls. Some of them advertise the sensory engagement their dolls and toys provide children. Exploring the extent of this physical play, it is questionable whether the body is actually highlighted or instead in some sense limited or even erased through prescribed forms of ritualized play. As with formalized fun, tightly controlled and prescribed ritualized play seeks to harness the subversive qualities of both play and ritual, whose free and creative nature may undermine both institutional and parental expectations.

Play subverts goals, religion intertwines with commerce, dolls mingle with politics, games become work, work enforces fun . . . and so it goes with every area we have explored during this project. The shifting boundaries and restructured relationships among religion, play, work, commerce, toys, and ritual are the principal themes of this book. Rather than simple answers, we found that the longer and deeper we looked the more complex the interactions became. Perhaps this is the lesson to be learned from our study of religious games and toys. Although it is easy to create divisions between religion and ordinary human endeavors, such partitions cannot hold.

The very existence of religious games and toys belies the dualism of religion vs. play, religion vs. commerce, play vs. work, and many of the other categories that are so easy and tempting to use in our thinking. There is no pure organized religion untainted by money, and no one right way of worship. Those are illusions of some academics and institutional authorities, who frequently wield power by controlling interpretations of text and who have traditionally sought to deny the validity and variety of lived religion, since it is harder to control. It has been in their interest to create a divide between proper and improper religion, between the great and little traditions, between elite and popular practices. But religions live through people's everyday practices, and religious games, dolls, and objects of every sort demonstrate this embodied religiosity.

Welcome to our world—the world of religious games, toys, and dolls.

1

LET THE GAMES BEGIN

Board games are cultural texts.

Sally Sugarman, "Children on Board,"
Images of the Child, 323

Games of the Gods

Games and toys reach back into the dawn of human history. Although we can only speculate about the playthings of our prehistoric ancestors, the artifacts of the Near East yield wonderful discoveries of ancient toys and games. Archaeologists find their depictions chiseled into temple walls and painted in murals on the inside walls of pyramids. These often illustrate scenes from everyday life, including adults playing games and children spinning tops. Dolls have been discovered entombed in ancient crypts in Egypt, Greece, and Rome, serving as faithful companions in the journey to the afterlife. Reflecting a time before the modern tendency to compartmentalize areas of life—and before the scholar's tendency to divide the world between things sacred and profane, or sacred and secular—these ancient games and dolls were an integral part of religious practice.

Commercially produced religious games in America date from at least the 1800s, when games such as *Mansion of Happiness* (1843), *Bible Characters* (1890), and *Bible Authors* (1895) were created. The stream of religiously themed games steadily gained

1

momentum through the 1930s and 1950s, with *Bible Lotto* (1933), *Bible Rhymes* (1933), and *Going to Jerusalem* (1955) occupying family leisure time on Sunday afternoons.

Today, an astonishing diversity of religious board games is available online and in specialty stores. Most are variations of familiar and popular games such as *Risk, Trivial Pursuit,* or *Monopoly,* using common game types such as race games, where winning is based on being the first player to reach the goal. *Monopoly* alone accounts for a host of religious imitations, including *Mormonopoly, Catholicopoly, Bibleopoly,* and *Episcopopoly*—as fun to say as to play. Other spin-offs of popular games include *Mortality,* a Latter Day Saints' version of *Life,* and a religious version of *Risk* called *Missionary Conquest,* which as its name suggests is not exactly a game of ecumenical goodwill. *Settlers of Canaan,* one of the newer spin-offs, is a religious version of Klaus Teuber's award-winning *Settlers of Catan* game, which demonstrates the efforts of religious game designers to keep current with the most popular trends.

Christianity is well represented in the world of board games and plays a major role in this book, especially given the relationship between Protestantism and commerce in American history. In addition to the above, other Christian games include *Vatican: The Board Game; Redemption: City of Bondage; Divinity* (the only game to have the *imprimatur,* the Catholic Church's official seal of approval); *Journeys of Paul;* and *Left Behind,* based on the best-selling novels. *Armor of God* comes as a board game as well as a play set that includes the Helmet of Salvation, the Breastplate of Righteousness, and the Sword of the Spirit in order to "play and learn about God's protection for spiritual battle."

Judaism and Islam, the other Abrahamic traditions, are also represented by board games such as *Race to the Kabah, Mecca to Medina, Exodus,* and *Kosherland,* a takeoff of *Candyland.* Many Muslim and Bible-based games are *Trivial Pursuit*–type games, requiring knowledge-based answers to move on the board and win the game. Not to be overlooked, Eastern religions also inhabit the realm of board games, with *Karma Chakra, BuddhaWheel,* the *Mahabharata Game,* and *Leela,* a New-Age version of the ancient

Kosherland game

game of *Snakes and Ladders*, which is also available online in Sikh, Muslim, and Jewish versions. A Sufi version of *Snakes and Ladders*, known as *Shatranj al-Irfan, Chess of the Gnostics*, exists as well. The well-known *Chutes and Ladders* is itself an adaptation of *Snakes and Ladders*, which has Hindu or Buddhist origins,[1] and is still known by that name in the United Kingdom today. Although unlikely to be a direct descendant, the new educational history game *Maharajah: The Game of Palace Building in India* is reminiscent of the ancient Indian game *Shaturanga*, in which armies vied to build empires under competing rajahs.[2]

Like religious texts, games lend themselves to interpretation, with the medium of the game shaping the content and context of meaning. For example, the game pieces may provide symbolism—as in *Catholicopoly*'s Bible, dove, and lamb playing pieces—the board a storyline, and the game play a running narrative or a rhetorical strategy. And like religious texts, contradiction and confusion sometimes emerge when playing the game, producing multivalent and even conflicting meanings.

Journeys of Paul is a case in point. The game board depicts a map of the ancient world circa 60 CE. Starting in Jerusalem, players move through the region by land or sea, emulating the Apostle Paul's journeys and collecting enough believers (Cell Groups) to build a church. The first player to build three churches and reach Rome wins, collecting Opportunity, City, and Event cards along the way. Since one player may not build a church in the same city as another player, there is essentially no interaction between them. On the one hand, this supports a noncompetitive atmosphere reflecting the need to create a Christian community by building churches in as many areas as possible. On the other hand, it contradicts the ideal of community itself, since there is no cooperation or meaningful interaction between players.

Game boards are carefully designed to illustrate particular religious narratives. In Hindu and Buddhist versions of *Snakes and Ladders*, positive and ethical actions are the ladders that climb upward to liberation (*moksha*) or enlightenment, while selfish and unethical actions are the snakes that slide the player down to rebirth as lower forms of life. Evangelical practices emerge in *Salvation Challenge*, which imparts clear judgments about proper Christian behavior. This game bestows greater rewards to those who jump up, put their hands in the air, and loudly proclaim "Jesus, Save Me!" when they land on the cross than to those players who merely say it. Sometimes the games present a straightforward, if limited, picture of the religion: *The Holigame* teaches about Jewish holidays, Bible games teach Scripture, *The Hajj Fun Game* teaches essential information about the meaning and practices of *hajj*.

Both the game pieces and the boards themselves are often highly symbolic, with illustrations, colors, and images carefully chosen to reflect aspects of the religious tradition. The board for *Karma Chakra*, a Buddhist game, has outer gates facing the four cardinal directions; mandalas representing earth, water, fire, wind, and space; Yama, the fierce-looking judge of the dead; and symbols such as the Bodhath Stupa in Nepal and the Bodhisattva Manjushri's Sword of Wisdom. Players must make their way through all five circles to be reborn, collecting good and bad karma cards on the way. In this game rebirth is determined by the total number of karma points. On each play, the short text corresponding to the space on which the player has landed must be read aloud, reflecting the merit gained in Buddhist practice by hearing sutras, even if one does not understand the language. The worst rebirths include "In intense heating hell for one-eighth of an eon" and rebirth as "a frog, born inside a boulder for 1000 years." Other possibilities include "Hungry ghost who perceives food and drink as pus," "King of the demi-gods," and "Bodhisattva of the first level (Great Joy)." The players aim for ever-better rebirths, with the goal of reaching the bodhisattva level and becoming a Buddha-to-be, but they do not compete against each other; there is no clear winner.

BuddhaWheel, another Buddhist game, has a board based on the Wheel of Life, with the primary causes of rebirth—greed, lust, and hatred—at the center. It also displays Yama, the Lord of Death, and the six realms of rebirth (hell-being, hungry ghost, animal, human, demi-god, and god). Outer circles represent the spiritual and subtle paths. Players are reborn over and over, collecting both good and bad karma cards. The aim of the game is to escape the wheel of rebirth; intermediate stages include being protected from lower rebirth and becoming a bodhisattva. Once you become a Buddha you are thereafter entitled to start the game as a Buddha, helping others. There is quite literally no end to the game.

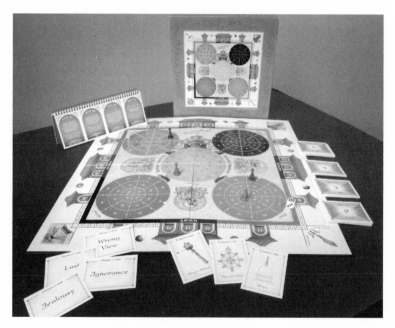

Karma Chakra game

Another game that brings religious symbolism and meaning to life is the *Mahabharata Game,* based on the epic Hindu myth. Players are aided by Kaurava or Pandava warriors, whom players pit against each other in battles, collecting coins as well as virtue and wrath cards while traveling around the board. To win, a player must collect at least one of several Celestial Weapons—mythical implements with divine powers bestowed upon their favorites by the gods. In the *Mahabharata Game,* the deep mythological significance of Celestial Weapons, as well as the game pieces and their movements around the board, all symbolically transmit Hinduism's beliefs and practices. There are 108 coins, a sacred number representing the 108 stages that the *atman,* or soul, goes through in its journey toward enlightenment. Players start the game at Auspicious Beginning, paying respects to both Vyasa, the author of the *Mahabharata*, and to Ganesh, the elephant god who "presides over all auspicious beginnings." Graphics are classic Hindu representations of deities and other mythical figures. And as we have found with many games, the complexity of directions for the *Mahabharata Game* echoes the complexity of Hinduism itself.

Religious board games not only exhibit varied ways of expressing doctrine, ethics, and myth, they have different aims as well. Both Buddhist games described above were created primarily for use by educators in order to teach about Buddhism. Chodak Tashi Ghartsang, the designer of *Karma Chakra*, says that each color and image were carefully considered so that the game would convey as much of Buddhism's meaning and philosophy as possible. Even the game's noncompetitive nature was intended to reflect and evoke the nature of Buddhist practice.[3] *BuddhaWheel*'s highly symbolic and beautifully designed board communicates through embodied play rather than explanatory text and succeeds quite well in conveying some of the essential truths of Buddhism such as karma and reincarnation. When asked whether a player could win this game, one student's response was "Well, yes, but it takes *so* long! You just keep getting reborn over and over and over again!" Exactly the point. And students who have played this game in class are unlikely to forget what they have learned from it.

But most religious board games are designed for children and utilized within a family and institutionally religious context. One impulse behind such games is to enculturate children into a religion's values. Yet while games may be instructive and revealing, they must also be entertaining—they are a form of play; they are fun. This is one of the principal motivations for offering religious games to children—they willingly participate in religion because they are having fun. In fact, the word *fun* is used frequently in the marketing of religious board games. Both fun and play are implied themes in all the games, but they are particularly emphasized in games for the Abrahamic traditions. And as we shall see in chapter 4, while fun and play suggest spontaneity and freedom, in the context of games played to educate, proselytize, or instill moral values, they instead take on a utilitarian function and become a kind of work.

Fun with God

In addition to board games, there are many other types of religious toys: stuffed torahs; Moses, David, and Jesus and the Tomb action figures; Noah's ark collections; and Resurrection Eggs, which supplement a young child's Easter book. "Lead your kids on a fun, faith-filled Easter egg hunt this year—one that teaches them about Jesus' death and resurrection! Each egg carton is filled with a dozen colorful plastic eggs. Pop them open and find miniature symbols of the Easter story inside."[4] One of the dozen plastic eggs contains a crown of thorns, another is empty, representing the disappearance of the body of Jesus from the tomb, and pointing to his resurrection. Muslim toys include a mosque building set, mosque jewelry cases, and a prayer practice chart. Jewish toys include dreidels, wooden Shabbat sets, toy *sukkahs*, and a Plush Plagues Bag that includes "all 10 Plagues!"[5]

Religious dolls are part of this wonderland of sacred fun. There are plush and plastic talking Bible dolls, pumped-up Christian action figures, dolls designed to support a Jewish girl's religious identity and conform to religious requirements, Goddess dolls designed for affluent young feminists, talking Muslim dolls that teach Arabic phrases, and "anti-Barbies"—Muslim dolls deliberately designed to compete with Barbie for the hearts and minds of young girls. There are plush Buddha and Śiva dolls, and cuddly Jesus and Esther dolls as well.

Madinah Salat Fun Game (Madinah, also spelled Medina, is a Muslim holy city; *salat* is the daily obligatory prayer of Islam.)

Numerous card games and puzzles teach a variety of languages, including Hebrew, Arabic, and Punjabi. The Christian Book Distributors Web site not only offers religiously themed educational materials, they also offer nonreligious toys that appeal to parents with religious consciences who may be looking for nonviolent toys, such as a food groups toy with hand-painted pieces in four wooden crates, a pizza party game with different toppings, and a car towing game.

Not all religious toys are meant for the edification of the young. Many religious games and toys are satirical or simply products meant to be amusing enough to sell in an era where we are over-satiated with things, and any cultural phenomenon is fair game for marketing purposes. These items amuse or appall us, depending on how clever or offensive the item is, and for whom it is intended. Some items—ones definitely not intended for children—undoubtedly push the envelope of taste, such as religiously themed dildos in a variety of faiths.[6]

Indeed, satire abounds online, in specialty stores, and even in these authors' offices. Peering down from the bookshelves in

Nikki's office is a Miracle Eyes Jesus, whose roaming eyes really do follow you around the room, while the movie *Dogma*'s infamous Buddy Christ grins and gives a thumbs-up sign from another bookcase. Hanging in Rebecca's office is a Ganesh air freshener that "smells like enlightenment," and a Holy Toast Bread Stamp that stamps an image of Mary praying onto a slice of bread, which appears once the bread is toasted:

> In the beginning . . . there was bread. Ho hum. Make that boring bread an inspiration by embossing it before you toast! Our easy-to-use HOLY TOAST stamper always makes a good impression. Press the stamper into an ordinary slice of bread, toast it, and behold a miracle![7]

Consider the Lookin' Good for Jesus items, which encourage girls to "Get tight with Christ!" These items include a Jesus mirror figurine, bubble bath, a coin purse, lip balm, and sparkle cream: "Easter-lily hand and body cream (with sparkle!). Now, easier to be redeemed in his eyes with a handy travel size 2 oz. tube!" All items are guaranteed: "Look your Sunday Best! Guaranteed to help you be worthy and get noticed by the King of Kings."[8] Also available at this site are a Jesus Saves car air freshener, Believe in God Breath Spray, and Convert to Judaism Breath Spray: "Can't speak a word of Yiddish and think Sabbath is an 80's metal band? Be part of this unique faith instantly, starting today! Peppermint Flavor."

Other popular culture trends are also mirrored in religious parody: Wristbands and T-shirts that ask What Would Jesus Do? also inquire about the preferences of Satan and Cthulhu and have even morphed into the antiwar slogan What Would Jesus Bomb? Nikki cheerfully received WTFWJD (yes, that's exactly what you think it is) buttons from a Lutheran minister with an obvious sense of humor, who couldn't keep enough of them in stock in her office. Rather than displaying a set of positive affirmations or inspirations worn as a sign of emotional support, altruism, or innate goodness of the wearer, one set of rubber wristbands commemorates the seven deadly sins: sloth, gluttony, greed, envy, vanity, anger, and lust.[9]

There are Hindu finger puppets; bobble-head Jesus, pope, and Buddha dolls; and punching rabbi dolls. Nuns have their own subgenre, with finger puppets; punching nun dolls; NunChucks, a toy that catapults small nun figures; and Nunzilla:

> Say your prayers! No one is safe from the wrath of Nunzilla! This fire-breathing wind-up sister trudges straight out of a Catholic-school student's nightmare like a determined disciplinary force, with green eyes blazing and sparks flying from her mouth. Wearing the traditional black and white habit and carrying a Bible in one hand and a ruler in the other, this holy terror will have you owning up to transgressions from as far back as birth.[10]

If you want practical items, you can order a Last Supper lunch box, any one of a number of Hindu lunch boxes including Kali or Krishna, or a Śiva snack box with Hanuman on the back. The Next-to-the-Last-Supper (packaged as a Chinese take-away meal) and Last Supper After-Dinner mints are available, as are Enlightenmints and Testamints (each mint wrapped in a verse of Scripture). Or there are After the Rapture mints, "for those of us who aren't going anywhere." By the way, according to the online retailer Amazon the mints are kosher.

Satirical board games are also represented in this category; prime examples are *Chutzpah* (1967), *Is the Pope Catholic?* (1986), and *Fleece the Flock* (1989).[11] For a more ecumenical satirical twist, consider the recently produced *Playing Gods: The Board Game of Divine Domination* (2008), with five fighting idols for game pieces—a particularly fierce-looking Kali, a smiling chubby Buddha with a machine gun, a wrathful Moses wielding a hefty tablet, Jesus taking an aggressive hold on the cross, and a vaguely Islamic-looking figure with a bomb and a scimitar—all reassuring us that parody and satire are alive and well.

Some items may be tongue-in-cheek for some buyers but serious for others. Testamints clearly fall into this category, since spreading the gospel is serious business for some folk, no matter what means are used. Jesus bandages might be seen to draw on his healing powers. Yet another example is the Dashboard Monk:

> Only when you grasp the essence of bouncing on a spring, will you truly understand the meaning of sitting still. Park this peaceful, 4-$\frac{1}{2}$" (11.4 cm) tall Dashboard Monk anywhere you

need spiritual inspiration. Each hard vinyl monk has an adhesive base and sways with the slightest provocation, reminding us that sometimes it is wise to bend like a willow.[12]

Cynical prose written by a marketing maven? Heartwarming holistic dharma reminder? It is left to the reader/consumer to interpret how serious the author is.

This need for interpretation makes it difficult for many people to recognize and appreciate the sincere educational and religious intentions behind many games. Serious games are not always understood as being serious, nor are some games immediately recognized as meant for children. Most people who see the games in our offices, or with whom we discuss the games, at first think they are *all* meant as jokes or adult satire, just as we did when we first came across them. This response affects how people react to the items as religious objects. As we will see with dolls in the next chapter, many people are made uncomfortable by the association of religion with fun and toys. Uncertainty over the intention of the games is one factor—are they satire or not?—but there is also a basic dualism underlying this unease, a division between religion and play that views them as distinct

Dashboard Monk, plush cuddly Buddha, and squeaky toy
laptop Buddha

and separate realms. Religion is serious, games are not. Religious games inhabit a liminal realm that cannot be easily understood or categorized. This form of religiosity, which reflects American cultural trends, causes obvious disquiet for many.

Toys and games are a medium for cultural expression—not only a medium in the sense of being a form or material mode of representation, but also in the sense that they mediate among potentially conflicting cultural and religious values. Some religious games, for example, display the value placed on charity and altruism on the one hand, and making a profit and taking care of the bottom line on the other. Another form of mediation is parody, as childhood studies scholar Sally Sugarman points out. "Parody and irony are elements in successful games which, through exaggeration, often provide a mocking commentary on some of the values they extol."[13] But because toys and games are often overlooked or devalued as the trivial and frivolous playthings of children, it is sometimes difficult to see how they can both exemplify cultural and religious norms and present serious resistance to those norms as well.

That play and fun have their dark sides can be readily seen in the marketing of games such as *Mortality* ("Finally, a truly fun, uplifting gospel game!") or *Missionary Conquest* ("One Giant Game of Laughter and Strategy"). Like the game *Life*, *Mortality* has inner and outer sections to the playing board. The inner section represents childhood, youth, and dating; the outer represents the adult world. The player must get engaged and married before being allowed to play the board's outer adult section. The first player to land on Temple Marriage gets to be a bishop and makes the rules for the rest of the contestants. Players win by collecting 150 Testimonies. Landing on a Trial of Faith square requires the player to draw a card, which adds or subtracts from their Testimony pile.

Mortality's successful or winning moves impart fairly clear judgments about gender, sexuality, and power. Gender stereotyping is overt, and there is a clear bias toward heterosexual dating, marriage, and the idea that you have to get married before you can be an adult. Simplistic or frivolous trials of faith trivialize the role of religion in facing the vicissitudes of life, e.g., a player freezes because he did not put wood in the fireplace. There is also an underlying theme of the importance of money: a "rich makes richer" mentality, money makes everything better, and testimonies "buy heavenly rewards." Winning *Mortality* means dying in order to go to heaven, a "winning strategy" used in *Bibleland* as well. But in the case of *Mortality* it directs us back to the name of the game and the play on the name of its predecessor—mortality rather than life.

The game *Vatican* contains a surprising number of game questions dealing with issues of molestation, violence, and kidnapping, according to the students who played the game as part of a special Liberal Arts and Sciences Frontiers of the Discipline course at Iowa State. This is apparently indicative of the highly political and sometimes perilous path to the Papacy. Navigating these questions takes some degree of skill, and simply trying to second-guess the answer that would yield the highest number of points seldom worked for the students. Students in the Introduction to Religious Studies course at Merrimack College who played and studied the games also noted that the answers to moral and ethical issues were not obvious, an element that they felt added to the value of this game.

This sensitivity to moral complexity is rare in religious games we have examined and used in classes. Its name more than suggestive of colonialism, *Missionary Conquest* displays stereotyped and arrogant attitudes that are no laughing matter outside of the world of board games and in the real world of global politics. The game provides players opportunities to earn money in order to finance missions. The player wins the game by establishing a certain number of missions or earning 700 Blessing Points. Some of the most expensive missions are in Iran, Iraq, and Saudi Arabia, because there a player can earn extra points by being stoned to death, for example, thus becoming a martyr. Fun and laughter, indeed! Although it is perhaps intended to be lighthearted, the game displays a frightening ethnocentrism that is quite dangerous given the political climate of the present day.

But perhaps we're being overly sensitive. After all, it's only a *game*!

It's How You Play the Game

"It's only a game." How often have parents said this to children upset over losing a game? Games and leisure activities throughout the ages have flown under the radar, so entirely woven into the fabric of everyday life that religious studies scholars seldom regarded them as worthy of examination. Against the serious business of scriptural exegesis and high ritual, religious games and dolls seem to express a trivial form of play. Until recently this meant they were often overlooked as subjects of scholarly inquiry. But as artifacts of religious practice, of what folklorist Leonard Primiano calls "vernacular religion,"[14] or what Nikki Bado-Fralick terms the level of "individuals-practicing,"[15] religious dolls and games serve an important pedagogical function: they educate and proselytize within the context of play—and that play raises serious questions.

As cultural and religious artifacts, games and toys not only *reflect* values and customs, worldviews and expectations, stereotypes and biases, but also transmit these through play. Games and toys also travel easily between religions and cultures—perhaps more readily than other practices—because they are so often regarded as harmless fun. What could be more innocent than playing a game?

But if they are just innocent games, why does the mere existence of religious games challenge and disturb many people's religious sensibilities? After all, the "cosmic duel on the board does not carry over into 'real' life."[16] Or does it?

Kingdom of Heaven is an example of a game where the "cosmic duel on the board" does carry over into life. This game was intended to "bring the revelation of salvation by grace," like the Bible. While the vehicle is entertainment, the aim is quite serious—this game is clearly meant to influence the players' lives. It is evident from the instructions that this pastime is no mere amusement:

> **Beware**: If a player, after getting a few negative "Witness cards," and [sic] is still without his "Predestination" card, stops on a death segment, **he is disqualified** from the game, being considered dead in his sins, without hope and lost eternally.[17]

In the case of religious games the division between real life and the board is not so clear. While games are certainly not the only source of religious information for impressionable young children, the games perform a serious pedagogical function. And because religious games and toys often reflect or serve as evidence of values, parents and religious institutions often reinforce the meanings created through playing games. Thus the meanings of playing *Missionary Conquest* or *Mortality* or *Bibleland* (a game in which only the winner gets to heaven thereby preventing the other players from reaching that goal) are worthy of scholarly examination.

Although they frequently disagree among themselves, scholars break down play and games into several categories. One of the most prominent groupings of play is Roger Callois' division of the subject into four categories: *agon* (competitive play), *alea* (games of chance), mimicry (or imaginative play), and *ilinx* (giddiness, self-loss). He further divides play into two basic types: *paidia*, the inner freedom or urge to play, and *ludus*, organized play, with its rules and boundaries. For Callois, ludic play focuses on satisfying outside conditions such as game rules, rather than simply focusing on the inner state of play.

Against this backdrop, games are traditionally divided into three types: chance, strategy, and skill,[18] although earlier scholars had more rudimentary divisions. Alice Gomme, for example, who did extensive work collecting and cataloging children's games in the mid- to late 1800s, used only two categories: dramatic games and games of skill and chance.[19] For her, a game had to have an element of winning or losing.[20]

Board games, as a distinct sphere of games, are sorted into several different types, depending on the scholar doing the sorting. H. J. R. Murray's division into five types—games of alignment and configuration, war games, hunt games, race games, and *mancala* games—was expanded into six by R. C. Bell—race games, war games, positional games, *mancala* games, dice games, and domino games.[21] In his book's second volume he adds three more categories—games of words and numbers, card games requiring boards, and games of manual dexterity.

Although typologies develop in the direction of ever more variation, religious games do not follow suit. Regardless of their apparent variation, religious games primarily confine themselves to two types: race games and war games. *Monopoly*-type games are race games, as are the various versions of *Snakes and Ladders*. *Missionary Conquest* is a war game because the players aim for control of territories. *Journeys of Paul* is also a war game because it is territorial and aspires to build churches around the Mediterranean.

Two of the Buddhist games, *Karma Chakra* and *BuddhaWheel*, look like race games but have problematic typological elements. Both games strive to educate and to embody Buddhist concepts and ideals in the game board and game play. American students who play these games in our religious studies classes tend to interpret both games as race games and try to beat each other. But in the rules it is clear that you play for yourself, and that the only competition—if it can be called that—is an inner one. The first player to finish is not necessarily the winner, nor does a better rebirth mean that a player has won the game. After all, a better rebirth is still a rebirth, and the player must go around again! And in *BuddhaWheel*, if you do manage to reach the highest level of spiritual development—a Buddha—then whenever you play the game thereafter you may start as a Buddha and help others. In other words, you can now play the game from the paradoxical position of not having to play the game.

These two games stand out because of their lack of interplayer competition, raising the question of whether they still qualify as games or are simply educational pastimes. Theoretically, competitive game playing would violate Buddhist ideals. But games seem to equal competition in contemporary American culture. In *Episcopopoly* it is not possible to win the game without helping others, and students often have a hard time digesting this and acting on it. Can there be games—or winners—without competition? This question is raised by another noncompetitive game, the Christian *Ungame*. The lack of competition here is not due to its religious association; the Christian edition is simply one of several versions of the *Ungame*, developed in the early 1970s era of peace and love. The name reflects its noncompetitive ideals and reveals the deep connection between games and competition—it is an "ungame" precisely because it is not competitive. In the classroom we find students so bored by games without interpersonal competition that they will even create it when it is not there, which says something about either the nature of games or the nature of our students, or both. Agreeing with Gomme, our students prefer games to have elements of winning and losing.

Competition is not the only problematic issue that arises from religious games. Game playing can be a problem from a doctrinal or theological perspective as well. One Muslim Web site[22] includes a discussion of whether it is lawful under Sharīʿa (Islamic law) to use dice to play a religious game, since it could be construed as a form of gambling—a very old game of chance, indeed. The prohibition against gambling, including playing cards, is one that is also echoed today in some denominations of Christianity.

The Die Is Cast

Because our prehistoric ancestors left little in the way of artifacts that have survived to the present day, it is impossible to determine accurately how far back into human history the impulse to play and to create games stretches. We could sensibly imagine that humans have always shared—with at least some mammals and birds—the capacity for and desire to play. And we need not suppose that games demand advanced designs and technologies, as evidenced by the recent induction of the lowly and unpretentious stick into the Toy Hall of Fame.[23]

As mentioned at this chapter's start, board games and other toys have been part of human culture for millennia. Archaeologists have unearthed treasure troves of games, dolls, and other toys in tombs in Egypt, Greece, and Rome. Like other aspects of everyday life, games were depicted in murals painted on pyramid walls and carved into Egyptian temple walls and roofs, dating back to at least the fourteenth century BCE.[24] Game boards have been found dating as far back as the sixth millennium BCE in Jordan[25] and to at least 3500–4000 BCE in Egypt.[26]

In addition, the history of games is intimately interwoven with religious rites and practices. Games were an integral part of religious life, and the movement of games from place to place may have accompanied the spread of religion, as in the dissemination of Buddhism from Northern India.[27] This contradicts a seeming disconnection between religion and games, a sense that is rooted historically in two things: outmoded scholarship and the characteristic way religions developed in the United States. Contemporary scholars of religious studies point out that the starkly drawn division between sacred and profane is largely an invention of a nineteenth-century scholarship now discarded as evolutionary, unilinear, and overly dualistic in nature. The compartmentalization of life into separate spheres, distancing secular from sacred, has uniquely American roots connected to the ways in which ideas of the separation of Church and State developed politically in American culture. How people actually live and practice their religious lives is far more interesting—and messier—than the tidy compartments suggested by the division between sacred and secular.

The interweaving of religion and games throughout history bears witness to the complexity and nondualism of lived religion. Ritual divination—determining whom the gods favor—provides one of the strongest historical connections between religion and games such as dice, cards, and sports, as well as games of chance in general. The power of today's modern tarot cards to divine the future and interpret the querent's place in the world is one shared by a host of games throughout history. The association between games of chance and supernatural forces is a natural one, as those forces affect every aspect of life—and death. Mihaly Csikszentmihalyi and Stith Bennett note that although this connection is clear, the transformation of divination from sacred activity to game is not.

> It seems clear from ethnological evidence that games of chance, like other games, were first played in a context of religious ceremonial activities, i.e., they served to relate the players with supernatural forces postulated to exist in the environment. . . . The purpose of divination is to secure guidance from the unpredictable powers that rule over the destiny of man and fill him with anxiety over the future. It is performed in order to discover the probable course of natural events and the outcome of human efforts such as war, hunt, planting, and

fertility. . . . It is impossible to know when exactly the sacred ceremony of quizzing the supernatural became a mere game of chance.[28]

Although the usage of games of chance is interpreted here somewhat functionally, games involving dice and divination have a long and important historical pedigree, going back at least as far as 3000 BCE. Divinatory games of chance—gambling—are likely one of the oldest and strongest connections between games and gods, as the die is cast and lots are drawn to determine whom the gods favor. An Akkadian die from the ninth century BCE inscribed with a prayer points us toward the origin of the Jewish holiday of Purim, which comes from the biblical casting of lots. The Chanukah dreidl is a close relation to dice, and though the modern interpretation of the letters on the dreidl simply refers to how much or how little money one can take from the kitty, those letters also represent the phrase "A great miracle happened there," referring to the biblical story of the Maccabees.[29]

Although dice have also been used for guidance in worldly affairs as well as religion,[30] the connection between games and a nonrational, nonordinary reality has always been strong. The link between dice and the sacred that is so overt in the Akkadian die is echoed by gaming practices a world away in Montezuma's court; Bell's description provides further evidence of the religious impulse behind dice games:

> Emperor Montezuma sometimes watched his nobles playing at Court. Duran describes these Mexican gamesters walking about with a patolliztli [game] mat rolled up under an arm and carrying a little basket containing coloured stones used as markers. Before a game they called for a bowl of fire and threw incense into it, or sacrificed offerings of food to their dice and then they would gamble with all the confidence in the world.[31]

This does not seem so very different in spirit from appeals to Lady Luck in today's casinos. While the language and actions differ, the impulse—calling on a higher power to influence the outcome—is the same. Because it seems sacrilegious to pray to God to intervene in a game, we do not quite think of Lady Luck as religious. Clearly though, she is a close relative of the gods of gaming found in numerous cultures, such as the Roman god Mercury or the Greek Hermes, the Mexican God of Sport and Gambling Macuilxochitl, or the Keres Indian's Iyatiko, the mother, the source of games.[32]

Games of chance and skill come together in the world of sports. Modern sports have their origins in myth and ritual, although this is difficult to discern today. One of the oldest continuously played sports in the world, the Aztec ball game *ullamaliztli*, was played at religious festivals to ensure the proper working of the cosmos.[33] *Ullamaliztli*'s bouncing rubber ball represents the journey of the sun in and out of the underworld, marking the continuing cycles of nature and cosmos. *Ullamaliztli* is still played today, now called *ulama*, and its offerings of incense and the occasional human sacrifice are a distant memory.[34]

Today's international and multisport Olympic Games descend from the Olympian contests of ancient Greece, which were religious in nature. As in many cultures, these games had their origins in religious myth. The Olympics were created by a god—Heracles—in honor of his father Zeus. The games were not just mere contests to be played before the gods but reflected the games of the gods themselves. They were a "representation of the life of the gods above."[35] From the media extravaganza that surrounds the Olympic Games today, one could make the point that the winners of the games not only were but still are celebrated as heroes and treated like gods.

Other contemporary games such as lacrosse, now divorced from any religious overtones, developed from Native American religious practices. The intensive training and food and sexual restrictions it formerly had clearly marked it as ritual behavior.[36] Implements from games such as the hoop-and-pole game were still found on Zuni and Hopi altars as well as on ceremonial clothing at the beginning of the twentieth century—relatively recent in historical terms—and the masculine and feminine symbolism of game implements used in ritual points to their role in fertility rites.[37] Of the seven games considered sacred in the Zuni tribe, one is a board game, and Murray notes that variations of this sacred game are played by many Native American tribes.[38]

Children's games of skill and sport are sometimes thought to be remnants of ancient rites. Gomme states that diagrams for some of these games have been found scrawled on Christian churches from the Middle Ages.

> Other games of skill are those played by two or more players on diagrams or plans. Many of these diagrams and plans are found scratched or carved on the stone flooring or walls of old churches, cathedrals, and monastic buildings, showing that the boys and men of the Middle Ages played them as a regular amusement—probably monks were not averse to this kind of diversion in the intervals of religious exercise.[39]

Even hopscotch is thought to have been a Christian adaptation of an ancient Roman practice.[40]

Another place where chance and skill intersect is board games, which have a long religious pedigree as well. The popular game *Chutes and Ladders* is reportedly based on an ancient Tibetan game about the stages to liberation or enlightenment. According to Mark Tatz and Jody Kent's book *Rebirth: The Tibetan Game of Liberation*, the original game was invented in the early thirteenth century in Tibet by the great Sanskrit scholar Kunga Gyaltsen.

> The Game of Rebirth reveals the Tibetan Buddhist map of the universe. The scroll painting or "board" lays out a cosmic geography, presenting one's possibilities of future rebirth, and demonstrates the paths to liberation and the forms of enlightenment. In the course of playing this game the players' tendencies toward certain destinations are revealed, and guidelines are presented for their transcendence of ordinary existence and attainment of future states that are free from suffering.[41]

This game was played as an educational game as well as for amusement. Tibetans had a long history of divination and enjoyed dice games; they even bet on the outcome. Hindu children play versions of the game in India today, and its basic structure continues to provide a foundation for all manner of games. *Rebirth* can even be played online.[42]

In addition to unlocking the keys to enlightenment, sometimes people played games to keep the spirits happy. Happy spirits would

Variations on *Snakes and Ladders*, clockwise from lower left: Sufi
Snakes and Ladders, a modern rendition of the original Tibetan game
of *Rebirth* (translated into English), Sikh *Snakes and Ladders* (rear,
standing up), *Leela* (lower right), and a contemporary Hindu *Snakes
and Ladders* (center)

presumably make certain that cosmic forces of nature would stay
in harmony—ensuring that crops would grow, animals would
reproduce, and the sun would continue to rise and set. Games also
represented these forces of nature; in the *Popul Vuh* the game symbolized the struggle between the forces of light and darkness and
may have been understood to influence those struggles by supply-
ing the gods with the necessary vigor. One Celtic myth even tells
of a game board where pieces move by themselves, and Irish fairies
regularly played games.[43]

The Egyptian pyramids yield some of the earliest board
games in the world, including *Mehen*, a game shaped like a coiled
snake, dating between 3200 and 2250 BCE, and *Senet*, which
resembles backgammon. While it is hard to say exactly how these
ancient games were played, their presence in the tombs clearly
marks them as religious artifacts. Game playing is portrayed in
the Egyptian *Book of the Dead*, "where the soul of the departed
plays a game in the other world." Egyptian gods and goddesses

also played games; one painting shows the pharaoh Rameses III playing a game with Isis.[44]

One ancient Egyptian game is called *The Game of the Sacred Way*, named for the central line or column on the board, i.e., the Sacred Way. This game involved "great changes of fortune" following unexpected moves of the pieces. One of the moves even gave rise to an expression: "I remove this from the Sacred Way," similar to saying that someone is "removed from the stage of life."[45]

Egyptian tombs are not the only places we find games associated with death and the afterlife. Dice games and board games have been played at funerals in the Celebes and are still played today in Ecuador, perhaps as a means of communication between the living and the dead.[46]

Both chess and the Chinese game *Weiqi*, more commonly known by its Japanese name *Go*, have roots in ancient cosmological play. Experts in the game speculate widely on its origins as a divinatory device, its black and white stones representing the forces of yin and yang and its lines the axes of heaven. China has a long history of various kinds of dice games with boards.[47] Some of the earliest sources on chess, a game with origins in Zoroastrian myth, are Arabic.[48] There are claims that the original game of chess, the game of *Asha*, was brought by Zarathustra (Zoroaster) to the bored King Vistaspa, and that Zarathustra demonstrated "all the laws of the universe and life" to the king through this game. The original game symbolized cosmic laws and the battle between good and evil, a fundamental aspect of Zoroastrianism.[49] Even the moves of the pieces had cosmic significance.

Clearly the relationship between religion and games is ancient and varied. It was not always uniformly positive, however, and could be quite contradictory within the same culture or religious group. The Arab world had many games by the time of the inception of Islam, yet the Qur'an forbade game playing, according to most official interpretations in the early years. Nonetheless game playing continued, and spread together with the dissemination of Islam.[50]

Conversation about the appropriateness of the intersection of games and religion continues into the present day, and not only in Islam. While gambling remains an issue in Islam and particular denominations of Christianity, the intersection between sports and religion is also a hot topic. Recent American controversies include the appropriateness of prayer at school athletic events,[51] a greater emphasis on sports than religious education,[52] and the effect of the 2002 Salt Lake City Winter Olympics on the Mormon image.[53]

Pick a Card, Any Card

As we have seen, religious games are multivalent and are used for a number of things: divination, determination of skill, entertainment, and farce. Some religious board games have education as their primary goal—as in the games *BuddhaWheel* and *Karma Chakra* or *Race to the Kabah*. The use of games and play for religious education is not a new concept—playing cards with religious themes existed in a number of cultures. Catherine Perry Hargrave's *A History of Playing Cards and a Bibliography of Cards and Gaming*, which includes wonderful black-and-white reproductions of many cards, contains a number of examples of religiously themed playing cards. She describes cards showing the history of Christianity in Russia, for instance, as well as a lavishly illustrated tarot deck called *The Golden Tarot of the Tsar*, in which the icons of the saints and biblical scenes have textured gold backgrounds. Hargrave, an authority on playing cards, also includes evocative descriptions of antique religious card games such as *The Spiritual Card Game*, here described by the Carmelite Reverend Father Joseph of St. Barbara in a book published in Antwerp in 1666.

> The king shows saints and the great of the earth, kneeling before God the Father; the queen shows two saints in adoration before Mary, the Queen of Heaven; the knave shows the rich and mighty before the throne of the crucified Christ. The ten shows Moses with the Ten Commandments, each one a heart upon the tables of stone; the nine shows nine choirs of angels; the eight pictures eight Christian virtues; the seven, seven works of mercy; the six, the goals to be striven for in human life; the five, the wounds of Christ; the four, the last ends, being the death and the ordeal, hell and heaven. The three pictures the Holy Family; the two, the worship of God

the Father and Mary the Mother; and the one, the Truth which must be in a Christian Heart.[54]

Christianity is not the only religion to make use of playing cards. In fact, the blessing, virtue, event, wrath, and obstacle cards—versions of which are part of most contemporary religious board games—are close relatives of ancient playing cards found in many traditions. The Chinese had celestial generals and evil forces on cards, "believed to bear so powerful and magic a charm that they are placed on the coffins of their dead," while Indian playing cards portrayed the incarnations of Viṣnu, one of the primary Hindu gods.[55]

The mysterious and magical qualities of cards with religious themes are apparent in the ways they have been used, not only in ancient times in cultures on the other side of the world but in relatively recent history in the West. Scriptural cards credited to Charles Wesley, containing some of his verses and biblical passages, quickly became used as a form of divination.

> "These people called Methodists" after "a dish of tea" would shuffle these cards and the one drawn would furnish a conversational text. It is amusing to find that they quickly took on the old-time significance of cards as a means of divination. Good men and women believed that Providence spoke through them, and many decisions were made according to the guidance of these little scraps of paper.[56]

This type of divination has a long history that continues today. Consider those who draw inspiration from the Bible by using it in this same way—randomly opening the Bible to find the passage that gives divine guidance on a particular question—the same method St. Augustine used in his famous conversion in the garden.

But just as we see parody and subversion in today's religious games and toys, so too in the past playing cards were used as a tool for religious satire. An early eighteenth-century set of Dutch cards presented a satire on the papacy: "All of the papal scandals are raked up and pictured, so that the use of the cards was forbidden to all good Catholics, and all possible copies were burned by the command of Rome."[57] Around the same time in England a deck of cards was advertised as "The horrid Popish Plot, lively represented in a pack of cards," picturing events starting from "'The Plot first Hatcht at Rome by the Pope and Cardinalls' and ending with 'The Tryall of Sir G. Wakeman, and 3 Benedictine Monks.'"[58]

Needless to say, this did not improve the attitude of those whose religious sentiments led them to disapprove of playing cards. Hargrave quotes an early writer (seventeenth- or eighteenth-century) who condemns them as a device of the devil. "The Playe of Cards is an invention of the Devill, which he found out, that he might the easilier bring in ydolatrie amongst men."[59] Religious standards were implemented in other ways as well. Early tarot cards, coming into Italy from the East, were Christianized with "Le Pape" and "La Papesse" cards, literally the pope and popess. Current English editions of tarot decks often show them as "The Magician" and "The Priestess"—a backwards move for those who Christianized the deck in the first place!

There are also a number of modern Christian tarot decks, such as the *Angel Voices Oracle*, the *Angels Tarot*, the *Master Tarot*, and the *Saint Deck*. Most of these are illustrated with biblical figures and include pieces of Scripture or episodes from Jesus' life. If you are playing cards "just for fun" but want to add a religious dimension, you might try one of several decks of religiously themed cards, such as the *Jesus Cards*, which supplement or substitute religious artwork for the normal suits and also include Scripture or Bible stories. The artwork in all of these decks ranges from simple and cartoonish, as in the *Soultidings TruthCards*, to beautifully illustrated works resembling medieval stained glass, as in the rare and out-of-print *Tarot of the Cloisters*.

Mere Child's Play

Historically, the games we have been discussing were part of the adult religious world; regardless of the fact that in the twenty-first century the market for adult and family games is huge, today we tend to think of games as belonging to the world of children. This shift is partly due to the development of the concept of childhood as a distinct and special time of life. In medieval times, for example, the concept of childhood simply did not yet exist. "Certainly there was no separate world of childhood. Children shared the same games with adults, the same toys, the same fairy stories. They lived their lives together, never apart."[60] The notion of childhood as a distinct category of life is a modern one, and the thought of childhood as a "safe space" in which children must be nurtured and protected from all the evils of the world is perhaps a peculiarly American one.

Thus, without a concept of childhood as a distinct time of life with particular needs for guidance and instruction, the morality of games related to larger religious issues rather than targeting children's morals specifically. As the idea of childhood developed, the morality of games in relation to children became a different issue. Through the sixteenth century there was disagreement over the morality of games; most accepted them, but "rigid moralists condemned nearly all of them out of hand and roundly denounced them as immoral, allowing scarcely any exceptions."[61] Compromise was found by the late seventeenth and eighteenth centuries, a compromise that demonstrates the changing attitudes toward childhood. This change "bears witness to a new attitude to childhood: a desire to safeguard its morality and also to educate it, by forbidding it to play games henceforth classified as evil and by encouraging it to play games henceforth recognized as good."[62]

Which games were moral and which were not might seem a simple question, yet a few hundred years have changed our perspectives significantly. And even as the concept of childhood was beginning to develop, pastimes that we would consider inappropriate for children were accepted. One colorful description of gambling from 1674 seems clearly to mark it as immoral.

> Gaming is an enchanting witchery, gotten betwixt idleness and avarice: an itching disease, that makes some scratch the head, whilst others, as if they were bitten by a Tarantula, are laughing themselves to death. . . . It hath this ill property above all other vices, that it renders a man . . . always unsatisfied with his own condition; he is either lifted up to the top of mad joy with success, or plung'd to the bottom of despair by misfortune, always in extreams, always in a storm; this minute the gamester's countenance is so serene and calm, that one would think nothing could disturb it, and the next minute so stormy and tempestuous that it threatens destruction

to it self and others; and as he is transported with joy when he wins, so losing he is tost upon the billows of a high swelling passion, till he hath lost sight both of sense and reason.[63]

Yet gambling and games of chance were not always regarded as dangerous or immoral pastimes. Around the same time as gamblers were indulging in "enchanting witchery" it was not uncommon for children to engage in games of chance, even losing money. Though it seems curious to us that there were no objections to this activity, our sensibilities are based on a contemporary understanding of childhood, not the perspective of the seventeenth century, when children's gambling was common enough to be portrayed in European engravings and paintings, in which children are depicted playing dice, cards, and other games of chance as well.[64]

As mentioned earlier, the idea of childhood as a distinct stage of life with particular qualities separate from infancy or adulthood is relatively recent, and according to Neil Postman, arose largely due to the invention of the printing press.[65] Once books became accessible to the population at large, a gap between those who could read (adults) and those who could not read (children) developed. At this point adulthood and childhood would have been partially defined by the ability to read rather than by age, a shift that was essential for the development of modern education.

Just as the invention of the printing press was a significant factor in the development of childhood, in *The Disappearance of Childhood* Postman suggests that childhood is disappearing as a result of newer forms of communication. Going back to Morse Code and the invention of electronic forms of communication, but writing before email was in general use, he argues that the need to read well and think is becoming obsolete, a point to which we will return in our discussion of fun.

While agreeing with Postman that the ability to think deeply and rationally about a subject is hampered by superficial education and media geared toward novelty and easily digestible sound bites, we also think that given the increasing complexity of modern life and the amount of information available through diverse media, the need to think clearly is more important than ever. Postman further argues that adults are more like children and children more like adults; they pick the same favorite shows when surveyed, and TV ads show different generations wearing the same blue jeans. Rather than a result of new communications, a stronger connection might be found in marketing strategies that target an increasingly younger demographic and in advertising that includes younger actors, especially women, in the marketing of products geared toward mature adults. It is also important to consider the role of class and socioeconomic status in terms of both access to and attitude toward communication technologies.

Yet regardless of how many factors we enumerate it is clear that the modern concept of childhood developed over centuries and is today a fairly fluid concept. The answer to the question of when one is considered a child and when one is considered an adult depends largely on the particular dimension of human experience being considered at the time. For example, at eighteen a person can vote and join the military but is not adult enough to drink a beer.

The blurring of boundaries between childhood and adulthood is pervasive in American culture. While games are generally thought of as children's activities, in twenty-first century American culture more adults are playing games than ever before. When people first see religious games and toys, they often ask who they are intended for and, as mentioned earlier, often misidentify children's religious games as adult satire. The fluid and shifting boundaries between adulthood and childhood may be one factor in this conceptual confusion, but considering that historically games were of the adult world, this perplexity seems to be a rational and reasonable reaction. With the exception of games designed specifically for very young children, it is often unclear whether religious games are children's items or not. The ones intended to be educational are meant to be used for many age groups; those with religious sources are generally targeted to specific ages. One maker has a series of moral choice games for children (*The New Kid's Choices Game, Kid's Choices Pocket Edition*), teenagers (*The New Teen Choices Game*), and even families (*Family Choices Board Game: Proverbs Edition*).

Games and toys not only transmit cultural values but reflect them as well. As we have seen in this chapter, games and religion have a long and complex history—they were used for divination and gambling, for this-worldly satire, and in the afterlife. Games were objects and methods used to interpret divine powers and influence supernatural forces. These religious and magical functions reflect the presence and movement of the sacred in the material world, indicators of a complex whole rather than a dualism where sacred and ordinary occupy separate realms.

Contemporary religious games have their roots in ancient practices, but their flavor —their style and substance—as well as their commercial focus reveal a specifically twenty-first century American form of religiosity. Dolls are also an intricate part of this complex history; in the next chapter we examine the magical nature of dolls and their use in contemporary religions.

2

WELCOME TO THE DOLLHOUSE

I think every Barbie doll is more harmful than an American missile.

Masoumeh Rahimi, Iranian toyseller

It's Alive! It's Alive!

Dolls. For some people they evoke the same reaction as clowns—abject terror. Popular culture is full of cinematic examples of dolls gone wrong. *Devil Doll, Death Doll, Attack of the Puppet People, The Dummy,* the nefarious Chucky in the *Child's Play* series, *The Puppet Master, Living Doll*—their names say it all and confirm what we have always known: dolls are alive, and they are watching us. Does magic lurk beneath their smooth plastic skin, threatening to escape with mischievous intent once our backs are turned?

What makes dolls so often the subject of horror movies and unforgettable *Twilight Zone* episodes? Historically they were often imbued with magical powers. Unlike games, which usually have no physical resemblance to what they signify, dolls look like humans. This seems to give them special abilities. Dolls that have their own consciousness, move on their own, and plot revenge with their cousins in crime—puppets and ventriloquist dummies—have been a staple of film and television since at least the classic silent movie *Der Golem* in 1913. Dolls are capable of evoking within us a deep psychological ambivalence rooted in the fundamental worry that our control over the magic in dolls just might be slipping.

Dolls and religion share a long and involved historical relationship with one another. As with games, it is impossible to determine the precise origin of dolls, although some scholars date the creation of dolls to prehistoric Stone Age ancestors over 25,000 years ago. Historically, doll artifacts were constructed out of a wide variety of materials limited only by availability and imagination, including clay, bone, bronze, stone, ivory, wood, wax, paper, cloth, and straw—some more durable than others. The earliest dolls were simple carvings or markings on stone, bone, clay, or sticks that were decorated with geometric designs, with hair constructed of strings of clay or beads. Naturally, the simpler the doll, the harder to identify it as such, let alone determine its purpose.

Objects scholars assume to be dolls have been found in some of the earliest archaeological excavations of Egyptian tombs. Artifacts are often determined to be dolls not only because of their miniature size but also their placement, for example within the crypts of children. In addition, doll-like artifacts with miniature tools have been discovered accompanying important mummies, as though to serve their master in the afterworld.

We might question the characterization of these artifacts as dolls. Were the tomb artifacts once cherished possessions? Gifts given by grieving friends to console and reassure the departed spirit? Miniature magical companions? Symbolic representations of power and importance? Theological statements about expectations for the afterlife? None of these possible meanings is exclusive, and we can probably imagine several others. But speculation about early doll artifacts transgresses parameters and expectations about what a doll is in contemporary American culture.

Today, dolls are typically defined as small three-dimensional figures resembling human beings and used as toys or playthings for children. But the earliest dolls were not exclusively or even primarily for children, and likely had numerous and multidimensional meanings, including religious or cultic ones in which they would have played a significant role in both mythology and ritual practice within their various cultures. Doll historian Max von Boehn suggests that for adults, the doll "possessed an occult significance with mystical-magical associations which in an inexplicable way united the present and the past and reached deep into the world of the unseen."[1] Dolls around the world have been adored as figures or idols of goddesses and gods and have acted as ancestors, offerings, fetishes, amulets, talismans, and scapegoats. Dolls have been sacrificed in place of humans and have been the instruments of both positive and negative image magic, a practice of using dolls or poppets to heal or hex particular persons. Clearly our modern conception of dolls as merely children's playthings needs adjustment.

But caution is necessary when identifying and interpreting doll artifacts and their use and meaning, especially artifacts dating from prehistoric times. Looking at these artifacts through the lens of modern culture and modern academic scholarship inevitably distorts their meaning and produces interpretations of material culture that often say more about the present than the past. For instance, there are lively and ongoing debates among contemporary scholars about whether female statues found at archaeological sites are goddesses meant for worship or figures used for some other purpose, including child's play or even pornography.[2] This debate in particular reveals a lingering underlying strain of sexism in classical Western scholarship that tends to identify male artifacts as statues of power representing deity, and female artifacts—diminutively *statuettes* or *figurines*—as "dolls" or other playthings. While much can be determined from placement of the artifact at the site, what the artifact meant to those who made it is nevertheless still largely educated guesswork.

Our interpretations of artifacts are on firmer ground in recorded history. For example, in ancient Greece dolls served dual roles as both playthings and offerings to deities. Greek girls played with their dolls until they married and then dedicated them to an appropriate goddess such as Aphrodite or Artemis, possibly to ensure fertility—a doll association that can be found in widely different cultures throughout the world. Greek boys seemed to follow a similar pattern, at maturity dedicating their dolls and toys to Apollo or Hermes.[3] The boundaries between things sacred and profane in ancient Greece were considerably more fluid than our more rigid compartmentalization would suggest, so dolls used in Greek ritual ceremonies were also afterwards sometimes given to children to play with,[4] suggesting a pedagogical dimension to the doll and doll play.

This exchange is reminiscent of *prasad*, Hindu offerings that are blessed through contact with the deity, a god or goddess. *Prasad* is usually food, which is offered to all participants after the ritual so they can share in its newly sacred quality. In this same way, the doll is made sacred through ritual, and the child participates in the divine through contact with it.

The use of dolls in love and other forms of image magic is particularly widespread throughout the world, from wax and wooden images used by ancient Greeks and Romans to dough dolls mixed with hair, blood, spittle, and nails buried at the crossroads by Transylvanian Rom to ensnare a lover, to Chinese wooden and paper dolls "animated with evil spirits by wizards" to deliver harm or vengeance.[5] According to Boehn, "a Japanese woman who finds herself betrayed makes a straw doll intended to represent the faithless man, bores it through with nails, and buries it in the place where he sleeps. Whether this is intended to draw him back or is conceived only as a punishment remains uncertain."[6] This particular image is likely a *wara ningyo* doll, which resembles a simple human figure made of straw and is used much like the well-known voodoo doll, for either good or ill. As a sign of the modern convenience of online shopping, you can even purchase a "home cursing kit" based on the Japanese *wara ningyo* doll. A wide variety of voodoo dolls with different themes is also available both online and in specialty stores.

Japan has an abundance of folk tales about the magical powers of dolls that remain an important part of religious and cultural practice today. Some of the earliest historical doll stories mention their use as substitutes for human beings in ritual self-immolation, *zyunsi*, a practice that was outlawed in the archaic period, between approximately 1000 BCE and 650 CE. Rituals designed to cast out evils and illness use dolls as scapegoats to carry away negativity from their human designates. Colorful dolls and toy animal figures made for children protect them from harm and sickness by distracting evil spirits. Dolls protect unborn children and expectant mothers, memorialize miscarriage or abortion, and are widely used in the worship of Jizo Butsatso, the bodhisattva of children and travelers, among others. As the protector of miscarried, stillborn, and aborted children, Jizo is the focus of *Mizuko Kuyo*, a healing ritual for the families of those children, and temples that practice this ritual may display hundreds of doll-like statues of Jizo, with offerings of toys and flowers. Buddhist monks also use dolls to illustrate points of the dharma, while Shinto priests position dolls and toy horses in places of honor on shrines.

There are many Japanese folk traditions about dolls magically assisting people in their undertakings. Folklorist Richard Dorson tells of a Japanese legend in which straw dolls come alive and help a lone carpenter build a small shrine on the borders of Bizen and Bitchu provinces. This magical monument exists today as the Kibitsu shrine.[7] On a somewhat more practical level, roly-poly eyeless daruma dolls, named for the wandering monk Bodhidharma, are still given at the start of a new year or the beginning of a project. Daruma dolls were not only named for Bodhidharma, they also take their rotund shape from the story that he meditated in a cave for nine years until his legs fell off. The daruma's right pupil is painted in at the beginning of the year or project, and the left is painted in at the successful conclusion, after which the dolls continue keeping watch to ensure that a task continues its proper course. Sometimes the dolls are ritually burned at the task's end—perhaps at Takasaki's Shorinzan Daruma Temple itself, famous for its daruma dolls.[8]

Dolls play important religious and ritual roles in India as well as Japan. In the north, dolls illustrate the birth story of Krishna. In the south, dolls help celebrate the festival of Navratri with a beautiful and elaborate ritual called Bommai Kolu, literally "doll displaying."[9] Navratri is a nine-day Goddess celebration of the defeat of the demon Mahishasura by the Goddess Durga. The first three days of the festival honor Durga for her heroism, the next three Lakṣmi for her benevolence and wealth, and the final three days honor Saraswati for her wisdom and knowledge. During this time, women and girls visit one another's displays and exchange food and conversation while admiring one another's skill and creativity in the design and execution of the Kolu. On the tenth day, worshippers celebrate Durga's victory over the evil demon Mahishasura, which ensures prosperity and new beginnings for the coming year.

The dolls displayed during Bommai Kolu are Durga's *durbar* or court assembly. They are arranged on a platform built in odd-numbered steps, usually no more than nine. Dolls are arranged in a hierarchy, with deities on top, followed by important figures such as gurus and saints, even Buddhas. The remaining steps are likely to reflect various social themes such as weddings or religious festivals, or national events such as the launch of India's moon mission Chandrayaan, and events such as the Olympics. The bottom shelf is usually given over to children to decorate with their toys and dolls, also illustrating a theme—anything from agriculture to Harry Potter to visiting a zoo.

While the Bommai Kolu was once an occasion to admire the doll-making skills of the women of the household, today's displays are usually mixtures of very old heirloom dolls along with commercially produced dolls, some specifically designed for the ritual. Most Kolus are likely to feature a pair of wooden male and female *marapachi* dolls, which are typically passed from mother to daughter when the daughter begins her own Bommai Kolu. Online discussion among Hindus sometimes bemoans the elements of Western culture that are becoming more a part of the Bommai Kolu, especially in the use of Barbie dolls, which are dressed to resemble various goddesses or other religious figures.

Doll play and religion seem to intertwine easily in religions such as Hinduism and Buddhism, but the relationship between dolls and religion is more problematic in the Abrahamic traditions—with the possible exception of the Catholic Church, which

> quickly turned to its own advantage the belief in idols which is deeply rooted in the instinct of the folk, skillfully transforming these into figures of mercy. The miracle-working images of Mary and of the saints, arrayed like dolls and covered with rich ornaments, were once to be numbered by the thousand. Several of the famous divine images possessed, and still possess, a rich and costly wardrobe.[10]

The root of the problem with dolls in Judaism, Christianity, and Islam lies in the biblical prohibition against making graven images, which is found in the Ten Commandments and reinforced in Deuteronomy. A Protestant version of the second commandment is usually rendered "Thou shalt not make unto thee any graven image." The fuller citation is "Thou shalt not make unto thee any graven image or any likeness of any thing that is in heaven above, or that is in the earth beneath, or that is in the water under the earth" (Exodus 20:4 KJV). Deuteronomy 4:16-18 is usually cited as a reinforcement of this prohibition not to make a graven image that is "the similitude of any figure, the likeness of male or female, the likeness of any beast that is on the earth, the likeness of any winged fowl that flieth in the air, the likeness of any thing that creepeth on the ground, the likeness of any fish that is in the waters beneath the earth." The central question of course revolves around how "graven image" is interpreted. The faceless Amish dolls illustrate the tendency for some religious denominations such as the Amish and the Old Order Mennonites to take these prohibitions quite seriously. Religious dolls may also pose theological problems for Orthodox Jews and strict Muslims for similar reasons.

The full citations of Scripture not only ban images of humans but of animals too, although stuffed animals do not seem to be as problematic as dolls. As noted earlier, perhaps this reflects the power invested in the human image, which is not only endowed with consciousness and will, but made in God's image. It may also reflect the biblical granting of human dominion over animals; as lesser forms of life, animals are not as dangerous.

One notable place where doll-like figures both human and animal make an appearance is in the Christmas tradition of Nativity scenes, or crèches. The manger, Jesus, Mary, Joseph, the magi, angels, animals, and other elements from the story of Christ's birth are ostensibly for display, even appearing theater-like in their orientation. Crèches come in many materials, and while more expensive versions may be protected from children's hands, many crèches are handled and played with by children during the Christmas season, with some nativity sets designed and marketed as children's toys.

Serious Play

In spite of the often historically problematic relationship between religion and dolls, toy manufacturers have clearly decided that dolls mean business, lucrative business at that. A search online or in specialty stores reveals a stunning variety of dolls explicitly designed to appeal to children in different religious traditions. Parents who wish to avoid secular dolls such as Barbie may purchase instead the Muslim-American Razanne doll or her increasingly popular Syrian counterpart Fulla, named after a type of jasmine that grows in the Middle East. Both dolls come accessorized with the *hijab* but may also include high heels, makeup, and a pretty floral dress for wear when out of the public eye. The Christian Messengers of Faith Virgin Mary and Esther dolls also teach modest dress and talk as well, providing 60–70 seconds of Scripture, advertised as "recorded in an easy-to-memorize style."

Gali Girls, providing religious role models for growing Jewish girls, are clearly designed as a wholesome alternative to Barbie. The Gali Girls Web site includes a video of a concerned Jewish Bubbi worried—"Oy ve!"—that her precious granddaughter is playing with "trashy, scantily clad dolls." Gali Girls "come to the rescue," providing "strong Jewish values and a proud Jewish heritage." They

Two versions of the Razanne doll, from left to right: In & Out Razanne, with indoor dress and toiletry articles, and Scout Razanne, in uniform with scout cheers CD, canteen, backpack, and binoculars

are "kind and compassionate, vibrant and curious, beautiful and intelligent." Gali Girls will teach girls Jewish history and show them how to light the shabbat candles and dress modestly—it's the "best Chanukah Gift Ever!" The ending of the Gali Girls video illustrates one of the overarching themes connecting the Abrahamic religious dolls: modest dress. In the video, a scantily clad Barbie-type doll asks what those Gali Girls have that she doesn't. A small teddy bear in the corner replies, "Uh, clothes?"[11]

Dolls are widely marketed to children and parents who practice religions outside of the Abrahamic traditions as well, including rather more unusual alternative religions in which, for example, a plush Cthulhu, for fans of Lovecraft and his *Necronomicon*, might be desirable. Lucky Japanese Buddhist children who receive a roly-poly daruma doll at New Year could see their wishes come true, while their American counterparts can cuddle with comforting plush Buddha dolls as they're learning the dharma. Hindu Goddess dolls serve the needs of fantasy and ritual play for both Hindu girls and their mothers. Dolls and statues of sacred figures such as Lakṣmi, Goddess of Wealth, and Saraswati, Goddess of Education, are widely available. Pixar illustrator Sanjay Patel and artist Leeanna Butcher have designed a Kali plush doll—complete with tiny skulls emulating Kali's symbolic attire and resembling a mix of Kali and a Powerpuff Girl—to accompany his line of Kali and Ganesha T-shirts for tots.[12]

A pocket-sized plush Kali, from Pagan fiber artist Kelli Lincoln, is already available online along with a wide variety of goddesses and gods from many pantheons and cultures. Her Dancing Goddess dolls represent a "perfect blend of playfulness and spirituality" that make "wonderful gifts for Menarche ceremonies, Blessingways, Cronings, House Blessings, Birthdays, and Solstice celebrations, and are a wonderful decoration for an altar or season table."[13] When asked what inspired her to create Pagan-themed dolls, Kelli replied that she "had a vision of many children cuddling their Goddesses for comfort as well as lugging them on errands with their moms. I believe strongly that our spirituality can be mundane . . . as well as something higher, and I love how my dolls blend the two sides. It has turned out that adults love the dolls as much as children, so they also allow us to honor the child within!"[14]

Affluent parents of young Goddess worshippers can obtain one of the newly created line of "Goddess Spirituality" dolls providing hours of fun with feminist spirituality (Aphrodite is the first in the planned series). Cintra Reeve, the CEO of Goddess Dolls, is hoping her dolls will empower young women. Looking much like a Barbie and dressed in a Grecian-like garment and cape, the dolls' high cost has sparked discussion in online sites such as that run by Tim Boucher:

> Best of all, this lovely doll can be yours for a mere $150, even though it's advertised as being [made] in China and which means that it's almost certainly not hand-made or custom built to warrant such a high price tag (although, it does say it has "realistically depicted breasts" so maybe that's the reason). . . .
>
> Cintra Reeve, CEO of The Goddess Dolls, started the company because she believes that children (and adults, too!) need a line of dolls that symbolize the positive and empowering aspects of the Goddess tradition, such as love, wisdom, and compassion.
>
> That's great, and I agree that there is a need for alternative spiritual role models, but why the cost? To me it indicates a certain disconnect between the pagan culture and the culture at large.[15]

The cost of religious dolls is an issue for some devotees of Mata Amritanandamayi, better known as Ammachi or Amma, the Hugging Saint. On her Web site, a variety of huggable deity dolls are available, ranging from about $80 to $250 for small or large versions of Kali, Śiva, Lakṣmi, Hanuman, and even Jesus.[16] Dolls of Amma herself range in price from $45 to around $80 and are made by volunteers using materials that Amma has either worn or blessed. While the site generated a lot of criticism from readers of political digest *Salon*'s online community,[17] the dolls evidently bring comfort to her followers:

> Amma might not see too many grown men bringing dolls for blessing, but without having to ask "your doll?" she knew it was a special gift for myself. She tilak'ed the doll—and me

too! I don't recall Amma ever sticking kumkum paste on my forehead before. Since the doll received Amma's blessings, it's not easy to let go of her. She is sitting on my lap as I work at my computer. I sleep with her, and reach for her when I wake up. I talk to her and hug her as if this doll is Amma herself. The doll is not only soft and nurturing to cuddle, but fills the longing for Amma's darshan during the long wait between her tours. It's like a murti of the Divine Mother. But while most murtis are made of hard metal or stone, this is very warm, fuzzy, huggable, snuggable murti. And now, other devotees ask me if they could hold my doll. . . . I think every little boy should have an Amma doll. And big boys too![18]

Those looking for empowerment through the Goddess need go no further than Barbie, who has had her share of religious incarnations. In addition to the collectible Goddesses of the Arctic (2001), Americas (2000), Africa (1999), and Asia (1998), and the Goddesses of the Moon (1996) and Sun (1995)—all clad in exquisite designer gowns by Bob Mackie—Mattel released a Diwali Barbie for Hindu girls in 2006. Considering the price of Aphrodite, the Barbie Goddesses of Moon and Sun are more "reasonably" priced at $195, if you factor in the collectibility of a Bob Mackie designer gown. The Barbie dolls are arguably more straightforward and honest in their overt commercialism, while Goddess spirituality dolls and other religious dolls available online offer empowering love, wisdom, and compassion at a price sure to be well above the reach of most.

Interestingly, the Barbie Goddess series, as well as the Diwali Barbie, have received criticism for something other than their cost: racial insensitivity and cultural stereotyping. The Asia Goddess doll sparked a call for a protest from the Asian American Legal Defense and Education Fund.

I call your attention to the exoticization that Asian women have historically suffered in the West. I call your attention to the racist violence that is integral to and a result of this grotesque fascination with Asian "femininity." I call your attention to the stereotypes that each of us carry as a consequence. "Fantasy Goddess of Asia Barbie" is obviously designed to satisfy the White male gaze that has promoted trafficking of Asian women by legitimizing industries such as the "mail order brides."[19]

The Diwali Barbie sparked a similar protest among bloggers:

"If we wanted little Indian children running around and worshipping a disproportionately tall woman whose skin is unnaturally white and lives up to the standards of exotic in the West, we would point them all to Aishwarya Rai. At least she does something," writes feminist blogger onebrownwoman.

A poster on SepiaMutiny.com noted that Barbie's costume is really more like "half a sari"—closer to a lehnga with chunari—and that her forehead ornament is a tikka, not a bindi.

At the end of Mattel's product description, the caveat "Doll cannot stand alone" has also inspired snickers in the blog community.

"Thank you Barbie for reminding us that at the end of the day, no woman should really be able to stand alone. Especially not the exotic ones," writes onebrownwoman.[20]

Racial issues are not new to the world of dolls. In the nineteenth century, after Harriet Beecher Stowe's *Uncle Tom's Cabin* came out, plays, dolls, toys, furnishings, and knickknacks, even foods, took advantage of the book's popularity. One such doll, the topsy-turvy doll, which the mother-in-law of one of the authors played with as a girl in the 1920s, had a head on each end of a single body with two sets of arms, but no legs, the heads covered by a long skirt. On one side, the doll is "Little Eva," white daughter of the plantation owner. But turned the other way, the doll becomes "Topsy," the black slave girl. Although we could look at this from a perspective of deep psychological play between self and other, the construction of the other often draws from highly loaded racial imagery and stereotypes.

Cultural analyst Robert MacGregor correlates the spread of racism with "capitalism, colonialism, and Christianity around the world," in part because the symbolic use of color was so strong in Christianity.

The perceived biological differences gave rise to a biological hierarchializing of different people based mainly on the colour of their skin. Eventually skin colour expressed a hierarchical religious evaluation which attained a widespread secular content within Western cultures. . . . This superior/

inferior dichotomy was a powerful foundational basis that appeared in ethnic and race relations.[21]

Advertising exploits the differences between the images of the golden-haired, noble Eva and her wooly-haired, goblin-like friend Topsy. One promotional throwaway for a play based on the book read in part

T   is for Topsy, impish and wild
             Only sweet Eva can tame this poor child
O's for Ophelia, a spinster unblest
             An angel to Eva, to Topsy a pest
P   is for platform, where Tom was on sale,
             And also where Eva saved Topsy from jail.[22]

The letters down the left-hand side eventually spell out TopsyEva. At one point in the poem Topsy is referred to as "the wickedest gal," drawing on the corresponding dichotomies of white/black, good/evil, angel/devil, spiritual/carnal, and even salvation/damnation.[23] Before you jump to the conclusion that this sort of marketing no longer occurs, the advertisement that sparked MacGregor's article was a 1991 Benetton ad depicting a "smiling, blond-haired white child juxtaposed to a very serious looking black child that appeared to have her hair styled in the form of two horns."[24]

We are far from the simple, warm and romanticized visions of a childhood of carefree play. Dolls conjure a bubbling brew of seriously disparate, powerfully conflicting, and politically charged meanings that engage issues of identity such as race and gender, and raise questions about the commodification of spirituality, as well as cultural hegemony and the ethics and psychology of religious conversion. Representing perhaps a sinister side of play, these significant issues are ones on which we will continue to reflect throughout subsequent chapters.

Competing for Converts

Clearly religions—and toy companies—are competing for converts in the marketplace, and one of their primary battlegrounds is what children do on the field of play. In addition to being a lucrative business, many designers of religious dolls are hoping that the dolls can be effective vehicles for transmitting the religion's traditions and promoting the faith, and many market the dolls in precisely this way.

The talking dolls, most of which recite bits of Scripture or prayers that children are expected to memorize or otherwise absorb, are an excellent case in point. Advertised as providing your child with "a fascinating learning experience," Little Talking Farah teaches Muslim children "eleven beautiful Islamic phrases in Arabic," some in praise of Allah. Pretty in pink—including a pink prayer rug and shoes—popular Fulla recites her evening prayers in Arabic. Orthodox Jewish children are included in the conversation with an adorable doll named Bubbaale Shimaale—"Simon the doll"—that outsells Barbie in ultra-Orthodox areas of Israel. Shimaale or Shimmi "avoids the traditional biblical prohibition on creating idols by having only four fingers on each hand and a clown's red nose. Instead of the latest fashion, he wears *tzitzit* and a yarmulke. Press his hand and he recites prayers in Hebrew."[25]

The Christian company one2believe produces a line of talking dolls under their Messengers of Faith series, each of which comes with accessories and sixty- to eighty-second sound bites of Scripture "perfect for easy memorization." These include talking Jesus, Moses, and David dolls, as well as two female biblical figures, the Virgin Mary and Esther, who demonstrate the expected modest dress along with easily memorized Scripture.

Designed to make scriptural faith "fun to learn," one2believe's talking dolls made news headlines internationally with the United States release of their talking religious dolls in retail giant Walmart—prompting a BBC story that claimed, "Instead of Spiderman or Bratz dolls, children in the US could soon be clutching a talking Jesus toy, a bearded Moses or a muscle-bound figure of Goliath."[26]

Interviewed for a BBC article, David Socha, founder of one2believe, spoke about the market for "God-honouring" toys that reflect Christian values.

> We get a lot of people, even people who are not of faith, don't go to church, saying "I've got a four and a six-year-old and I

don't know what to get them any more," he said. If you go in a toy aisle in any major retailer, you will see toys and dolls that promote and glorify evil, destruction, lying, cheating. In the girls' aisle where the dolls would be, you see dolls that are promoting promiscuity to very young girls. Dolls will have very revealing clothes on, G-string underwear.[27]

Clearly Scripture isn't the only religious value the talking dolls are supposed to communicate, although it is a central one. Morals and modest attire are also central themes that run throughout the marketing of the dolls.

In examining how well they deliver their key religious talking points, results vary. In some cases, the doll's sound bites don't accurately reflect their scriptural source, as is the case with the Holy Huggables version of talking Esther, whose bits of Scripture bear little or no resemblance to the original. Although some news articles about this line of dolls claim they recite or even teach Scripture,[28] accuracy is not a necessary ingredient according to the Holy Huggables Web site. "With reaching children's hearts as our first priority, we chose many different translations because we wanted to speak to a child on his or her level. Some verses are paraphrased for children to understand better."[29]

Soft talking dolls, left to right: Holy Huggables Jesus, Farah (teaches Arabic), and Holy Huggables Esther

Even when accurate, the dolls' sound bites are nevertheless just that—sound bites—tiny pieces of Scripture taken out of context and disconnected from the totality of the biblical story. Esther's story, which is far more extensive in the Bible than Mary's, takes place in complex historical, mythological, and biblical context that is arguably open to multiple levels of interpretation—including both feminist and nonfeminist readings. Are any of these interpretations even remotely transmitted or suggested in seventy seconds of disconnected text?

Similar questions may be raised about the talking Virgin Mary doll. While there is not much written about Mary in the Bible, does her story *really* boil down to a few easily memorized sound bites from Luke? Sally Cunneen, author of *In Search of Mary: The Woman and the Symbol*,[30] might argue that it does not. Examining a wide range of materials on Mary, from extrascriptural stories to iconographic and artistic representations, Cunneen explores the many meanings of Mary as she moves and changes through historical time and space—none of which is captured in a seventy-second sound bite.

The point is that biblical stories occur in a larger context, one that changes in meaning both through the passage of time and as the stories move throughout different cultures in the world. Rote memorization of Scripture isolated from its historical and deeply embedded cultural contexts does not capture the full range of meaning that scriptural sources hold. Reduction of complex sets of interwoven and sometimes conflicting meanings and interpretations to easily memorized sound bites seems to do a disservice both to Scripture and to children, who learn at an early age to treat text one-dimensionally and literally, entirely missing nuances of meaning.

We might question to what extent a talking doll's simplified sound bites will affect children's understanding of Scripture and hinder their ability to develop a more mature and nuanced understanding of religious concepts. The idea of saying prayers to a huggable Jesus doll seems equivalent to young children's beliefs that pets can pray, a concept they can grow out of with age and appropriate spiritual direction. Given proper adult guidance, children come to understand prayer as part of a human system of religious belief and practice that is culturally specific or culturally accepted.[31] But what kind of mature religious guidance can come from a grandmother who buys a huggable talking Jesus for herself and who cherishes it too much to give it to her grandson? "I bought this for myself! I love it. I listen to it often to remind myself of the truths it says. I will play with it with my grandson, who is 3, but it's too precious to me to hand over to him."[32]

Perhaps these concerns are inconsequential, like worrying that children who grow up with Little Talking Farah will think that Arabic is just eleven handy phrases, or that dolls that say just "Mommy" or "Daddy" or "Math is hard" will limit a child's linguistic or career choices. Some groups nevertheless do take these concerns quite seriously. Readers may remember the controversies over Mattel's 1992 release of Teen Talk Barbie, which said things like "Will we ever have enough clothes?" and "I love shopping." But it was Barbie's "Math class is tough!" utterance that prompted the American Association of University Women to file a lawsuit in protest, causing Mattel to withdraw the offensive phrase. Surely children who play with talking Esther or Virgin Mary dolls will quite likely be exposed to religious Scripture in a fuller sense, so perhaps we are overestimating the effect dolls will have on their development. After all, it's only a doll. Everyone knows it's not real.

We'll come back to that.

Battle for the Toybox

In addition to scriptural sound bites, dolls transmit a religion's values with respect to gender roles and behavior, providing an interesting intersection of religion with identities of race, gender, sex, and politics. Some religious dolls, especially ones for boys, are consciously marketed as wholesome alternatives to popular toys with darker themes, such as predatory aliens, scary monsters, and demonic Hellboy action figures. One action figure quite possibly designed to stimulate the more puerile imaginations of little boys is the Job christian action figure from Train Up a Child, Inc.— complete with realistic sores. Although Job's boils do not actually seep or pop, he could nevertheless satisfy children who might

Biblical action figures, left to right: Judah (1984), Peter (1991), and
Job (2001), complete with sores on his face, arms, and legs

otherwise play with dolls such as the Impaled Mummy action figure, whose "skull head and visible, blood-covered internal organs"
are played with by "putting a spear through his back and watching the effects."[33] Whether Job the doll succeeds in illustrating
God-honoring values by suffering with a skin disease, or simply in
occupying boys who might otherwise be drawn to "demonic toys"
is unclear.

Parents worried about the possible "effeminizing" effects of
their little boys playing with dolls—even talking Jesus dolls—
have a line of manly religious action figures from which to choose.
The terms *action figure* and *moveable fighting man* were coined
in the 1960s by toy entrepreneur Don Levine and Hasbro as a way
to describe their newly created G.I. Joe doll and avoid the potential
"stigma" of little boys playing with dolls.[34] More recently, Levine
has created the Family Values LLC's Almighty Heroes collection,
a line of Old Testament action-hero and heroine figures complete
with appropriate accessories and Bible stories. Notably, these toys
are marketed as gender-specific. They include Samson, Joshua,
Noah, Moses, David, and Goliath—plastic electronic sword sold

separately—"action figures" for little boys, and "fashion dolls" Queen Esther and Deborah the Warrior for little girls—charm bracelet sold separately.

Today's parents can retire G.I. Joe to the doll reserves and enlist a veritable platoon of brave Christian soldiers in the war against evil. In addition to the Almighty Heroes, parents who are both religious and patriotic might consider the Latter Day Saints' Captain Moroni action figure. Advertising informs us that "Moroni was a strong and mighty man, a man of perfect understanding, a man whose soul did joy in the liberty and freedom of his country" and who "became commander of the Nephite army at the young age of 25." Action figures representing the lazy but ferocious Lamanites—essentially Native Americans marked for their wickedness by a darker skin—and the 2000 brave Stripling Warriors are sold separately. The characterization of the darker-skinned Lamanites offers another example of the way in which the intersection of religious and racial identity provides a potentially controversial political dimension.

Parents who want to purchase "big tough toys that boys will love to play with," toys that are sure to withstand the rigors of the battle between good and evil, may find what they're looking for in one2believe's Spirit Warriors collection. One2believe's Web site is now dedicated to winning the "Battle for the Toybox"—a militaristic addition to their narrative that was absent when we began our research in 2006.[35]

In fact, their Web site contains a Battle for the Toybox link that takes the consumer to two versions of a downloadable flyer for the battle. One flyer, featuring a steroid-pumped Samson battling an equally enormous Goliath, is titled "Join the Battle," a contest not mentioned in any biblical narrative. The other flyer has Samson battling Goliath in the center, surrounded by illustrations of the company's other toy lines, and announces "One2believe is in a Battle for the Toybox," asking "Which side are you on?" Customers are encouraged to download the flyers and distribute them to friends and family.

While assembling your platoon of soldiers for the big battle to come, why not enlist the help of the heavenly angels themselves?

The successful animated movie series *Angel Wars Guardian Force* tells the story of adolescent angels learning how to protect the earth from evil demons and deciding whether they will submit to the will of the "Divine Master King." A child interested in the series can now own the Archangel Michael action figure, complete with impressive sword-like weapon. Michael battles the Fallen Angel Morgan action figure, sold separately, which changes into the evil demon Morg, also equipped with impressive weapons. Since there are no fallen angels named Morgan in the Bible, the question arises whether this may be an attempt to demonize Celts, whose mythologies and religious folk practices are significant in some forms of Contemporary Paganism.

To be sure, toy advertising, like sports, is replete with militaristic narratives, especially in the marketing of toys for boys. According to Eric Clark's *The Real Toy Story*, "good fighting evil is a major psychological element in boys' play";[36] "combat sells action figures," making violence "common in ads for boys' toys."[37] War metaphors permeate the toy industry, if online articles like "Islamic Doll Kicks Barbie's Ass" and "Fulla the Muslim Doll Conquers Land of the Nile" or chapters like "Barbie Goes to War: Battle of the Dolls" and "War of the Aisles: The Retail Battleground" in Clark's *The Real Toy Story* are any indication.[38]

According to toy tycoon Don Levine in reference to his *Almighty Heroes*, "The Battle of Good vs. Evil is what makes these characters stand out."[39] The theme of the grand battle between good and evil is echoed by *Angel Wars Guardian Force* creator Chris Waters, who stated in an interview with *The 700 Club* that the tragic events of 9/11 inspired him to create the series as a tale of Christian salvation. According to the interview, Waters created the *Angel Wars* superheroes to bring salvation to a fallen world upon hearing the story of a child who asked his mother, "Where was Superman?"

Salvation from evil seems to preoccupy Waters, who said in the interview, "I realized there was a whole generation of kids who didn't understand salvation and who didn't know salvation was available to them. They need to know they can participate in the *real* battle—the spiritual battle we face every day, without having to walk in fear."[40] Waters notes the special importance of saviors for boys who grow up without fathers: "They fill a void. . . . We're looking for a savior, and we're looking for something outside of ourselves to save us from ourselves."[41] The salvation theme is echoed in an interview with Kendall Lyons of the online newsletter *Animation Insider*: "We gravitate to stories with salvific characters because we're looking to be saved from a fallen world. *Angel Wars* offers this hope both as an allegory, and for some, as a concrete reality, and for this reason we have had a great reaction from a broad audience."[42]

But placed in the context of increasingly violent and militaristic narratives emerging from the religious right, a disturbing amalgam of war, religion, and play emerges. Chris Hedges, in *American Fascists: The Christian Right and the War on America*, makes this chilling observation about the eagerly anticipated apocalyptic battle between good and evil:

> The yearning for this final battle runs through the movement like an electric current. Christian right firebrands employ the language of war, speak in the metaphors of battle, and paint graphic and chilling scenes of the violence and mayhem that will envelop the earth. War is the final aesthetic of the movement.[43]

Are toys like the Spirit Warriors or Almighty Heroes harmless and wholesome alternatives to more destructive toys, or are they helping to prepare children for religiously sanctioned violence against those "left behind?"

Spirit Warriors and Almighty Heroes seem to fit into a broader battle for the toybox that extends beyond the world of religious dolls to include board and video games. Although video games and animated movies are outside the scope of this book, they are here worth a brief examination, as quite clearly the toys and games market is multidirectional, its merchandise overlapping and tightly knit with products targeted to as many age ranges as possible. Some toy empires begin as dolls or action figures and then expand into board or video games, movies or anime, or, more rarely, novels. Others— like *Angel Wars Guardian Force*—begin as movies or animated videos and then expand into action figures or board and video games.

"Religious warfare" and "dehumanization" are precisely the accusations leveled against video games such as *Left Behind: Eternal Forces*.[44] The series of novels written by Jerry B. Jenkins and Tim LaHaye has been wildly popular. But the release of the video game *Left Behind: Eternal Forces* in 2006 made waves internationally and sparked calls for a boycott of Walmart and other sellers, from groups as varied as atheists, Muslims, and progressive Christian groups including the Christian Alliance for Progress and Talk to Action, which describes the game as follows:

> [Y]ou are a foot soldier in a paramilitary group whose purpose is to remake America as a Christian theocracy, and establish its worldly vision of the dominion of Christ over all aspects of life. You are issued high-tech military weaponry, and instructed to engage the infidel on the streets of New York City. You are on a mission—both a religious mission and a military mission—to convert or kill Catholics, Jews, Muslims, Buddhists, gays, and anyone who advocates the separation of church and state—especially moderate, mainstream Christians. Your mission is "to conduct physical and spiritual warfare"; all who resist must be taken out with extreme prejudice. You have never felt so powerful, so driven by a purpose: you are 13 years old.[45]

Early reviews of the game noted its complete absence of minorities and the tendency for characters that are converted by the Tribulation Forces—the "good guys" who wreak God's tribulation on the rest of society—to transform into nerdy white men with poor fashion sense. Women characters, when they appear at all, are excluded from many career paths, including builder, soldier, disciple, and musician. But perhaps more important than the privileging of race and gender is the assumption of militaristic violence and Christian dominion. Zach Whalen, one of the game's early reviewers, points out that because "we can see in our current political environment the effects of a worldview in which proponents literally believe that, any day now, they will be exempted from apocalypse while the rest of the world suffers," it is "important that we identify and call attention to the ways this ideology is built into its fabric." Whalen calls for us to "understand and explain how the game's systems structure its version of reality around a conservative, dominionist view of the world that extends from the Fundamentalist version of Christianity and does not accurately reflect the views of mainstream Christians."[46]

Connecting the game to the empire and dominionist agenda of megachurch pastor Rick Warren, author of *The Purpose-Driven Life*, groups such as Talk to Action voiced concerns that prompted one of Warren's top aides to resign as advisor to Left Behind Games and provoked removal of the Purpose-Driven name from the game's Web site.[47] While Warren has been dubbed "America's minister" by *Time*, Talk to Action notes that his agenda goes far beyond America and traditional ministry. "He sees himself as the CEO of a global marketing enterprise, and as the Commander in Chief of a stealth army of one billion Christian foot soldiers."[48] And enlistment age is getting younger all the time, with religious toys and games targeted at ever-younger groups of children.

At least some educators and psychologists are concerned about the level of violence in these toys and games, a paradoxical problem since much of the motivation for creating religious games and toys in the first place was to have nonviolent alternatives. Critics of the violence of toys and games have pointed out that the products are marketed to younger children through links to video games and movies clearly meant for adolescents, teens, and young adults.

> Many of the movies are rated PG-13 or even R, but their toys are marketed to children ages 4 and up. Often, toys linked to these movies are also linked to other media such as TV, video games, and comic books. This cross-feeding starts with toys for the youngest children and begins the cycle of children's involvement with entertainment violence.[49]

How do religious toy manufacturers conceptualize children playing with their products? One2believe enlists what it calls a form of "kinesthetic learning" that occurs when children play with the dolls and act out their stories. The dolls and their messages are part of one2believe's vision of bringing children to "a place of spiritual discovery" and "introducing them to the Lord" by "stimulating their creative imaginations" through fun.[50]

> A young boy and his little sister are sitting on the floor in their living room. With eyes wide open, they look up expectantly

at their parents. While Dad opens the Bible to the story of David and Goliath, Mom holds a Bible character doll. The doll is fashioned after the character David, holding in its right hand a sling and a stone. Dad reads in a bellowing voice, "Am I a dog that you come to me with a stick? said Goliath." Mom then asks, "How do you think David answered Goliath? Let's push the button and find out what happens next." As the children activate the doll's voice, the scriptures come to life!

The purpose of this family activity is to pique their children's imaginations and turn their hearts toward God. But don't tell their kids that . . . they're having too much fun![51]

In the above scenario, a highly choreographed form of embodied education supposedly operates through play to convey a Bible story and possibly instill the moral value of courage in the face of impossible odds. But in this idealized script, complex religious texts and narratives are oversimplified and reduced to easily memorized short phrases. The kinesthetic learning seems to be limited to handling the dolls and pressing their talk buttons, a ritualized—but severely restricted—form of play and performance.

A major question immediately arises: what happens to the enculturation of moral values when children go "off script" and create their own play scenarios? Play is wonderfully interactive and ambivalent—even subversive, as we shall see in chapter 5. Children seldom stick to scripted actions in play, no matter how solidly both they and the script are rooted in religious values. In fact, one2believe's rosy vision of family values through fun and play only produces more questions.

For example, what is the larger relationship of kinesthetic learning to religious practice and ritualized behavior? The constrictive nature of one2believe's imagined scenario—pressing talk buttons to a scripted doll play—seems likely to limit the range of richly embodied and sensual ritual practices found in religion, rather than engage the body with religious practice. Instead of being highlighted through physical engagement, the body is hardly implicated at all—perhaps even erased—in this form of play, except as the passive receptor for a set of narrow and idealized actions.

The Politics of Plastic

The body as passive receptor for and object of morality is particularly stressed in some of the female religious dolls—especially those marketed as "anti-Barbies" and emphasizing the ubiquitous modest dress. For example, a devout Muslim parent who wants something wholesome for her daughter to play with might replace secular Barbie and Bratz with the Muslim-American Razanne doll, produced in Michigan by NoorArt, Inc. Reflecting the international and multiracial composition of the Muslim community, Razanne is one of the few dolls we have encountered that is successfully presented in different ethnicities.

Muslim dolls have even been designed and developed by government agencies hoping to counteract what is perceived as the pernicious influence of Barbie. The Institute for the Intellectual Development of Children and Young Adults, an agency affiliated with the Ministry of Education in Iran, designed sister and brother Muslim dolls, Sara and Dara, available in traditional regional outfits, to compete with Barbie.[52] They are promoted on the Web site "Islam for Today."

> Meet Dara and Sara, Iran's answer to Ken and Barbie. The Muslim dolls have been developed by a government agency to promote traditional values, with their modest clothing and pro-family backgrounds. They are widely seen as an effort to counter the American dolls and accessories that have flooded the Iranian market. Toy seller Masoumeh Rahimi welcomed the dolls, saying Barbie was "foreign to Iran's culture" because some of the buxom, blonde dolls have revealing clothing. She said young girls who play with Barbie, a doll she sees as wanton, could grow into women who reject Iranian values. "I think every Barbie doll is more harmful than an American missile," Ms Rahimi said. . . . Another toy seller, Mehdi Hedayat, said: "Dara and Sara are strategic products to preserve our national identity."[53]

While not directly marketed as "anti-Barbies," one2believe's lines of "girls' dolls" promote a "religiously appropriate and morally grounded positive body image and role model" for young girls. In addition to talking Virgin Mary and Esther dolls from their

Messengers of Faith series, they also produce Abigail, Leah, and Elisabeth dolls in their P31 Series, which appears to do a lot more than just provide positive body images. The P31 dolls are based on the teachings of Proverbs 31 and are designed to "encourage young girls to pursue biblical womanhood."

What "biblical womanhood" entails is a focus of the Proverbs 31 Ministry, started in 1992 by Lysa TerKeurst and Renee Swope as a monthly newsletter and now including a daily radio show, monthly magazine, books, speakers, courses, and an active online ministry. A clue to P31's orientation can be found in a speech titled "A Special Word for Proverbs 31 Tomboys" given by Rebekah Zes at the Vision Forum Ministry 2003 Father and Daughter Retreat in San Antonio, Texas, and posted on Vision Forum's Web site.

> [T]he strength for a woman is found in her femininity, and in her embracing and fulfilling the role that God has given to her as a young lady. Growing up, I was very much what one would call a tomboy. . . . But the Lord . . . began to show me . . . that true young ladies should be gentle in speech, in voice, in manner, that they should be full of love for home, yet they should also be firm, and decided in their convictions. This is where a woman's true strength lies, because real femininity is anything but weakness. My beliefs about femininity while I was growing up were all lies. But the Lord has shown me that a woman can be just as strong as a man, but that those strengths are manifested in different ways. The means of a man's strength is different than the means of a woman's strength. We are both warriors and soldiers for Christ, but we have different dominions that we are to take.[54]

Proverbs 31 Ministry suggests not only "appropriate and modestly dressed" dolls for little girls but provides advice to both girls and women about the seven principles that make for virtuous feminine (and not tomboyish) behavior.

The testimonials that accompany Proverbs 31 sites are arresting and even a little sad. Some are written almost as confessionals, along the lines of "I was a heroin addict until God showed me the error of my ways." Substitute the word "feminist" or "tomboy" for heroin addict and you see the not-too-veiled statement this makes about gender roles—with even a hint about sexuality.[55]

The P31 dolls are accordingly not only attired in modest dress, but *feminine* dress that will induce the appropriate behaviors of service and submission—women's strengths—in young women. The text would seem to indicate that only women who are submissive "girly girls" can attain the status of warrior and soldier for Christ, and they need to start their training early.

One2believe's talking Esther and Virgin Mary both depict the body, insofar as the dolls vaguely resemble average human women who wear what we are supposed to assume are traditional and historically accurate articles of clothing, including sensible shoes and sandals for their sensibly flat feet. (No Barbie tippy-toe high heels here.) While the Virgin Mary's position as mother of Jesus is fairly well known, Esther's role is less so, thus representing a potentially powerful teaching moment for both young children and students in the religious studies classroom.

For instance, many college students in women and religion classes can readily name the "bad girls of the Bible"—Delilah, Jezebel, and the easily tempted Eve, among others—but very few of them can come up with the "good girls." If they are able to name a few—Deborah, Ruth, Esther—they usually don't have any idea what the women did to make them good. Talking Esther affords both young children and students an interaction with a moment of the text in which the actions of a woman on behalf of her people were not only valued but also heroic. But will heroic religious dolls like Esther or the modestly clad Muslim Razanne provide children with viable role models strong enough to counter Barbie, Britney, Paris, or other "girls gone wild"?

The worlds of Barbie and her Muslim counterpart Fulla in particular engage two uneasy and seemingly incompatible partners—play and religion—in a dance of creative, contested, and performed meaning. Both the American-based Razanne and her Syrian colleague Fulla are designed to offer wholesome alternatives to Muslims looking for a corrective to the moral laxity of Western culture epitomized by Barbie[56]—the quintessential hussy banned by the Saudi Religious Police as that "Jewish doll, whose revealing clothes and shameful postures . . . are a symbol of the decadence of the perverted West."[57] The dolls are extremely popular with

Fulla dolls, from left to right: Original Fulla that came with prayer rug and prayer beads (in front), Singing Fulla in evening dress, Talking Fulla that says the evening prayer, and a walking Fulla with purse, luggage, and luggage cart

Muslim parents and children; in particular, the Fulla doll generated over two million sales in the first two years after her creation in 2003 and outsells Barbie in Damascus toy stores by about forty to one.[58]

Both Razanne and Fulla are consciously marketed as contrasts to Barbie and are designed to appeal to Muslim values. Usually this translates into modest clothing accessories and "more realistic" body measurements. Razanne's accessories, like her clothing, are relatively modest. For example, she comes in a scout version with a canteen, backpack, and CD of Muslim scout cheers; her "In and Out" version includes a perfume bottle and other vanity articles. But Fulla comes fully accessorized and marketed in a manner similar to Barbie, in spite of their differences.

On the other hand, the Messengers of Faith talking Virgin Mary and Esther dolls do not come with additional wardrobe pieces or posh accessories. Indeed, it is difficult to imagine much in the way of accessories for the Virgin Mary—certainly nothing on the order of Barbie's convertible or her Malibu Beach House. But more than the lack of accessories, their scripted, historicized, and biblical nature both limits the range of accompanying product and seems likely to reduce the field of creative play to a fairly narrow set of possibilities.

Could the style and scripting of these dolls really affect children's play that much? While we have some concerns about choreographed play or narrowly prescribed roles, one of the principal insights to come out of our research on religious games and dolls is the potential to fall into lines of thought that too easily divide experiences into opposing dichotomous pairs, as for example sacred and secular, or religion and play. These divisions usually prove to be illusory, vanishing under more direct scrutiny, and the classification of dolls into those that are better and those that are worse for creative play may be one of these mirages.

Filling Emptiness

Certainly, one important feature that Barbie and—to a more limited extent—Fulla share is status as cultural icons. In her book *Barbie Culture*, Mary Rogers notes, "No icon represents only one dimension or axis of a culture. Instead, icons become such because of their versatility, thick folds of meaning, adaptability to diverse individuals' needs or interests, ultimate ambiguity, and open-ended nature."[59] In order for an artifact (and its attendant marketing) to succeed as an icon, it must be ontologically "empty." As such, Barbie becomes the medium for fantasy, capable of bursting "cognitive and emotional limits on consciousness"[60] through imaginative and interactive play. Being ontologically empty allows the doll to be filled with the complete range of fantasy in play.

Rogers reminds us that—like a "fetish"—Barbie has supernatural powers. "An object like a Barbie doll becomes a magical presence and wondrous force in one's world."[61] This is not surprising given dolls' historical connection with magic, as noted earlier in the chapter. Barbie might have a "backstory" to go with a particular set of accessories, but Barbie the doll may become *anything*—

teacher, doctor, princess, racecar driver, astronaut—accessories sold separately, of course. Ruth Handler, Barbie's creator, has always insisted that the doll is a canvas on which children paint dreams of their own futures as adult women.[62] As a cultural icon, Barbie participates in infinite dreams, multiple meanings, and endless stories.

Fulla, marketed as the "moral Muslim choice" for young girls, has a similar open-endedness built into her marketing. At the moment, she occupies herself at home and in being a good shopper. But career options and accessories are emerging; by late 2008 Fulla dentist and teacher sets were on the market. It will be interesting to see what other stories Fulla will be encouraged to tell in the coming years, and what stories children will develop on their own that are not on the approved list.

In contrast, it would seem that the talking Virgin Mary doll can become, well, Virgin Mary—and a significantly reduced and selectively scripted Mary at that, especially if the parents are watching. Her narrowly written role is in marked contrast to the increasingly important position Mary plays in the religious lives not only of Catholics but of all other Christians, including Protestants, Coptics, and Orthodox. That Barbie should be a more successful icon than the Virgin Mary is an interesting irony that speaks volumes about the consumerist nature of today's society and highlights Russell W. Belk's 1995 observation that the "hope for transcendent magic [is] shifting from religion to science to consumption."[63]

The need for dolls to be essentially empty of meaning in order to become successful (and profitable) cultural icons points to an interesting conundrum for religious doll makers. Religious doll makers count on the power of dolls to influence behavior and instill religious values. Yet the more dolls are used to script the behavior of children through a limited and rehearsed notion of play, the less likely the dolls will succeed—and the more likely children will deviate from the approved script. Children always move away from set rules and preorganized ways of playing, even if they do so merely out of boredom. As feminist writer Linda Scott notes in *Fresh Lipstick,*

"Playing Barbie" was . . . more like a grand adventure you made up in spontaneous collaboration with a small group of playmates. Each girl provided the voice for her doll, moved her about in response to the action, and helped spin the narrative as the group went along. You could play your Barbie as a witch, starlet, mermaid, angel, criminal, or wicked stepsister, just as you could pretend to be another character when you played dress-up. The claims of today's feminists that children were indoctrinated to be Barbie underestimates both the imaginative range of doll-playing and the rebelliousness of the Baby Boomer girls.[64]

Princess Virgin Mary—rock star astronaut, anyone? Why not?

Dolls allow for the magic of play, the ability for children to create and tell their own stories. A doll's religious identity is not necessarily an obstacle to play for children, who are not limited by the doll's given characterization. Playmobil makes a Nativity playset complete with camel, frankincense and myrrh, Jesus, Mary, Joseph, and the guiding star—all the necessary elements are there. But these pieces are not limited to reenacting a narrow telling of one sacred story. As seen with the Hindu Bommai Kolu, G.I. Joe and other dolls like Playmobil firemen, Santa, Roman centurions, racecar drivers, and Snoopy—virtually any toy character you can imagine—can and do make their appearance at the manger as well. Even Darth Vader.

The relationship between children and dolls is not a one-way dynamic; while children use dolls in powerful and imaginative play to create fantasies and tell stories, dolls also can and do have an influence on children. This two-way dynamic creates many contradictory expectations among adults who are concerned about the effects of play on children: too many accessories could hinder children's imaginations, but a lack of accessories could also hinder their imaginations. Should we buy complex Erector sets or something simpler like Legos or Lincoln Logs—or simply give them a cardboard box? In the context of our dolls, should we purchase the well-accessorized Fulla or the Virgin Mary?

The same kinds of arguments occur about violence and toys, as well as sexuality and dolls. Barbie's effects on young girls' body image and ideas of self have been studied by everyone from psychologists to advertisers. Barbie has been accused of everything from promoting anorexia to sexualizing young girls. But just as violent toys will not necessarily mark children for prison later in life, being accused does not make Barbie guilty. Brian Sutton-Smith, perhaps the foremost psychologist of play and toys, notes that people's concerns are not necessarily based in realistic assessments, and can result in amusing speculation:

> Some years ago a new version of Barbie was created, called Growing up Skipper, who could be made to grow up from a flat-chested child to a bosomed teenager by rotating the left arm. A writer in Ms. magazine wrote, "The mind reels at the possibilities for 'creative' play—eight-year-old girls trying to grow their own (breasts) and thereby twisting one another's arms into a mass of torn ligaments, small boys staging neighborhood porno exhibits. . . . One wonders whether men would tolerate a comparable male toy. Can't you see it: Growing up Buster—twist his leg, his penis grows and his testicles descend."[65]

On the other hand, the example of Cindy Jackson shows the unquestionable influence that dolls can have on body image . . . and shape!

> Cindy Jackson, the Fremont, Ohio-born founder of the London-based Cosmetic Surgery Network, may be the ultimate Barbie performance artist. She has had more than twenty operations and spent $55,000 to turn herself into a living doll. She has had chemical peels, tummy tucks, facelifts, eye-lifts, breast implants, and liposuction. She has even had two nose jobs. . . . But no longer is she satisfied merely remaking herself. Her mission, which evolved while assisting other women through Barbie-izations, is to create "a bionic army."[66]

Fear of Barbie's apparently magical sexualizing powers is widespread. As anti-Barbies, Fulla and Razanne are deliberately marketed to emphasize and appeal to personal qualities other than external beauty and sexuality. According to the founder of the Michigan company that creates Razanne, "The main message we try to put forward through the doll is that what matters is what's inside you, not how you look. . . . It doesn't matter if you're tall or short, thin or fat, beautiful or not, the real beauty seen by God and fellow Muslims is what's in your soul."[67] At the Online Islamic Store, Razanne was marketed as

> The perfect gift for all Muslim girls!
> Builds Muslim identity and self-esteem.
> Provides Islamic role models.
> Promotes Islamic behavior.
> Shapes interactive play.

While Barbie is characterized as a morally lax whore or slut with her "improbably pneumatic curves and lanky legs," Fulla is described as "modest," her assets "never officially on display."[68] Moreover, Fulla is "honest, loving, and caring, and she respects her father and mother."[69] Fulla is "popular because she's one of us. She's my sister. She's my mother. She's my wife. So as a parent, I'd like Fulla for my daughter."[70]

Now if you think that Fulla and Barbie must look drastically different from one another, you'd be wrong. They are made of the same material and are the same height. They have the same tip-toe feet designed for high-heeled shoes. Both dolls are made by the same subcontractor in China, using the same plastics and the same doll molds—with one measurable difference . . . The only change made to the doll's basic physique is to flatten out Barbie's less-than-modest breasts to produce Fulla.[71]

The bodies of the female dolls become interesting signifiers for morality and deserve extensive treatment on their own. The bodies of the Muslim dolls, as well as talking Esther and Mary, appear to reveal their moral value precisely in what they conceal—the form of the female body. In particular, the expression of positive moral values is perceived through absence, in other words, in terms of what is lacking or missing in comparison with Barbie—to wit, the size and display of the breasts, a concern apparently shared by other religious groups.

> I had to beg for a Barbie from my Southern Baptist family because of those boobs. My sister and I didn't know the word for it, but we could tell from the reaction of our parents that Barbie was a slut. Nobody ever told me I "had to look like Barbie," as feminists often claim. Instead the message came

through loud and clear that I was never to show up anywhere looking like Barbie.[72]

Muslim parents who buy Fulla dolls perhaps hope their daughters will choose the ways of the good Muslim girl over notorious party-girl Barbie. These ways include the *hijab*. "If the girls put scarves on their dolls when they're young, it might make it easier when their time comes. Sometimes it's difficult for girls to put on the *hijab*. . . . Fulla shows girls that the *hijab* is a normal part of a woman's life."[73]

Here again Fulla and Barbie share something in common: winning over consumers when they are young. Fulla's creators hope that she will influence girls early on and lead them to adopt the *hijab* when they are older. Barbie's creators count on their merchandising to grab children when they are very young and hold on to them until well into adulthood.

> There is a mass of "psychographic data" about girls of different ages, about how they play, their hobbies, the television programs, music, and clothes they like, their favorite singers. It pours in from focus groups worldwide, including Mattel's own test center where children are observed through one-way mirrors. Mattel researchers visit children's homes to watch girls play.[74]

But doll play is notoriously interactive and multivalent; little girls and boys are seldom simply passive consumers of marketing messages. Children produce and perform an incredible array of potentially conflicting meanings—along with the occasional unintended (and sometimes hilarious) consequence—through play. Children have been known to do all sorts of things to their Barbies, including decapitating them, shaving their heads, piercing various body parts, and cross-dressing Barbie and Ken. Quoting research from Dr. Agnes Nairn in a Bath University study of one hundred children, journalist Tom Parry reports "girls hate Barbie so much that many torture, maim and cut her head off." "It's as though disavowing Barbie is a rite of passage," says Nairn. "Kids, who spend about 3 billion pounds a year, also hate being targeted by advertisers."[75] As adults, they go on to create anti-Barbie clubs and produce an almost unlimited number of "transgressive" Bar-

bies, including Exorcist Barbie, Drag-Queen Barbie, Transgender
Barbie, Trailer Trash Barbie, and Big Dyke Barbie.

The marketed message for religious dolls such as Fulla can
itself be problematic: while some Muslims think Fulla is a positive
influence, others are concerned that the doll will coerce young
girls into a conservative and repressive form of Islam that some
fear is becoming more widespread. Feminists, many of whom have
long criticized Barbie for some of the same reasons Muslims con-
demn her, might be expected to see Razanne and Fulla as positive
role models that deemphasize women as sexual objects. But that is
not automatically the case, says Zoepf.

> Maan Abdul Salam, a Syrian women's rights advocate, said
> Fulla was emblematic of a trend toward Islamic conservatism
> sweeping the Middle East. "Though statistics are hard to
> come by," he said, "the percentage of young Arab women who
> wear the hijab is far higher now than it was a decade ago, and
> though many of the girls are wearing it by choice, others are
> being pressured to do so."[76]

Consumers and feminist critics are not the only ones taking
dolls seriously. In the fall of 2008, a Fisher-Price doll from the Little
Mommy series, which cooed and said "mama," was thought to utter
"inappropriate" phrases as well. Video after video of news reports
on YouTube show concerned Americans listening hard as they try
to decipher what this doll is saying, most of them extremely concerned when they are told it says "Islam is the Light." Reaction to
this grew to the point where parents were "outraged."[77]

After people started complaining, some Walmart and Target
stores stopped carrying the dolls. Fisher-Price sent original audio
files to news outlets to prove that there was no subversive message in the original. Sound quality is relatively poor with these
items, especially when generated through a computer. From our
attempts to hear this, and judging from the reactions of those in
the videos, we would say that a person would be hard-pressed to
decipher the phrase.

The fallout from this speaks volumes. Chattanooga, Tennes-
see, TV station WDEF has a large banner in their YouTube video on
this topic that says "Un-American Doll?"[78] and those interviewed

made it clear that a doll should not say that phrase in America, especially at Christmas time. One WBAL-TV (Baltimore, Maryland) newscaster stated, " 'Islam is the light'; those four words are igniting controversy and confusion across the country." One interviewee was concerned that "some people will probably laugh but some people I think would be very offended"; another considered it problematical "especially when kids are so young and pick up on things so easily." Fisher-Price was blamed, and even the muffled quality of the sound was seen as evidence that there was an attempt to hide the words.[79] Just a doll? Not, evidently, when dolls can be used to spread religion and undermine patriotism even through incomprehensible phrases.

One of the newscasters presented a more open-minded attitude about dolls promoting Islam: "There is religious freedom for everyone, that's not the problem. The problem is the boxes are not clearly marked."[80] In other words, it is fine for a doll to support Islam, as long as people are warned.

Apparently, problems with subversive dolls occur around the world. Saudi Arabia, whose religious police removed Barbie from the shelves, is one of a number of countries that perceive Barbie as a dangerous and threatening influence. Iranian officials, mentioned earlier, attempted to launch their own modestly attired anti-Barbies, and so have Egyptian officials who are part of the Arab League in Cairo. Russian attempts to ban Barbie were on the grounds that "she has harmful effects on the minds of young girls. The doll has been accused of awakening sexual impulses in the very young and encouraging consumerism among Russian infants."[81] Dolls bring modernity or American pop culture to these countries, sometimes supplanting their own traditions. But as antagonistic as Barbie and Fulla seem to be in many countries, interestingly, in Jordan they happily share shelf space in toy stores.

Fulla has had her own share of problems with officials. In September 2006, Tunisian security forces removed Fulla from stores because of her *hijab*,[82] again due to concern over radical forms of Islam. Since her creator, NewBoy, is based in Syria, she was on the State Department's terrorist list and was not allowed in United States markets. For the U.S., Fulla remained largely on the "do not fly" list for years, although a recent revisionist history moving her creation to Dubai may have helped break the ban, as in 2009 she is now available online through a U.S. distributor based in Virginia.[83] Fulla's potential earning power here may have something to do with the lifting of the ban on importing her.

This suggests that business sometimes trumps politics—and religion. As discussed earlier in this chapter, religious dolls raise serious issues, including concerns over the commodification of religion and the fear that the bottom line has the upper hand. While the obvious consumerism, or perhaps even greed, of the religious doll business should come as no surprise in our twenty-first-century consumer-oriented society, there is a more critical issue that emerges in the marketing of religion through dolls. The business of religious dolls may perform a double disservice: it cuts dolls off from their religio-magical origins, and it does so in the name of promoting or supporting religion. By severely controlling and restricting play, the commercial marketing of religious dolls potentially compromises the power of the dolls to signify meaning. This ironically severs the living exchange between dolls and religion, extinguishing the energy on both sides of the relationship. In the next chapter, we explore the complex connections between money and religion, and the tensions that arise in the marketing of religious toys and games.

Perhaps all dolls are ontologically empty, blank mirrors. This may be the source of their ultimate power and the source of our fear. As blank mirrors we project whatever we need onto them. They become sluts, serve as ideal sisters, preserve national identity, embody goddesses, and facilitate rituals. They become politically, sexually, commercially, and religiously charged. Their emptiness becomes filled with imposed and creative realities that must then be taken seriously as they manifest in our world. Religious dolls still possess powerful magic—magic that is too often concealed by the view "it's only a doll."

3

HOLY COMMERCE, BATMAN!

Freedom's just another word for lots of things to buy.

Twitchell, "Two Cheers for Materialism," 283

The Religious Marketplace

What can the study of religious games and toys tell us about the relationship between religion and commerce, or religion and consumerism? Clearly these toys are material evidence that such a relationship is alive and well—consider that in 2008 Walmart decided to carry a line of talking religious dolls. Yet at the same time, judging from the extensive number of books and articles written on the subject,[1] the tension between religion and almost any aspect of money makes us profoundly uncomfortable. Underlying this tension is the idea that religion is "tainted" by coming into contact with money or commerce, as though there were an ideal religion, pure and unspoiled, isolated from the seamier sides of culture: money, sex, and entertainment.

American perspectives on the relationship between religion and money range from one extreme to the other—from "profound discomfort"[2] with the connection between religion and commerce to the idea that religious consumerism is "liberating and democratic."[3] In between is a range of diverse views, including some seeking to mediate between religion and consumer society, usually seen as naturally antagonistic to one another.

The relationship between religion and commerce has always been present, and even thrived, in religious practice. But there seems to be an indistinct line that must not be crossed, which determines whether or not certain religio-commercial practices are ethical, or even tolerable. Hindus making statues for the Ganesh Chaturti festival, stores in Rome selling robes and rosaries, and the significance of Mecca as a marketing center at the dawn of Islam do not especially bother American sensibilities. But selling indulgences, the practice of exchanging money for forgiveness of sins—one of the factors that led to Martin Luther's protest and the rise of Protestantism—seems clearly to cross the line. So does selling religious relics such as saints' bones or "pieces of the true cross," items that for many violate sensibilities of taste as well as ethics. The fact that Japanese Buddhist priests make such a good living from funerals that they can support car dealerships, while not necessarily unethical, troubles Americans who romanticize Buddhism. And talking Jesus dolls or the Internet-marketed Job-with-boils action figures are religious commodities that make many Americans squirm.

Religion and commerce have been interwoven in diverse ways, not just in selling ritual necessities or other religious items. For example, tithing, giving one tenth of one's income or produce, is a religious practice rooted in Jewish traditions of the Old Testament that is still practiced in some Christian institutions. At times this was voluntary, at other times mandatory. While today this is thought of in terms of money, in earlier historical periods one would have been required to donate one tenth of one's harvest, or of one's production if a craftsperson. For those merely eking out a living, this created real hardship. From an idealistic perspective, the aim of tithing might have been to redistribute goods, but this practice was used to increase the wealth of institutions and those in power. St. Peter's Cathedral in Rome was built partially on the backs of those who could least afford it. Forms of tithing still exist today; the collection plate in church is a close relative, and in some European countries state-sponsored religion leads to legal church taxation.

Islam also has something to say about the relationship of money and religion. One of the Five Pillars of Islam, the fundamental practices that all Muslims are expected to perform, is *zakat*, which requires Muslims to give 2.5 percent (1/40) of their income or production as alms. Redistribution of wealth is important; the members of the Islamic community, or *ummah*, are expected to help each other. Islamic law also regulates other monetary practices; for example, Muslims are not allowed to charge interest. The Muslim business model thus differs from the Western, Judeo-Christian model, though it is true that some Muslims have found ways around the laws so that they can charge a fee while not calling it interest.

In Buddhism, the rule that monks and nuns must beg for food is a form of control of commerce, since commerce involves exchange. While this practice does not involve money, it does entail an exchange of spiritual value. The monks and nuns receive food, and in return the villagers who donate the food receive merit, which accumulates and results in a better reincarnation. For a villager, taking care of the needs of the monastic community is a form of investment in one's future lives and eventual enlightenment. Buddhist tradition also regulates monetary practices; monks and nuns are forbidden to handle gold or silver. As with other religious traditions, bending the rules is not unknown; in China in 2006, a Shaolin monk was given the gift of a luxury car valued at US$125,000 for promoting tourism.[4] This gift, and other apparently lucrative practices among Shaolin monks, have created a fair amount of criticism.

Clearly the problematic relationship between religion and money, or religion and commerce, is not limited to recent American cultural perspectives. Islamic law regulates interest in order to maintain an ethical and just relationship between lender and borrower, but also to keep wealth from becoming a barrier to a proper relationship with God. Buddhist monastic laws forbid the handling of money both as a form of discipline and because being in contact with money can interfere with monastic aims and practices.

American religious history is largely, but not exclusively, a story of Protestant Christianity. The forms and practices of

American business and consumerism were initially shaped mainly by religious needs. To understand the complex connections among religion, money, and commerce in the United States requires that we examine the particularly Christian aspects of this history. The development of religious games and toys in the form we know them today proceeds from this same set of relationships; as a result most games and toys available today—online and in specialty stores— are Christian, and this chapter focuses primarily on these items.

The history of religion in the United States, along with contemporary consumer culture, gives rise to particular kinds of concerns about the relationship of religion to money. The roots of this tension lie in the New Testament; a well-known passage regarding money and religion clearly states that wealth and spiritual life are at odds.

> Jesus said: "If you want to be perfect, go, sell your possessions and give to the poor, and you will have treasure in heaven. Then come, follow me." When the young man heard this, he went away sad, because he had great wealth. Then Jesus said to his disciples, "I tell you the truth, it is hard for a rich man to enter the kingdom of heaven. Again I tell you, it is easier for a camel to go through the eye of a needle than for a rich man to enter the kingdom of God."[5]

How did Christianity get from an ideal of poverty and discipline to the Christian theme park Heritage USA and the megachurches of the twentieth-first century? In part this was due to the separation of Church and State, which requires churches to promote themselves, to attract "customers." Religious games can be viewed as a new way to accomplish this, as illustrated by the various versions of *Monopoly*: *Bible-, Catholic-, Mormon-* and *Episcopopoly*. State-sponsored religion, in contrast, has some advantages. "A state church does many things. Most relevant here, it relieves religion from market pressures, from the need to maintain its financial solvency through commercial self-promotion."[6]

Protestants are responsible for developing much of the marketing of religion that has taken place in the United States over the past few centuries, though Catholics and Jews have also had a hand. "Catholics invented many of the business tricks of the Christian world. American Judaism, from orthodox to reform, was a veritable training ground for success in commerce and the entertainment world."[7] And it was certainly not just the wealthier churches or synagogues that engaged in business practices: "Churches of the poor carried religious competition to extremes undreamt of by middle-class congregations. Inner-city pastors looking for customers lined up their storefront faiths side-by-side down city blocks."[8]

The affinity between Protestantism and business was natural, due to the need for self-promotion and the call to spread the word of God, but this kinship was also complex and, according to historian Douglas Carl Abrams, led to some unintended results. "The encounter with modern culture affected their values . . . they adapted to the business ethos of the 1920s and in doing so contributed to the process of economic modernization. Unwittingly, perhaps, they prized secular values such as efficiency, a mechanistic perspective that centered on results, and increasingly they lost sight of a purer spiritual vision."[9] And while capitalism was arguably a logical development for Protestants,[10] it still needed to be learned.[11]

It has definitely been learned. Promoting Christ is big business, and experts are available to help ensure that this continues to be the case. The Christian Book Association (CBA), which sponsors a huge industry convention each summer, the largest annual gathering of Christian retailers and suppliers in the world, also offers services to Christian retailers. CBA's Web site as well as its journal, *CBA Retailers+Resources*, provides retailing advice about merchandising, sales, and marketing as well as

> in-depth, insightful coverage of the latest market trends; vital CBA initiatives; industry news; reviews of the newest products; regular columns on marketing and sales, operations and systems, human resources, business law, and merchandising written by experts in the industry; and insightful feature articles that provide real-world solutions to tough topics Christian retailers face each day.[12]

Churches have also become big business, with megachurches functioning as centers in which to consume Christianity. In an article on New England megachurches, Frances Fitzgerald describes her visit to one in New Milford, Connecticut:

The doors open onto a spacious and well-lit reception area with wall-to-wall carpeting, plasma TV screens, and sofas, where people can watch the service going on in the sanctuary. . . . While I leafed through four-color brochures advertising Bible-study classes, a day-care center, a pre-K-12 school, and a variety of ministries, she asked if I wanted to fill out a card with my contact information and gave me a gift for newcomers—a beribboned package containing a coupon for the church's coffee shop, more brochures, and a CD of a sermon by the senior pastor. . . . Did I want information about small groups? There were groups for single women, basketball players, scrapbook-makers, museumgoers, and a group led by Susan herself for people learning to trade on eBay.

I passed a bookstore and found myself in a hallway decorated with comic-book-style murals of a street scene in an old-fashioned town. At a registration desk, parents were lining up at a computerized check-in system to get name tags for their kids before sending them in to the schoolrooms for children's church, which offers Bible lessons, worship, playtime, and snacks. At the "Sonbucks" coffee shop down the hall, volunteers were working an espresso machine. When a band began to play, people drifted into the sanctuary, some carrying their Styrofoam cups with them.[13]

Megachurches and Protestant religious commerce of the twenty-first century seem a far cry from the origins of Christian worship in community and vows of poverty. If you earn your money spreading the gospel, can you still get to heaven?

But although these contemporary religious forms, which reflect modern cultural modes of exchange, seem distant from more economically subdued perspectives within Christianity, the fiscal interests of religious institutions are not new. Organized religion and money have always been entwined. "No organized church, in fact, ever imagined itself as a totally non-secular institution."[14] To the contrary, churches have long imitated business models and continue to be quite successful at it. It was not just the need to attract members that motivated business models, but also the mundane needs of institutions, such as paying ministers or organists and maintaining physical structures.

Play Money

Many Christian games reflect the economic reality of churches as institutions. The importance of these worldly concerns is evident in the number of game cards devoted to these issues, expressing problems such as the need for promotion in order to bring in new members, or the expense of building upkeep. This game card from *Catholicopoly*, for example, charges depending on how many chapels the player has built:

> Make general repairs
> on all property.
>
> $25 per chapel.
> $100 per cathedral.

Episcopopoly includes similar cards within an entire category of such expenses: Operating Budget cards. These are practical, noting the need for roof repairs, as well as silly, trying to be contemporary and relevant like many of the other games.

> Organist joins
> heavy metal rock group.
>
> Go back 3 spaces.

The attempt at relevance is a form of promotion, trying to attract young people through appearing tuned in to youth culture. Other *Episcopopoly* cards point as well to the need to market one's institution and religious "brand," a need that seems to be felt by religious institutions across the United States.

> Your church begins
> a Marketing Program.
>
> Advance to Episcopal
> Media Center.

Another significant economic issue is raising money for missionary work—obviously a central theme in *Missionary Conquest*. In this game, Financial Opportunities cards allow players to earn money for missions. These opportunities include, for example, a pharmacy, golf course, hot dog stand, oil well, and the stock market. Players roll a die to see how much they will gain or lose through these enterprises. In some cases their gains raise ethical issues: a "pharmacist" can receive $4000 because of the sufferings of others during cold and flu season, or $5000 for being the first store in town to stock a new muscle drug. But the principle is clear. Missionaries need money to finance missions, and that money must be earned somewhere. Though money does not win the game, raising more money means that a player can go on a mission to a more expensive area, with the opportunity to gain more Blessing Points and thus win the game.

Missionary work is based on the Christian obligation to spread the gospel, the word of God, a motivation that is behind a number of the Christian games. While most of these games fulfill this aim through their educational role, teaching the Bible for example, a few of them are divinely inspired; God may even suggest through visions ways to carry out this obligation. Réal Breton, the creator of the French Canadian game *Kingdom of Heaven*, explains how the game came to him in a vision:

> A few month [sic] ago, as I was praying to the Lord for a stable job, I asked Him in these words: "Lord, give me something that will, primarily, glorify your Name and will allow me to live in a secure way, while bringing help to your children in difficult situations." One night, as I laid in wait of Him, the idea of making His Kingdom known through a christian [sic] game, crossed my mind. I could easily explain the Kingdom of heaven, but, to reveal it in a game, was a totally different matter.
>
> I couldn't conceive a drawing that would best represent the Kingdom of heaven. So I explained my problem to the Lord and, as I meditated in prayer, I heard a gentle voice from within inspiring these words: "You are in the world, but you are not of the world." That was it! A big crown immediately came to my mind showing the state of the world with all its covetousness and miseries. . . .

All who have tried the game have expressed the desire to own one. . . . The results have stunned me. I could see the influence this game could have on the unsaved family members of christian [*sic*] brothers and sisters. Through curiosity and, by the grace of God, they might come to know their Saviour.[15]

Games are simply one more way to bring the gospel to the world.

That a game can be used to proselytize, to spread the gospel, points to the fact that this message can be carried through diverse means, and many ways of promoting churches and the word of God have been used. Indeed, the push for churches to attract members was partly through economic necessity and partly through the proselytizing spirit; the connections between Christianity, money, and evangelism are complex.

The link between Protestantism and business has deeper roots than simply the need for churches to survive in a competitive religious economy. The need for financial resources, whether to fix the roof or pay salaries, is one side of the practical relationship between religious institutions and money in any tradition; in Christianity, particularly Protestantism, the obligation to support missionary work strengthens that need. Another practical element

The Kingdom of Heaven game

in the connection between religion and money in the United States is the need for institutional growth driven by the separation of Church and State; a necessity that gave rise to practices leading to consumerism itself. Many of the competitive methods developed by various Protestant denominations to attract new members form the core of consumer marketing today.[16] Evangelism and proselytizing are, after all, ways of selling Christianity to people, of bringing the gospel to the world. In adopting business models, churches were also fulfilling religious obligations.

But churches did not just adopt business models, they created them as well. Advertising, the force that drives consumerism, has links to the history of evangelism in the United States. "Nineteenth-century revivalists with their appeals to profess Christ helped sanctify choice: choosing Christ yielded emotional well-being. Similarly, happiness could result from selecting a product in the marketplace."[17] In the twentieth century, Protestant adaptation to the business ethos contributed to economic modernization, and at the same time this adaptation changed their vision as values such as efficiency and results replaced a purer spiritual vision.[18]

The new vision came to include the idea that living well in this world was an indication of a positive spiritual state; there is a clear link in some Christian views between living right in the eyes of God and having adequate (or more than adequate) income. While church doctrine glorifies God over mammon and contrasts this world and the next, "Elaborate church architecture was a visible sign of 'worldly success'"[19]—a concrete sign that one was right with God. Worldly goods are symbolic of one's spiritual state; thus God is concerned with management of personal wealth.

Missionary Conquest imparts this message of financial responsibility, though rather than gaining or losing money one gains or loses Blessing Points, which are required to win.

> The bank called!
> You had checks returned
> for insufficient funds—again!
>
> Lose 50 Blessing Points.

Fiscal responsibility is not the only economic activity that concerns God; He also apparently punishes harshly those who practice vocational independence.

> You did not consult God
> concerning a major job change.
> The results were disastrous.
>
> Lose 50 Blessing Points.

The complex relationship between religion and money also wends its way through *The Richest Christian*. On the one hand, this game is based on proverbs that convey ethical approaches to money. On the other hand, clearly God's will is for Christians to be not only ethical but smart in their fiduciary affairs:

> "He becometh poor that dealeth
> with a slack hand . . ." Prov 10:4
>
> Your house needs a new roof.
> You take the first bidder and
> he overcharges you. Lose $800.

Other themes relating to spirituality and money are also portrayed in religious games. Translating these ideas into play can result in rather literal interpretations, however, as is apparent in *The Richest Christian*, where spoiling the soul is equated with losing $800.

> "Rob not the poor, because he is poor . . .
> for the Lord will . . . spoil the soul of those
> that spoil them." Prov 22:22, 23
>
> You hire a new maid who desperately needs
> work, and you pay her less than the required
> minimum wage. The Lord is grieved and allows
> you to lose $800.

In this game, players not only tend to their worldly concerns in order to safeguard their money, they can also amass Eternal Treasures for proper and ethical financial behavior.

> "Do good, and lend, hoping for nothing again; and your reward shall be great . . . " (Luke 6:35)
>
> You have the opportunity to lend $600 to the player, other than yourself, with the least money. If you do, receive 20,000 ETERNAL TREASURES. (The money is never repaid.)

If the player knows that 20,000 Eternal Treasures are the reward for giving this money, then does it qualify as money freely given, "hoping for nothing"? In any case, the link between ethical behavior and financial reward and punishment is made clear in this game.

Financial incentives are integral to many of the games, though they are not necessarily used to reinforce ethical understanding. In some places religious games incorporate religious themes, while in others they mirror secular games with simply a change of language or context, as demonstrated in this example from *Catholicopoly*.

> Your Last Supper painting won 1st place at the parish fish fry.
>
> Collect $200.

Often, secular game play translated into a religious framework mixes with religious doctrine or ethics; there is apparently no contradiction in the combination of secular and religious play.

In many games values and morals emerge through ethical situations provoked by random choice of cards. In *Journeys of Paul*, Obstacle cards present situations such as being arrested by Romans. Depth and subtlety vary greatly among different games. *Journeys of Paul* is a teaching game targeting an older population; the variety and sophistication of its cards reflect this. The *Armor of God Board Game*, on the other hand, is aimed at children ages five and up, which is reflected in its lessons. For example, a player who picks this card is punished for mistreating others.[20]

> You know that God can help you stop teasing
> other kids, but you choose to make fun
> of them anyway.
>
> Give back the Shield of Faith.

In *Mortality*, Trial of Faith cards portray values, making an effort to be homey, humorous, and relevant to children's lives, while at the same time teaching lessons such as forgiveness:

> Your daughter's pet gerbil gets out and
> your neighbor's cat eats it.
>
> If you have 30 or more Testimonies, you forgive
> and forget and gain 15. If you don't, lose 15.

If not forgiveness, then perhaps the player needs to learn that domestic skills are also religious endeavors:

> Your visiting teacher just drops by
> unannounced and your house is a mess. If you
> have less than 30 Testimonies, you are
> offended and lose 10. If you have 30 or more,
> offer her a piece of banana bread and gain 10.

In *Mortality*, the more moral a life you have led, the more Testimonies you have. The more Testimonies you have, the easier it is to get Testimonies. Spiritually speaking, it is not possible to pull yourself up by the bootstraps in this game. But maybe all it takes is getting the family in a better mood.

> Everyone in the family is crabby for
> Family Home Evening,
> and no one listens to your lessons.
> If you have 25 or more Testimonies gain 10.
> If not, lose 5.

Here, as with other cards we have seen, the game designers attempt to be amusing and relevant, and there is something to be said for this approach. An overbearing or didactic manner would hardly lend itself to game play. The acknowledgment of how people live and their everyday relationships is one of the ways that games reflect lived religion, but it also draws people into play. Rather than *telling* children what they should be doing, games demonstrate it through lightness and fun, as though the players could be infused with a religious ethos through play.

Not all games take this approach. As we have noted, religious games teach more than ethics; many games are knowledge based, and often these use a more instructive style. Christian games that teach Bible knowledge or the life of Christ are examples, as are Muslim games, which are often based on the *Trivial Pursuit* structure. Answering questions about *salat* (prayer) or the *hajj* (pilgrimage), for example, determines whether or not one can move forward. The *Hajj Fun Game* asks questions such as "How many days must a pilgrim spend in performing Hajj?" and "What is the name of the sunset prayer?" Many Jewish games are similarly knowledge based. In *The Holigame: A Celebration of Jewish Holidays*, one question card reads: "During which holiday is it customary to stay awake all night to study the Torah?"

In a similar effort to educate, Buddhist games aim to demonstrate the working of karma through the roll of the dice—a different way of conveying knowledge. *Karma Chakra*, intending to educate players not only about karma but also about basic Buddhist concepts, includes the reading of Buddhist texts as an integrated part of play. *The Mahabharata Game* takes game-playing knowledge to another level; it comes with a thirty-eight-page instruction booklet that includes an extremely abbreviated version of the Mahabharata, one of Hinduism's most fundamental and significant myths.

Some games make an effort to bring a light touch to imparting knowledge. In *Let My People Go*, for example, players move forward or back by picking up cards with rhymes about the origins of Judaism. . . .

> A burning bush
> Moses did see
> The start of redemption
>
> Move up three.

. . . or the exodus of the Jews from Egypt. . . .

We're slaves in Egypt
There's so much to do.
You get tired

Move back two.

Pharaoh is surprised
there are frogs in his bed.
Another plague's starting

Move seven ahead.

In this game, moves are not dependent on the player's knowledge; this is perhaps because it is aimed at younger children (ages four to eight). It attempts to teach about Jewish history and the origins of Passover, but it does so through humor.

The *Exodus* game is another game that teaches about Passover. Note the wheel of plagues at lower right.

Religious games, tied into popular culture, religious promotion, and evangelism, not only use diverse methods of teaching but also teach diverse aspects of religion. Ethics, financial issues, Scripture, and other aspects of religious life and practice are conveyed not merely as separate elements: they relate to each other through game play. This form of transmission communicates their interconnectedness.

The medium of game cards can also be multidimensional. Even cards that seem relatively simple may be able to transmit different aspects of religiosity to different players, depending on their experience and maturity. For example, the *Armor of God* card, displayed earlier, teaches a very young child about not teasing others. But it also speaks to one's relationship with God and the place of human will—both highly sophisticated issues.

Religious games and toys also present the opportunity to communicate in different modes at the same time. *Episcopopoly*, as we have seen, includes a variety of financially oriented game cards. But it is also the case that the game itself was created as a fundraising project. Churches that donated to this project are featured on the game board, and the instructions for the game include information about this effort.

Christian *Funtastic Fitness Game*

Religious games convey lived religion—religion that weaves itself through all aspects of daily life: finances, jobs, relationships, and more. Rather than focusing on textual religion, these games naturally encompass all aspects of life as the focus of their religiosity . . . including fitness and weight. It is not just your financial activities or morals that interest God; He also wants you to be thin and fit. The Christian *Funtastic Fitness Game* makes this perfectly clear.

> If God should one day ask you to account
> for the stewardship of your own physical body,
> what would be on your ledger?
> Remember he is a kind Father!
>
> Answer then advance 1 space.

If you need evidence that God cares what size you wear, just check your Bible:

> Do Christians have a source of power
> to become Fit that non-Christians don't
> possess? John 15:7 is powerful!
>
> Answer then advance 1 space.

The Christian *Funtastic Fitness Game* playing cards propose that looking good and being in shape are qualities that Jesus "wants in order for you to be an effective servant." With this in mind, "What are some of the things YOU might have to do to Get Fit for the King?"[21]

The *Tales of Glory* talking Jesus doll could provide a model for Christian fitness. He is as muscular as any he-man action figure—upon seeing this doll one student exclaimed, "Whoa, Jesus is really buff!"

At first glance, this convergence of twenty-first-century evangelism and body cult appears strange. Doesn't God care about one's spiritual life rather than physical appearance? But as we have seen, according to these games God cares about your finances and your job choices; fitness is just one more element of daily life that can be included in a Christian lifestyle. Sacralizing seemingly mundane activities can also be understood through the lens of a sacred universe, the world made sacred. As in Islam, as in Hinduism, there is nothing in the world that is not part of the sacred or outside the realm of religion. In this case it includes fitness; in others it includes finances and commerce . . . or toys.

A Sacred Investment

As we have noted, the majority of religious games are Christian. Christian toys emerged from a long history of Christian retailing and from what media scholar Heather Hendershot, in *Shaking the World for Jesus*, describes as the development of a commercial approach to evangelism. This change included a reversal of attitudes toward religious imagery and a transformation from generally inferior products to those of decent quality or better.[22] She disagrees with the outlook that commercializing religion is a sign of superficiality, noting that "American religions have always been players, in one way or another, in the marketplace of culture."[23] Even targeting children was a logical approach, since they were considered "the group most vulnerable to the lure of secular culture's pleasures."[24]

But as natural as the evolution may be, there are still aspects of the marriage of religion and commerce in promoting religious toys that do not always sit comfortably. Just as the association of religion with fitness is disconcerting for many, the strength and tone of marketing of religious games and dolls sometimes strikes an odd chord. While many of these items aim to convey and instill ethical values and religious ideals, sales are also important. For example, marketing material for the *Kingdom of Heaven* game covers several bases, promoting the game as a miracle, an excellent gift, a powerful evangelistic tool, and an invaluable investment.

> This game is a **miracle**. Mr. Réal Breton had seen the power of God. He was sick even dying. He had no idea. He had no money. Yet in all, God had answered his prayers. He was given new health, a new project and the necessary financing.
>
> This game is an **excellent gift** for the family and the friends. You will have a good time playing the game together while learning the Bible. Also, you might eventually lead one of your dear ones to the kingdom of Heaven.

This game is a **powerful evangelistic tool**. In playing the game, a person may be led to the Kingdom of Heaven. . . .

This game is an **invaluable investment**. It worths [*sic*] $40 plus taxes. But we had made a special price taxes included: $25. If buying 2, it will be $20 each. For a modest amount, you may receive an invaluable return, even a harvest of life eternal, that is when someone is led to Christ. Is there a better investment?[25]

Although the association of life eternal and advertising language may sound jarring, the marketing of *Kingdom of Heaven* is sincere; the more that are sold, the greater the possibility that more souls will be brought to Christ.

Nonevangelistic religions do not have the same proselytizing push; nonetheless, they also promote sales: "All *BuddhaWheel* Buddhas are entitled to start future games as a Buddha. . . . Get your own *BuddhaWheel* and become a *BuddhaWheel* Buddha yourself!"[26] Here, as with the juxtaposition of eternal life and investment in the *Kingdom of Heaven* example above, the combination of sacred transformation into Buddhahood and promotion seems oddly dissonant.

Dolls join in the sales game as well. We have already seen in chapter 2 the extravagant cost of many of the religious dolls. But the profit motive behind religious dolls goes even deeper than that, especially in Fulla's case. Although seemingly worlds apart, Barbie and Fulla are equally invested in capitalist consumerism and advertising strategies. Marketing for both Barbie and Fulla enthusiastically participates in the "razor and razor blade" business strategy, a marketing approach originally developed by Ruth and Elliot Handler of Mattel.[27] "The doll is analogous to the 'razor,' and the accessories are the 'razor blades' that continue to sell long after the doll."[28] Once even one doll is purchased, the consumer has a huge variety of accessories to choose from—each sold separately, of course. Handler's strategy is widespread throughout the world of dolls.

Fulla has a range of merchandise rivaling Barbie's, including an extensive line of clothing and fashion accessories designed and sized for both dolls and little girls, including lunch boxes, silverware, stationery, backpacks, and luggage. Originally produced with her very own pink prayer rug, prayer beads, and pink shoes, Katherine Zoepf observes that now

> it is nearly impossible to walk into a corner shop in Syria or Egypt or Jordan or Qatar without encountering Fulla break- fast cereal or Fulla chewing gum or not to see little girls pedaling down the street on their Fulla bicycles, all in trade- mark "Fulla pink." . . . Children who want to dress like their dolls can buy a matching girl-size prayer rug and cotton scarf set, all in pink.[29]

Fulla's Syrian creator NewBoy uses Western-style television advertising methods to create "a profitable buzz among little girls across the region, who—like their Western counterparts—compete to be first in the playground with the latest spin-off product."[30] "On the children's satellite channels popular in the Arab world, Fulla advertising is incessant. . . . If you've got a TV in the house, it's Fulla all the time."[31] Clearly, if the advertisements on Arabic satel- lite television are any indication, Fulla is a seasoned shopper who could give Barbie a run for her money—she even has shag iPod pil- lows in different colors (large or small), and Bling Bling, a beaded jewelry craft set whose on-box promotional hype rivals any.

> In this kit we Bling you everything you need: Metal Beads, Glass Beads, Elastic Thread, and easy to Bling instructions! That's enough to make 24 Blinging Bracelets and 12 Rings! Bling your friends over and have a Bling Bling bracelet and ring party!

Ironically, Fulla is marketed as a parent's answer to, and in con- trast to, Barbie's consumerism. She is meant to represent modesty in all respects. Perhaps her manufacturers and marketing team are not familiar with the meaning of "bling bling" as ostentatious jewelry, with ties to hip hop culture.

There is no clear demarcation of where good taste is left behind in the drive for profits. For many Americans the annual commer- cialization of Christmas, the most obvious place where religion, toys, and marketing come together, definitely crosses the line. Christmas goods seem to be advertised earlier each year—with Christmas marketing occurring as early as October. There are even "Christmas in July" shopping extravaganzas on television's home shopping channels.

An early contributor to the commercializing of Christmas was John Wanamaker, a religious Presbyterian who in the early twentieth century "turned the Grand Court of his Philadelphia store into a veritable cathedral, replete with stained glass, stars, and angelic statuary,"[32] evoking religious sentiments so strongly that "many men reportedly removed their hats in a gesture of instinctive reverence."[33] When protests arose over the commercialization of Christmas, "[t]he cries that churches carried to the Protestant-founded department stores of Macy's, Wanamaker's, and Marshall Field's to 'put Christ back in Christmas' only served to stir up a market for manufactured crèches, cards with religious messages, and recorded sacred music."[34]

In protest at the almost overwhelming message to buy, buy, buy, some people simply choose not to celebrate the holiday. The Christmas Resistance Movement promotes awareness of alternatives on its Web site:

> You know holiday shopping is offensive and wasteful. You know Christmas "wish lists" and "gift exchanges" degrade the concept of giving. You know Christmas marketing is a scam, benefiting manufacturers, stores, and huge corporations, while driving individuals into debt. You know this annual consumer frenzy wreaks havoc on the environment, filling landfills with useless packaging and discarded gifts.
>
> Yet, every year, you cave in and go shopping.
>
> The relentless onslaught of advertising exerts constant pressure. So do the unified bleatings of herds of shoppers, who call you "Scrooge" if you fail to enthusiastically join their ritual orgy of consumption. Friends and family needle you with gift requests, store windows beckon with shiny colorful packages, the same "classic" holiday jingles are piped constantly through every speaker in town.
>
> How can you resist?
>
> Join the Christmas Resistance Movement![35]

Another online protest site is Redefine Christmas, which aims at channeling money that would have been spent on gifts to charity. "It's not about reinventing the holiday. It's about changing the way we look at gift giving and receiving. It's taking money we usually spend on obligatory gifts with little meaning, and creating gifts of charity that give in multiple ways, to the receiver, the giver, and people who truly need."[36] While the intention may be commendable, the language of this Web site contains allusions meant to massage the reader's ego, such as references to uniqueness—which in the United States today is considered an essential quality that, ironically, everyone should have.

> With millions of charities, there are undoubtedly at least a few related to your unique interests, beliefs or hobbies.
>
> Give Charitably Now![37]

If you would like friends to make these charitable donations in lieu of gifts to you, you can send a card to let them know your favorite charities, wishing them a "Merry Redefined Christmas"; you can even link to a variety of social networks such as Facebook to share or post your wishes.

Redefine Christmas does not reference religion in calling for a charitable alternative to Christmas giving; it appears to be simply a humanistic call to spend money on others who need it. "Imagine if there was more charity and less materialism in Christmas giving."[38] But in a manner similar to the association of eternal life with investment or Buddhahood with sales seen earlier in this chapter, the promotional approach and advertising techniques used at this site hit a peculiar note, seemingly contradictory to their altruistic aims. In the same way that ads for profit-making ventures manipulate our desires and aspirations, this site plays on sentiment. In early 2009 the Web site featured a heartwarming video clip of musician Buddy Guy declaring that this year he is supporting the Prostate Cancer Foundation, with "Oh Holy Night" playing in the background. All the emotional stops are pulled out in order to make the most of the Christmas spirit. Marketing and consumer culture are so pervasive that it is difficult to escape their framework, as will be discussed further in chapter 4.

While The Christmas Resistance Movement rests on an anti-consumption message and Redefine Christmas aims to redirect holiday spending to charity, the most common attitude of protest is still the call to "Put Christ back in Christmas," often seen during the holiday season on billboards for churches or related organizations such as the Knights of Columbus. Organizations like Buy Nothing Christmas, started by Canadian Mennonites, call on consumers to boycott consumerist Christmas traditions on the basis that the "real" message is being lost, that the true tradition is being sullied. They even have a "Buy Nothing Catalogue": "Finally, a Christmas catalogue with things you really want . . . and already have!"[39] This is a manifestation of the ideal of pure religion and authenticity, though in this case it comes from a grassroots effort rather than from the religious powers that be.

Religion Takes Practice

Until recently, lived religion was regarded as a lesser or lower form of religion, the little tradition, in contrast to the great tradition, religion of study and text. Scholarship on religion focused on the traditions of the educated and literate elite, as if those represented ideal examples of the religion separate and distinct from—and better than—the "lesser" traditions of common people.[40] But such a narrow focus on organized and institutional religion overlooks and even dismisses religions as they are lived and practiced by people every day (including playing with religious games and dolls). Although some religious narratives seem grounded in a dualistic distinction between sacred and profane or between secular and worldly, for most of history religion reflected how human beings understood and lived in the multiple dimensions of their world.

The little tradition, also called "folk religion" or "popular religion," often referred to what was thought of as women's religion, practices that frequently centered around home or family. These forms of religiosity did not focus on books; throughout most of history in most places few people could read. These were therefore the religions of people practicing in a way that related directly to the needs of their everyday lives. As such, these traditions included men as well as women, as archaeologist and anthropologist William Dever points out.

> [M]ost men in ancient Israel were in the same boat as virtually all women. The folk religion, or "popular religion," that we are trying to reconstruct here, despite its major emphasis

on women's cults and their role in family rituals, was the religion of nearly all men as well. At least it was for all except the fraction of 1 percent of men who happened to have written the Bible. They were "folk," too.[41]

Religion was simply how people lived, including all aspects of their lives—from birth and death to family and social relationships to food choice and preparation to trade and commerce.

The scholarly distinction between "higher" and "lower" forms of religion has roots in Christianity, where there is a long history of struggle between the religion of the elite and so-called popular religion. The notion of an ideal or pure religion was historically encouraged by the institutional hierarchy of the Church, which attempted to keep Holy Scripture from being contaminated by dissemination among the general public through print, especially in languages of the people—languages other than Latin. "Reading . . . was deliberately discouraged in Christian Europe" in order to preserve the orthodoxy established by religious councils.[42] Scholarship itself was closely tied to religious elites in the West—literacy being initially the domain of the clergy.

Another connection between the dualistic view of religion and Christianity is that Christianity is exclusive, in the sense that being Christian excludes being anything else. While it is certainly not the only religion that requires this, to be Christian means taking Jesus Christ as the Savior and the Way, which gives it a particular flavor. Exclusivity is not a quality of all traditions. In Japan one can have a Shinto wedding and a Buddhist funeral with no contradiction.

Partly because of the exclusive nature of Christianity, Christian leaders have tried to eradicate local practices that appear to conflict with Christianity—or at least to keep them separate from Christian practices. When people cannot or will not simply stop their traditional practices, variations in worship styles occur—sometimes even erupting in conflict. These variations may take the form of differences in singing, movement, or other physical expressions during worship services, or styles of symbolic imagery, but they can also be more extreme.[43] The question of how Christianity interacts with preexisting religious practices and beliefs is an active one. Rather than being erased, traditional practices often become transformed; older deities become saints, for example.

Christian missionaries, priests, and nuns living or working in non-Christian cultures often have complex relationships with those of other traditions. These relationships can be marked by deep respect and learning, rather than dominance. Where the contact between Christianity and other cultures emerges in the games, however, it is sometimes marked by stereotypical and patronizing points of view.

These types of attitudes arise in *The Richest Christian*:

> For ye . . . took joyfully the spoiling of your goods, knowing in yourselves that ye have in heaven a better and an enduring substance."
> Hebrews 10:34
> You have the opportunity to be a missionary to an uncivilized tribe. If you do, the natives there steal your clothes and dishes and you must pay $1000 to replace the necessities.
> Receive 40,000 ETERNAL TREASURES.
> (Purchase the items from the player on your left.)

In the interest of humor, odd pieces of irreverence and ignorance also surface, here from *Missionary Conquest*:

> The food is bad but so is your attitude.
>
> Lose 25 Blessings.[44]

Another example from *Missionary Conquest* is a Saudi Arabia card, which speaks about proselytizing in Mecca; but Mecca, the most sacred city in Islam, is closed to non-Muslims. Christian missionaries would not be allowed in. Furthermore, to preach conversion on the holy ground of another tradition is, at best, disrespectful.

Political issues arise not only between competing religions and cultures, but also within religious traditions. *Vatican: The Board Game*, designed as a teaching tool, portrays the process of choosing a new pope and does not hesitate to address issues of political and religious institutional power. Players start as cardinals with points awarded or subtracted for country of origin, age, and health. Moral choices made along the way allow players to gain or lose influence as they move toward the conclave and the vote for the next pope. The game simulates the real processes of gaining influence: "A cardinal can be appointed by the pope to various high profile positions" and can also "achieve fame in the pastoral realm." As honest as the designer, Stephen Haliczer, is about the realities of Catholic institutional maneuvering, he also places players within the realm of play by including a Spiritual Perfection space as well as the Cesspool of Sin. In addition, there is a Confessional box where the cardinals perform penance after they have fallen into the cesspool.

This game demonstrates the possibility of achieving a balance between teaching and play. Doctrine is not compromised in the interest of sales. The Spiritual Perfection space, for example, is reached through a ladder showing the purgative, illuminative, and unitive stages of ascent. And while the instructions state that the game "assumes no theological biases," Haliczer clearly did not play fast and free with the material. Control of information is a central feature of institutional religion, and although this is "just a game," even in play it is dangerous to toy with doctrine. As we will see in chapter 5, play is not always harmless. Play, like ritual, can be subversive; it can undermine existing structures.

Institutions maintain power through exerting authority, and for the Catholic Church this is done through regulating doctrine as well as practices. We have already mentioned that with the invention of the printing press, orthodoxy was threatened. It was thought that if ordinary people could read the Bible then they would interpret it for themselves rather than accepting the interpretations that came from those in power in the Church; in this way the truth, at least the truth as understood by those in power, could be contaminated.[45] Control of words and access to text was an attempt to safeguard the purity of the tradition, based on a conception that there was only one true interpretation, and that there was a pure form of the religion that could be protected from corruption.

But objects as well as words can be interpreted; the struggle for control over the *correct* interpretation of truth includes the control of material culture. In the past, in the Catholic Church, this included very detailed lists of sacramentals, how to use them, and what their benefits were.[46] It also applied to the effort to define "taste" and proper Christian art, which among other things meant a proper masculine image of Christ, and images of the Virgin that were beautiful yet not sexually arousing.[47] Mary and Esther dolls embody reflections of this attitude.

Religious imagery conveys sacred ideals and experiences directly to the worshipper. In Buddhism and Hinduism, and also in certain forms of Christianity, such as Eastern Orthodoxy, Coptic Christianity, and Catholicism, images are a significant and integral part of worship. In Hinduism, being in the presence of a holy image means participating in a sacred exchange. Contrastingly, Judaism and Islam forbid certain sacred images, such as images of God or Muhammad. Within these traditions it is understood that the sacred cannot be conveyed through sensory imagery; images of God would reduce the transcendent to a limited form and could potentially distort a worshipper's relationship to the sacred. In forbidding images of the sacred, their potential impact is revealed.

The power of religious imagery is also evident in attempts to regulate it. Control of images was a central aspect of the Reformation; not only was the veneration of images questioned, statues of saints were destroyed as well. The power of Buddhist imagery can be seen in the fact that in 2001 the Taliban found it necessary to destroy ancient Buddhist statues in Afghanistan. If these images had no power, they would not be dangerous and would not have needed to be destroyed.

Echoes of past attitudes of control over images exist today in the United States and can be seen with religious toys, especially with dolls. In chapter 2 we noted how proper body image and attitudes toward modesty are central elements in promotion and marketing of religious dolls in general. This control of and through religious objects reflects the transformation from a focus on text-based religion to an understanding that religion includes many diverse practices.

The Materiality of Religion

No religion exists in a book. Religion exists in the lives and practices of embodied, sensing, feeling, thinking beings. Because we
are sensing, feeling, and thinking beings we need to experience
and express our religions or spiritualities through our bodies, and
one way we experience religion is through objects. Objects convey
meaning and symbolism, and enable people to come into relation
with the sacred. The need for this relation, for this connection,
moves people to bring the sacred into all facets of their lives. Religious objects in the home link the ordinary and sacred worlds.[48]

Religious games and toys are part of a whole world of religious
objects that range from ritual implements, which can only be used
(or in some cases even viewed) by initiates, to religious key chains
and even socks—everyday items with religious symbols printed
on them. Sacred symbols and objects have entered popular culture
through avenues such as Madonna—whose name and use of Christian imagery in sexually arousing videos caused controversy—and
the growth of the T-shirt market, an industry ever hungry for new
images.[49] One notable example is a Christian T-shirt that states
"Body Piercing Saved My Life," with an image of a block of wood
with a hand and a large nail through the center of the palm, clearly
meant to represent the crucifixion.[50] The irony of the message is
the association of a secular practice, body piercing (often regarded
as non- or even antireligious), with a message of salvation, but it is
lent further impact by the image's gruesome quality.

The use of religious images in irreverent or sacrilegious ways
draws on the power of irony or contradiction as well. The further
from its traditional role, the more powerful is the impact of the
reinterpreted symbol. While the aim may be simply to show that
a symbol is not the reality and can be reimagined, using religious
symbols in contexts that are taboo shocks and displeases more
conservative viewers. But the value of long-standing symbols goes
much deeper than the commercial interests that feed the urge to
create a popular new style. The meaning of a symbol is embedded
in and draws on history, social relations, cultural context, family and individual experience, and much more. Symbols are deeply

implicated in personal and cultural identity. This is why the intentional "mis-use" of religious symbols is so potent.

Perhaps this also underlies some of the queasiness over the use of religious themes and images in toys. Such usage feels out of place, decontextualized, inappropriate. One example of this is the label on the Messengers of Faith "Tales of Glory" talking Jesus doll box, which identifies the contents in large type as

Jesus
God's Son

producing a strong dissonance in some people.

An example of seemingly out-of-place symbols in games is the Fruits of the Spirit cards from the *Kingdom of Heaven* game.[51] In this case the symbols of the Fruits of the Spirit are not being intentionally misused, but the application is still disconcerting. Game cards of "souls won to the Lord," or "Fruits of the Spirit," take deep theological concepts and reduce them to collected or manipulated objects. But to save souls, any means is allowed. The symbols and concepts of salvation need to be put out into the world in order to bring the influence of another world into this one. Game cards are fair game, so to say, in the quest to bring others to salvation.

Sometimes the effort to make sacred concepts into play as game pieces has odd results, as in the *Inheritance* game, which uses "lamb chips." Though these sound like something from *Gourmet* magazine, they are a reference to Jesus as the Lamb of God. This connection is further developed in the instructions "The Winning player rings the bell and declares, 'Worthy is the Lamb!! Worthy is the Lamb!!' "[52]

As we have seen in chapter 1, the playing pieces of the games are symbolic. *Catholicopoly* and *Episcopopoly* have wonderfully evocative pieces, exactly the same style but slightly different symbols. Both have angels, for example, but one has wings spread. The ark, dove, Bible, donkey, and bishop's mitre are also represented. *Episcopopoly* also uses small wooden offering plates during play.

The symbolic and emotional value of these items calls on more than just representational meaning. Small playing pieces have magical qualities for children. They invoke other worlds, as does ritual, and even in adulthood this special quality can be recalled.

In combination with tactile input and religious symbolism, the magic of play may deeply embed those symbols in children's feelings and psyches.

But games are only one place where we see these symbols. Some of the Christian goods available include beach towels, candy and cookies, socks, wallets, blankets, golf balls, ties, T-shirts, caps, checkbook covers, key chains, mugs, jewelry, umbrellas, switch plates, totes, backpacks, luggage, and items for indoor and outdoor décor. These come primarily with crosses, the fish symbol (with or without crosses), and Scripture quotes. People use these items to identify themselves as Christians, both to themselves and to others, but they also are a means of interaction between people: "Artifacts become particularly important in the lives of average Christians because objects can be exchanged, gifted, reinterpreted, and manipulated."[53]

Indeed, the use of religious symbols on everyday goods raises interesting questions about changing meanings. Looking at these items as an outsider, some are more perplexing than others. Mugs, key chains, and T-shirts have become common ways to convey messages, but beach towels and socks present some problems. Beach towels are used in the most casual of settings. Is it appropriate to sit on a crucifix or bit of Scripture in a bikini? Harrods, the famous London department store, was forced to remove a line of designer underwear and bikinis with images of Hindu deities on them.[54]

Socks are worn on the feet, the lowest part of the body, which in some traditions are symbolic of the lowest part of the self. In Sikhism one must not point one's feet toward the holy book, the *Guru Granth Sahib*. In Christian practice, the ritual washing of feet on Holy Thursday is a reminder of humility. And although the symbols themselves are not on the sole of the sock, it would seem to debase the symbols, and by association the religion, to wear religious symbols on the feet. Though it seems that way to outsiders, religious studies scholar Colleen McDannell has found that for Christians who use these items, these symbols cannot be lowered by association with the everyday.

> Families who use Christian merchandise do not find it sacrilegious or in bad taste to wear baseball caps with "Jesus

Christ, He's the Real Thing" stitched on them. Nor do they think paper napkins decorated with blue ducks and the phrase "Praise the Lord" inappropriate for a ladies' luncheon. Children get combs imprinted with "Can't bear to be without Jesus" as party favors. When I point out to Christians that baseball caps get sweaty, napkins are thrown in the trash, and combs get coated with dandruff, their attitudes do not change. The objects—caps, napkins, combs—are good in themselves. The phrases are excellent Christian sentiments. Sweat or dirt or dandruff cannot profane either the object or the ideas. Holiness is achieved through proper behavior and not normally through the intrinsic meaning of an object. What is important is the promotion of the Bible. Fashion, advertising, popular culture and style are merely the medium for the message.[55]

Perhaps the sacred nature of the symbols sanctifies these everyday items by association. They are no longer merely ordinary, they are now Christian, and imbued with greater meaning. But the items we use in our everyday lives *are* ordinary. We use them automatically, hardly looking at them except when they are new and exciting. When religious symbols are used on everyday objects, they become part of the ordinary materials with which people interact during the day. Symbols can lose their ability to evoke deeper meaning.

Nonetheless, as McDannell notes, the purpose of wearing and displaying these symbols is not the search for deeper meaning, it is to promote the Bible and the Christian way of life. And promotion is deeply embedded in American religious life.

Consuming Ideals

Religion and commerce have always had a necessary interrelationship. The form that relationship takes varies depending on the particular historical, cultural, and religious context. The separation of Church and State, evangelism, and contemporary consumer culture are among the factors that have created the specific flavor of religio-commerce in the United States today. And although the tension between religion and money has deep roots in Judeo-Christian-Islamic and Buddhist traditions, it is not the relationship between religion and money that is the problem, but rather the relationship between religion and a consumerism perceived as wildly out of control—buying and having as a way of life—that unsettles many of us.

While it is not clear to some Americans, especially the young, why consumerism is a problem, others see consumers as passive and without agency, manipulated by corporate greed and commercial interests. Consumer culture is self-absorbed, driven by shallowness—the self as the object of consumption as well as the subject who consumes. Consumer culture is all about indulgence and self-gratification, which replace traditional religious teachings about self-discipline and restraint. The perception of an overwhelming commercialization and commodification of society, in which everything is for sale—even spirituality—causes the unease.

The mixture of consumerism with religiosity is apparent on some Web sites. Christianbook.com, besides the many Bibles, crafts and educational materials, clothing, and other items, sells not one but two toy ATMs.[56] The connection between these toys and Christian ideals is obscure, if indeed it exists at all. The same question applies to another toy, the *Little Spender* game,[57] which teaches children how to spend money.[58] Perhaps consumerism is so inextricably bound to religious culture at this point that for some people the presence of toy ATMs on a Web site ostensibly selling religious goods is not an issue.

Religious Web sites sell nonreligious consumer-oriented goods, but more disturbing to many is that religious items themselves seem to have become simply consumer products. Under a consumerist lifestyle, religion becomes just another shopping experience, in which individuals can pick and choose from an attractive display of religious beliefs, objects, and practices removed from their contexts. They become mere "lifestyle choices," or even hot new looks, as this online promotion claims:

> Bindi on forehead! As old as tradition and as new as the times, the bindi has come of age. With a change in perceptions about beauty and adornment, the aboriginal Indian Bindiya, the symbol of inner shakti, the fabled red dot "kumkum" that the women wore in the center of their forehead has now become a fashion statement.[59]

Dream catchers, Zen alarm clocks, and other religious goods are available online and in drugstores, supermarkets, or the local Wal-mart. Some of these were (or still are) sacred items, part of deep traditions that relate humans to the cosmos and to each other. But what meanings do they hold when separated from that tradition? Theologian Vincent Miller argues that the result of this separation is fragmentation and loss of coherence.

> Thus, the commodification of culture causes a number of problems for religious belief and practice . . . the most fundamental of these: a dissolution of the coherence of religions reducing them to a palette of "cultural resources" that can be employed in any number of ways—even ways fundamentally at odds with the basic logic of their original religious tradition. This fragmentation also divorces faith from practice. Symbols, beliefs and even spiritual disciplines become free-floating cultural objects ready to be put to whatever use we desire. Buddhist meditation serves as a stress management tool in a capitalist business world devoted to endless acquisition; Yoga is reduced to a physical fitness regimen; the crucifix becomes a brand symbol for niche marketing of Catholic education.[60]

Driven by what Miller terms "corporate cultural production" and a mass consumer society, everything becomes possible material to be used to make money.

Some religious items for sale are clearly inventions of postmodern culture, where anything can be linked with anything else. The Zen alarm clock, while somewhat absurd, is not particularly harmful. But a rather more striking example is a Mayan-themed resort in the Bahamas, featuring a temple waterslide as a main attraction. "The Leap of Faith slide offers the daring and adventurous, a 60 ft. almost-vertical drop from the top of the Mayan Temple, propelling riders at a tremendous speed through a clear acrylic tunnel submerged in a shark-filled lagoon." Perhaps the customer would rather try the five-story corkscrew Serpent Slide, where "guests travel on a tube at high speeds through the darkness of the Temple's core. The twisting and turning ride culminates with a leisurely pass through a clear acrylic tunnel submerged in a shark-filled lagoon. Located at the Mayan Temple."[61]

Mayan temples have been linked with human sacrifice. Though this connection is somewhat controversial, it is still difficult to understand how the idea of a resort linked with human sacrifice became a reality. Perhaps the driving need for novelty, for ever-more-unusual fusions, has dulled our sense of appropriateness. The ride through the shark-filled lagoon echoes the blood rituals of the past, a "leisurely pass" to some perhaps, but hardly a comforting one for those with even superficial familiarity with ancient Mayan practices.

As society has increasingly become a consumer culture, consumed items are not only separated from their sources but from the conditions and communities that created them as well.[62] This results in particularly ironic situations, such as children's games meant to teach Christian ethics being produced in China, notorious for its poor working conditions. And it is not just Western or Christian consumers that demand these goods. A quick look around a few Jordanian toy stores reveals that their wares are virtually identical, with many of them also mass-produced in China. Consumer society is often enabled by appalling working conditions in countries where workers lack options or alternatives to slave-like conditions. For those underpaid and exploited laborers, consumer choice is the least of their worries. Global ecology is another serious ethical problem connected with rampant consumerism. A culture based on built-in obsolescence is filling garbage dumps with nonbiodegradable materials and depleting world resources, a fact noted by The Christmas Resistance Movement[63] Promotional material for religious objects often endorses ecological awareness and compassion, yet these commodities add to the problem, as does the heavy promotion of plastic toys on religious Web sites. These ethical dilemmas are particularly poignant when one considers that we are discussing the manufacture of children's toys and games—and not just any toys and games, but ones created and marketed in order to teach ethical behaviors.

Educational toys have grown into a huge industry; after all, the consumer way of life expands into all areas of human activity and thought. As a subset of educational toys, religious toys and games cater to parents' aims for their children. And with the need for ever more specialized items, it is no surprise that these articles are market driven as well. In an article about the mainstreaming of religious toys, Jacqueline Bodnar writes,

> Toys like this couldn't come at a better time. Parents are increasingly searching for higher quality programming and entertainment options for their children. This demand is creating a whole new market for those companies that want to fill the need for wholesome toys that deliver positive messages.

> MarketResearch, an organization that provides market research analysis, reports that during 2004, the retail market for religious-themed products was about $7 billion. In fact, the demand for such products has become so strong that they are available beyond just Christian stores. With such demand for these items, powerhouses like Target and Wal-Mart are now routinely stocking their shelves with them. With this line of products, parents can give their children toys that come from stories and lessons that they are familiar with. Up until now, this has been somewhat of a rarity. But this is changing, as the demand for wholesome and positive toys strengthens.[64]

Is Religion Going to Hell?

Although there are worries that religious toys somehow separate religion from its roots, it is also possible to see the industry's growth as a revitalization of religion. Since religion is no longer as controlled by institutional monopolies, individuals are freer to practice and express religion in a "deregulated" market.[65] Religion is practiced in new ways by new people, reflecting their needs in contemporary contexts.

One reason behind the concern about religious toys may be the great vs. little tradition opposition mentioned earlier in this chapter. For those who view text-based religion as the true religion, religious games may appear frivolous, misleading, or even a corruption of traditional doctrine and values. But religious toys and games are examples of contemporary lived religion; they demonstrate the influence of popular culture on religious practice. As we have discussed, high religion was controlled by the religious and literate elite. Religious toys are a move away from text, to religious practice that takes place in the home, among friends or family, and with familiar materials and modes of representation, namely games and dolls. This move shifts power away from institutional oversight and into community relationships and the realm of everyday practice, and can be seen as a positive movement, transforming religion into an integral element of people's daily interactions and environments.

Arguably, there are other positive ramifications as well. For example, increasing sales of these games is partly due to the ease of access provided by online retailers. No longer do you need a religious store nearby. For members of minority religions this is a great advantage. American Sikhs, for example, have easy access to games and educational materials that are difficult to find in the United States.

Moreover, with all the worries about consumerism, it is still true that consuming provides meaning; it also forges social bonds. Family and community ties may even be one of the primary uses of religious games and dolls. Rather than the educational or ethical intentions that are voiced, it may be that the primary use is gift giving and exchange,[66] to cement social relationships within a given religious network. In other words, the primary value of religious games and dolls may simply be as *objects* and not as instruments of religious transmission.

All religions use objects and images to convey, manipulate, or otherwise come into relation with the sacred. "Things," in and of themselves, are not contradictory to the nature and aim of religion.[67] So the worry that the abundance of religious commodities signals a degeneration of religion seems unfounded.

But there are other concerns as well about consumer culture and religion, especially surrounding issues of choice. Consumer culture presents us with an overwhelming variety of goods, reflected in the increasing number and diversity of religious toys. Many choices are available, and we are free to choose as we wish and to use items as we see fit. To be denied adequate choices now feels to many, at least in the United States, like a denial of a basic right or freedom. Choice is understood to be a fundamental good in a consumer society, and this applies not only to religious goods but also to religion itself.

Throughout most of human history and in most cultures, religion and culture were synonymous. There was no such term as "religion," no concept of religion as something separate from culture as a whole. Many people around the world are now free to follow a different religious tradition than the one in which they were brought up, the one their family follows, the one associated with their village or national identity.

This worries those who feel that consumerism makes conversion just another lifestyle choice, but that is not necessarily the case, as Miller argues:

> There is no denying that there are shallow seekers out there wandering from community to community and tradition to tradition, consuming experiences in the selfish attempt to get their "needs" met. Studies show, however, that a substantial proportion of those who switch religious affiliation do so for considered reasons (indeed, perhaps with greater consideration than those who remain in the traditions in which they were raised) and stick with their decisions.[68]

David Lyon, a sociologist, adds that the individual search and need for connection might result in a deeper personal relationship with a chosen tradition: "today's religious choices may reflect a seriousness of faith that did not figure in the lives of those involved in organized religion from the cradle."[69]

The changes taking place in postmodern American religion, such as the shift away from institutional control or the adaptation of popular cultural forms, appear to many to be the breakdown of tradition. Since religion is not being practiced the way it is "supposed" to be practiced, some think that it is a sign of the secularization of culture.

But there are good reasons to think that this is not the case. In the first place, religion is more visible than ever in the United States today. Second, all religions change. The illusion that traditions remain the same is just that, an illusion. Change may proceed very slowly, but it does proceed. Another misconception is that there is some original "pre-cultural" form of a religion, which is yet another version of the idealization of a pure, unsullied tradition. Every religion arises within a specific historical time and place: "There is no original, pure form of Christianity. Syncretism and cultural mixture mark it from the beginning."[70] Fundamentalisms often develop from a sense that a religion is too far from its roots. But the fundamentals to which fundamentalists wish to return are contemporary ideas of what those origins were, which are quite different from what actually existed in the past.

Is religion being reduced to just another commodity by our consumer society? That conclusion comes easily given the marketing of religion in the media, online, and in stores in the twenty-first century. However, religion still fulfills a unique and essential need in culture. In *Selling God: American Religion in the Marketplace of Culture*, historian R. Laurence Moore makes this point quite clear:

> the very importance of the phenomenon of commodification, its capacity to fixate our attention, requires us to stop for a moment and remind ourselves that religion is much else besides a commodity. Religion is not for sale at the local handy mart. You cannot find the daily price of religion in the *Wall Street Journal*, even if some religious leaders organize private enterprises that issue stock. The average American religious service does not try to provide on Sunday morning what people had wanted on Saturday night.[71]

As Moore puts it even more succinctly, "In American life, religion had to become a commodity, but that did not make it peanut butter."[72]

Our assumptions about what religion, culture, and society are or should be affect our ability to understand the changes that are taking place.[73] Social forms are changing, as are economic realities, for individuals and institutions. Consider the conceptual shift from nation-states to the kind of global commerce and information sharing that is taking place. Is there a similar shift happening on the religious landscape? Perhaps the older forms of religiosity are not the only possible forms. Yet it is also true that the forces pressuring us to consume take us away from an inward look, force us outward to acquire, and train us to desire novelty, distraction, and fun.

4

ARE WE HAVING FUN YET?

He who has the most fun wins.

Lake Compounce family resort billboard advertisement

We're Going to Have Fun Whether We Like It or Not

Presenting papers on religious toys and games at conferences frequently requires bringing along samples of the items that are part of our research project. Once we were carrying a pile of games through the lobby of a large conference hotel, and a family with a young boy passed us. The boy's eyes immediately fastened onto the games, and he kept his eye on them as he followed his family down the hall in another direction. Games have that effect on adults too. At a recent party, not only the children but also many of the adults were drawn to the toys and dolls on display. And we have found that students and colleagues go out of their way to spend time in our offices, playing with the many games and toys—serious and satirical—that line our bookshelves.

There is more to this attraction than simply the sensory pleasure of bright colors, although sensory engagement is certainly part of it. Colleagues and students feel good in the atmosphere of our offices. They smile when they see the games and toys, often commenting on which games they would most like to play, or wondering aloud what the creator of the toy or doll had in mind when he made it. Some of the toys invite touch and occasionally evoke

Hajj Fun Game

surprised laughter when the person discovers the joke behind a satirical piece or a parody. All of this goes to the heart of what *fun* is—the carefree fun of childhood, of free play, and playful discovery of the world. Whether this concept of fun is rooted in reality or romantic nostalgia, religious-board-game manufacturers not only rely on this attraction but also actively use it for marketing, in some cases producing rather odd results.

For example, the *hajj* or Islamic pilgrimage to Mecca is one of the five pillars of Islam, required of all able-bodied Muslims at least once.[1] The *hajj* is a serious and sacred obligation that expiates sins and brings the pilgrim closer to Allah. Although the impulse to educate children about the rituals and meaning of *hajj* is understandable, the word "fun" in the title of the *Hajj Fun Game* seems inappropriate and out of place.

Or take *Missionary Conquest*, a game that evokes colonial domination in both name and play, yet whose cover claims that it is "One Giant Game of Laughter and Strategy!" Attempting to hit as many hot buttons as possible, the marketing strategy for this game is clear.

Conquer the world—for Christ! This challenging board game tests not only your navigational skills as you travel around the world on mission trips, but also your ability to finance these expeditions by making wise investments. "Temptation" and "Blessing" squares add to the fun and keep the action going. Everyone can play because no Bible knowledge is required![2]

Several things are remarkable about the above passage, including the tight association between missions and money and the assurance that "no Bible knowledge is required," something we will examine shortly. As mentioned in the chapters on games and dolls, the militaristic and colonialist slant to this game is troubling, regardless of the maker's intention. It would be easier to laugh off or dismiss if the makers or promoters of some of the toys we are studying were not themselves engaged in a form of dominionist theology in which the battles for the toybox take on a real religious and political dimension. For these folks, missionary conquest is more than simply the name of a board game.

In addition, the incongruity of the pairing of fun and conquest is troubling, certainly as odd in its way as the pairing of fun and the *hajj*. The cognitive dissonance that emerges reflects a somewhat

Missionary Conquest game

recent understanding of fun in the culture at large—everything is better if you have fun doing it, and you should be having as much fun as possible.

In fact, if we are to believe advertising, marketing, and the media in general, we are simply not fulfilling our duties as human beings unless we are having fun all the time. The term *fun* is used indiscriminately to refer to so many different states that it has become almost meaningless. What exactly is fun? Is fun the same thing as play? We think we know what these terms mean, but when we try to define them, they become slippery and elude our grasp.

What kinds of activities do we consider fun? No matter what our idea of fun, someone is bound to disagree. For example, one of our colleagues considers primitive tent camping to be great fun. But for us, camping is about as fun as a root canal. Clearly all recreation is not fun, nor would all of us agree on what constitutes recreation. In terms of emotional states, we might wonder if happiness and enjoyment go hand-in-hand with fun. Can we assume that if we are happy or enjoying something, we are having or doing something fun?

Fun encompasses widely differing experiences and emotional reactions. However, those experiences and emotions are not necessarily identical with fun. For example, one element of fun might be joy, but a person can experience joy without having fun—joy in the birth of a grandchild, for example, or in witnessing the beauty or ferocity of nature. Other than sharing the common quality of being a positive experience, this joy is completely different from the fun of, for example, shopping at Jordan's furniture, as described by Ivor Morgan and Jay Rao:

> Brothers Barry and Eliot Tatelman built Jordan's, a Boston-area company with four stores, by breaking industry rules and injecting fun into everything associated with the company. Each Jordan's store has a unique way of making the shopping experience positive. The small original location, established in 1918 by the Tatelmans' grandfather in Waltham, offers freshly baked cookies and serves coffee, tea or hot cider. In Nashua, New Hampshire, visitors are treated to live music

and free balloons. The Avon site is home to the Motion Odyssey Movie—"MOM"—which boasts moving seats, laser shows, rock music and clouds of smoke. In Natick, visitors are greeted with Mardi Gras beads and twice hourly are treated to a New Orleans-style street performance in a replica of Bourbon Street. The fog-filled, strobe-lit performance features singing robots of Elvis, Louis Armstrong, the Supremes—and the Tatelmans. In August 2002, a giant IMAX 3-D theater was installed that drew 2,500 people on its first weekend.[3]

Not everyone, of course, considers this kind of shopping experience fun. Some people simply want to shop for furniture when they shop for furniture. And if you arrive unprepared for the performance, it is intrusive, even demeaning, to be treated like a child who needs to be amused. It is not fun.

What is fun for one person is not necessarily fun for another. What is considered fun in one culture or during one historical period is not in another. Rebecca Sachs Norris argues in "The Paradox of Healing Pain" that the experience of pain is shaped through enculturation;[4] this is also true of fun. While for some people fog-filled, strobe-lit Elvis performances are fun, for others they are not. Even a few decades can make a large difference in how people perceive play and fun. Consider the incredible growth of computer and video games. Would we have considered sitting in front of a computer "fun" a few decades ago?

Or take the style of play of *The Peacemaker Game*, produced in 1974, which is quite different than the religious games created now. This game focuses on influential Catholic figures such as Pope John XXIII, Mother Teresa, St. Paul, St. Francis, and Dorothy Day. Some game cards move the players forwards or backwards:

> John, you wrote a great encyclical (letter)
> called *Pacem in Terris* (Peace on Earth),
> which gives people courage and strength
> to carry on the Christian's work of peacemaking
> with all people.
>
> *Advance three spaces.*

Many other cards call instead for contemplative action, so to speak.

> Mother Teresa, you are a great reconciler.
>
> *Stay where you are and think about why*
> *Mother Teresa is a great Christian reconciler.*

Others call on players to think about how Dorothy Day is like Jesus, how St. Francis so loved Jesus that he made Nativity scenes popular, and so on. While it is possible that a few children in the 1970s might have been content to sit and meditate on the lives of model Christians as a game, it is hard to imagine that many American children of the twenty-first century would consider it fun, or would even consider engaging in it at all. It is difficult to imagine nine- to eleven-year olds who are used to Nintendo Wii considering this game fun.

Even without addressing personal, historical, and cultural differences, it is tricky to define fun and nearly impossible to capture its meaning by using other terms. Synonyms abound: amusement, antic, ball, blast, clowning, diversion, enjoyment, entertainment, festivity, gaiety, game, glee, happy, hilarity, horseplay, jest, joke, laughter, merriment, mirth, nonsense, play, pleasure, recreation, sport, tomfoolery, and many more. None of these carries quite the same feeling as the term fun. And as recently as the mid-1900s, there were seemingly no equivalents for this English term in other languages.[5] Current use of the word is relatively recent and is culturally determined.

Leisure activities and experiences inevitably reflect cultural mores. Having fun implies a particular view of the individual, of what a person is. In Western culture, that view usually includes some emphasis on individualism or individual autonomy. Fun is understood to be a personal experience, although it often occurs in social settings as well. The emphasis on the individualistic aspect of fun and the value that aspect is given may seem quite natural to most contemporary Americans. But this emphasis opposes religious ideals in some cultures that disapprove of the Western focus on individualism, which is often coupled with liberal politics, pluralism, democracy, and a scientific or rational approach to the world, and it may even be seen as a threat to traditional family values.

As with play, one important characteristic of fun as an individual experience is that it entails a lack of control. It is free and therefore unpredictable. Fun may lead to both questioning and questionable behavior that challenges institutions of power as well as social mores. It may produce creative thinking, laughter, or even derision and mockery. Fun is pleasurable and may be habit-forming or addictive. As in the song, people—not only girls—just want to have fun. It may cause something called "overstimulation," which seems to be a concern of parents of small children. Without supervision, fun may lead to "unwholesome" or unapproved activities—perhaps even sex or vandalism. Fun can get out of hand. In short, fun is dangerous.

This is another reason that fun and religion—like play and religion—occasionally come into conflict, since a central concern of religious institutions is control. That concern is shared by nonreligious or secular institutions as well, because fun can undermine the power of authority, whether religious or not.[6] The freedom, spontaneity, and lack of control essential to the spirit of fun are reasons why parents worry about unsupervised fun, why some Christian fundamentalists warn about the dangers of playing with "occult" toys, and why religions—and corporations—control fun.

Perhaps one reason that fun is so ubiquitous throughout American culture in the early twenty-first century is that if fun is promoted and controlled by authority, then fun cannot be out of control or subversive. Religious toys and games demonstrate this impulse in part. They provide an outlet for fun that is monitored and restrained. Overseen by parents, tolerated and promoted by religious authorities, fun becomes a tool of regulation and control, a "safe" outlet for children's energies in which their behavior can be cultivated and directed toward productive, educational, or moral goals. Control of fun in today's society ensures social and economic control. And since fun is a major aspect of American culture, the control of fun is serious business.

Formalizing Fun

Of course, one method of regulating fun is to institutionalize it, to incorporate it in an organized way within non-play contexts. The inclusion of and insistence on a domesticated form of fun at work is a fairly recent development. Play scholar Janet Cliff observes, "One can suffer for behaving too playfully or too seriously. Individuals are reprimanded for their playful behavior at work, often without consideration of whether or not this overt behavior affects their performance."[7] This is the case today in many work environments, but the intrusion of controlled fun into the workplace is a movement that has recently picked up speed, giving birth to professional fun consultants—funsultants—who guide hapless employees in fun activities—funtivities.

The use of fun in the corporate world is resonant of certain religious rituals. For example, in the Hindu ritual of *Holi*, religious participants turn the normal relations of authority and discretion upside down, splashing red paint on people seemingly indiscriminately, among other activities. But as anthropologist Victor Turner notes in his works on ritual processes, such ritualized chaos and subversion is temporary and serves to emphasize the importance of the world order as it stands. When the festival of *Holi* is over, order returns—stronger than ever. This pattern of engaging in activity and attitudes outside normal constraints, followed by a return to order, is common and is found around the world.

Likewise, in the corporate world of today, normal authority is also temporarily revoked and subverted by sanctioned fun. Matt Labash describes one such activity in his 2008 article "Are We Having Fun Yet?" in which the pattern looks much the same:

> One of the most popular funtivities involves a manager's face-off, where the bosses must grab a partner, and toss water-balloons back and forth to each other, wearing pirate patches on one eye to distort depth perception. They must also utter "Argghhhh" before each throw just to further humiliate themselves, cueing the hoi polloi that everyone has "permission to play."[8]

Unlike ritual traditions, there is no communally understood script or pattern for corporate funtivities. Rather than emerging out of traditional stories and ritual practices, this is an innovation imposed on a group of employees, created to make use of group psychology and to increase productivity. As a recently concocted managerial device, the rules and expectations of funtivities are neither clearly understood nor agreed upon.

In some cases order does not return to its proper place, and employees do not know when the next "kiss the monkey" moment will occur, a phrase that comes from the following true scenario, which serves as an example of some of the difficulties inherent in workplace funtivities. Upon finishing a big project, a company brought in a funsultant in a monkey suit, with balloons, to congratulate the employee who was responsible and acknowledge his contribution. Although he tried his best to avoid the whole situation by staying in his cubicle, his coworkers and manager insisted he emerge and literally kiss the monkey before being allowed to withdraw. Is it still fun if it is a forced activity? Most would agree that it is not.

According to Neil Postman in *Amusing Ourselves to Death: Public Discourse in the Age of Show Business*, the insistence on including fun in all aspects of life is a direct result of TV culture.[9] Postman is not referring only to sitcoms and similar programs, but to the whole world of TV:

> For those who think I am here guilty of hyperbole, I offer the following description of television news by Robert MacNeil, executive editor and co-anchor of the "MacNeil-Lehrer News-Hour." The idea, he writes, "is to keep everything brief, not to strain the attention of anyone but instead to provide constant stimulation through variety, novelty, action, and movement. You are required . . . to pay attention to no concept, no character, and no problem for more than a few seconds at a time." He goes on to say that the assumptions controlling a news show are "that bite-sized is best, that complexity must be avoided, that nuances are dispensable, that qualifications impede the simple message, that visual stimulation is a substitute for thought, and that verbal precision is an anachronism."[10]

In other words, even the news, which many look to for television with substance, is based on amusement, distraction, and entertainment, coupled with a lack of effort and a lack of depth. TV culture is easy, enjoyable, and fun. Advertising and news look much the same.

While it might be easy to place the blame for this substitution of *fun* for *fundamentals* solely on television, it is worth considering the market forces that drive television programming. The people who promote corporate fun are largely driven by the desire for substantial profit margins in everything from sitcoms to reality shows to news programming. If televised news has become *infotainment,* as the coined phrase goes, this might have more to do with the ownership of both print and media news outlets in fewer and fewer corporate hands. From fifty in the 1980s, the number has dropped to six major corporations[11] that control most of the media industry, and competition is fierce to land the next megahit that will attract the highest numbers of viewers and drive profits over the top. The limited number of players and the pressure to increase viewers and profits inevitably lead to a sacrifice of nuance, depth, and quality and an emphasis on novelty, accessibility, and superficial entertainment—even in the news.

The reduction of literacy, the ability to listen and/or read deeply in order to capture nuance and comprehend complexity, is not just rooted in the prevalence of television and the messages of marketing and media. It is also reinforced by institutions as widespread as an educational system that requires teachers to "teach to the test" under "no child left behind" policies, and religions that require their worshippers to read and interpret Scripture in a narrow and literal manner.

Reflecting this avoidance of knowledge and nuance in the repeated mantra "No Bible knowledge required," many of the religious games we have studied can be played without knowing anything about the religion. Indeed, students who played the games in our classes wondered aloud if the games were purposely designed for people who possessed absolutely no knowledge of religion. And the more students learned about world religions, the more likely they were to discover mistakes in the games, either in the way questions were framed, or in the answers.

In the case of religious dolls, a child does not need to know anything about the religious character the doll portrays but needs only to push the button to hear the Scriptures. As noted in chapter 2, the Scripture need not be complete or even accurate. *Just push the button. It's easy, and it's fun!* As long as the game has a religious theme, as long as the words sound like Scripture, as long as they make the child or, more likely, the parent, feel good about the Bible, the toys have served their purpose.

Susan Jacoby notes a similar superficiality in her chapter on "Junk Thought"[12] when she states that "the simplistic slogans of junk thought are perfectly suited to modern mass media, which must fixate on novelty in order to catch the eyes and ears of a public with an increasingly short attention span."[13] Like the religious dolls with their scriptural sound bites, religious games feed a short attention span by presenting simplified "belief bites." They represent moments embedded in a complex historical, cultural, and religious context that are increasingly watered down for mass consumption and reduced to an afternoon of easy and carefully regulated fun. Attempts at relevancy and humor in game cards also play into this mind-set, where accepting and adapting to popular culture are primary aims of social interaction and even education. The medium is the message; to be successful the social persona or commodity must draw from popular culture, participate in it, and reflect it.

The thirst for fun is so all-pervasive in American culture that at times it feels like a form of social lunacy. Life imitating art imitating life. How else can one explain Republican vice presidential candidate Sarah Palin's appearance on *Saturday Night Live* during the 2008 presidential campaign? Contemporary American culture, its media permeated by advertising and marketing, is a living form of *Alice through the Looking Glass*, where many can no longer tell seriousness from levity, news from advertising, information from entertainment, or authenticity from gloss. Reality shows distract people from perceiving the reality of their own lives. Games of conquest and war are played for fun, mirrored by television newscasts that carefully block the reality of war from their viewers. Speaking about the reporting of the Iraq war and the infotainment that passes for news, political journalists Amy Goodman and David Goodman note,

> The media have a responsibility to show the true face of war. It is bloody. It is brutal. Real people die. Women and children are killed. Families are wiped out; villages are razed.

> If the media would show for one week the same unsanitized
> images of war that the rest of the world sees, people in the
> U.S. would say no, that war is not an answer to conflict in
> the 21st century.[14]

But that would not be fun. It might even make us rethink the marketing of a game of conquest as "one giant game of laughter and strategy" in which the fun never stops.

In the corporate world, the culture of superficial, easy fun and junk thought has produced a shift from skills to personality. Rather than testing for literacy or the ability to perform a job, potential employees are given personality tests. Barbara Ehrenreich, author of *Bait and Switch* and *Nickel and Dimed*, concludes that as far as she can tell, the personality tests were given to "weed out the introverts," and that perhaps a college career spent "playing poker and doing tequila shots" was the key to passing the personality test and getting and keeping a job now.[15] Don't we all want to have fun colleagues?

One question to consider is whether the emphasis on fun in the workplace is simply a distortion of a need to integrate our lives, so that work, enjoyment, and family are not compartmentalized in separate spheres. In "How to Create a Place Where People Love to Work," Leslie Yerkes explores this question. Using examples such as barn raising, she states that "for long periods of time, fun and work coexisted."[16] While they were social occasions and likely provided a sense of deep satisfaction in participating in a community accomplishment, it is unlikely that barn raisings were regarded as fun in the sense this word is used now. A romantic view of the past, based in nostalgia for a time that never was, may be evidence of a need for something we are lacking in our lives. Perhaps religious games and dolls are a small attempt at integrating parts of our lives as well, breaking down perceived lines of division between play and religion, or fun and religious education.

But does combining fun with work, or fun with religion, really make us more whole? Is it really fun that we are seeking? Or is it a deep satisfaction with our work—that we have done a good job, that our jobs matter in the world, that we matter at all? It seems to us that these things cannot be replaced by formalized fun. The superficial concerns created by marketing and media keep us distracted from the reality of our lives, ever looking for a new diversion when the current one is no longer fun enough.

The Cult of Fun

The emergence of fun in both the workplace and religion is also indicative of a more general development in contemporary American culture—the cultural ideal of fun as a necessary good. Although this seems like a recent development, as far back as the early 1950s Martha Wolfenstein observed the roots of what she termed "fun morality" in child-rearing advice and practices.[17] Surely it is no coincidence that the seeds of positive psychology emerged around the same time with Abraham Maslow, although Martin Seligman developed this into a major branch of psychology in the late 1990s. Positive psychology and happiness studies have flowered and infiltrated corporate group think during the same period that the cult of fun has become all-pervasive.

Religious games are not the only things marketed as fun. Look around. Listen carefully to ads. Once you start noticing it, you see and hear allusions to fun all around. For example, JN Phillips, a Boston-area windshield replacement firm, ran radio ads in the spring of 2007 that stated that "real fun" was being able to set up your own appointment for windshield replacement online. We are expected to have fun no matter what we are doing, whether relaxing, or working, or taking care of windshield repairs.

The converse is also true: we can no longer have fun just to have fun. Fun is supposed to provide practical results, to produce some measurable good as well. A recent *New Yorker* cartoon expresses this point exactly, with a father telling his daughter that he does not ride his bike to have fun, he rides it to raise his pulse rate.[18] We take vacations to promote family togetherness, in order to produce more well-adjusted children. Or we go to spas for our health.

The move to make fun functional arose in part from the perceived need to make play safer, to protect children from the dangers, physical or otherwise, of unregulated play. Soon it was not enough for play to be safe, it also needed to prepare children for success. Historian Howard Chudacoff observes not only the types of activities that middle-class parents arranged for their children, but the way in which less-advantaged children were protected from play's seamier side.

> Upwardly mobile parents wanted their preadolescent kids to be better than average in all things, so they tried to provide them with professionally run activities that would enrich their minds, tone their bodies, inculcate physical skills, and enhance their self-esteem. To these ends, they enrolled their daughters and sons in gymnastics and karate academies, language and drama programs, music lessons, after-school science and math clubs, organized sports leagues—all with the goal of satisfying parents' aspirations for their offspring. Concomitantly, parents and social agencies concerned with the welfare of less advantaged children and with preventing such youngsters from being lured into gangs, drug use, and other antisocial behavior, steered children into organized activities sponsored by churches, schools, YMCAs and YWCAs, and boys' and girls' clubs.[19]

The overstructuring of children's time does not go unnoticed. Some see this as a problem: a disservice to childhood and a way of life that will stunt children's development. A 2006 article in the *Boston Globe*, "The Hidden Power of Play," discussed how overscheduled children are and the need for children just to have fun.[20]

Even the huge market in family and adult games may be linked to the trend toward structured fun. Family games, such as the popular *Blokus* or *Apples to Apples*, abound, and there are more adult games than ever before—drinking and sex games, for example. The adult games appear to be another way to formalize fun. Rather than being spontaneous and unstructured, sex and drinking are now regulated.[21] But the prevalence of both adult and family games points also to the regulation of leisure time in general. We should be having (structured) fun in our leisure time. Otherwise we are wasting it.

We are so used to having fun pushed on us that we hardly notice it anymore. Do we think twice when we see ads showing people apparently having the time of their lives? How many of us see a disconnection between the ad product and the apparent ecstasy of those in the ads? Or the improbability? Bob Geiger gives an example of using the concept of fun in marketing condos:

> The young people depicted in the ads are shown jumping, dancing, shaking their hair, wearing leather pants and leading active lives. They crisscross the Twin Cities to work and play.
> Take the text of an ad showing a leaping party girl:
> "Martini happy hour Thursday in St. Paul, then dinner at the new Thai place. Friday it's clubbing in the Warehouse District. Saturday? Latin salsa night in Dinkytown. Lucky for me, I live close to it all. The Metro Lofts. Follow the fun."[22]

Will she be able to afford her mortgage after having so much fun night after night?

We watch people having fun in television shows and advertisements and wonder why our lives don't measure up, never hitting quite the same high notes. Much of the pressure to keep up the level of fun comes, really, from the need to keep up production and profits. Marketing specialists are concerned that etailers don't make online shopping fun enough.[23] Not to worry—they're working on it, as demonstrated by Emily Rayson's article "Capturing the Joy of Online Experiences."

> Savvy online marketers have a challenging mandate to capitalize on customer delight and deliver truly invigorating online experiences. . . . Today, more than 16 million Canadian households shop online and expect their time spent to be "fun," "intuitive" and "simple" . . . it's about engaging more sophisticated users who expect smarter sites that not only work, but also excite and delight. . . . Customers remember and value great experiences—experiences that demonstrate a deep respect for their needs and a strong understanding of what is emotionally appealing. . . . It's about looking at the experience holistically and deftly converting a first-time user into a frequent and loyal visitor. Above all, it's about profitably achieving tangible results.[24]

Consider that last part. Can marketers really have a "deep respect" for customer needs and at the same time aim for "profitably achieving tangible results?"[25] Does the "strong understanding of what is emotionally appealing" really benefit the customer? Or does it instead use deep emotional and psychological needs to turn a profit, given that "savvy online marketers have a challenging mandate to capitalize on customer delight and deliver truly invigorating online experiences"?[26]

When words like "excite" and "delight" are used to describe online shopping experiences, they become watered down, losing their ability to describe genuinely intense emotional states. We receive such a tremendous overload of information and sensory input every day that marketers are forced to use increasingly stronger language in order to get our attention.[27] In the context of advertising, words are not meant to communicate rational thoughts; they appeal to feeling in the same way as does visual imagery. Dramatic and highly evocative language is necessary because so much of advertising is graphic, communicating directly to the senses and emotions through images.

Like advertising, games are also graphic, their varied styles designed to catch the eye. As we saw in chapter 1, the game board for *BuddhaWheel* is a sophisticated representation of the Wheel of Life, just as *The Mahabharata Game* board portrays highly detailed mythical imagery. The 1950s-style images on *The Richest Christian* board evoke "traditional family values," while the symbolic *Karma Chakra* board is colorful and highly abstract.

Close-ups of two parts of the *Bibleland* game board, showing the crucified and resurrected Christ

But images can communicate messages different from their associated text. The cartoon-like images used in some games are a case in point. While cartoon-like games are aimed at younger children, and religious games are not the first or only use of cartoons in religious education, one still has to wonder about the effects of these images. Because images work directly with emotions and senses, they can become deeply embedded elements of the psyche. What effects will result from *Bibleland's* anime-like, chubby-cheeked, cheerful images of Christ?

There is a certain logic in producing Bibles or religious games with cartoon-style images. Children love both print and animated cartoons. If you want them to love religion, or at least pay attention to religious stories, then why not present them in cartoon form? Hindu myths are presented in cartoon form, as are Muslim religious stories. Neither are uncommon; they appear on YouTube.[28] However, as we saw with religious dolls, there are limits. A cartoon version of the Qur'an is unlikely since images of Allah and Muhammad are forbidden. Nor does Chaya Burstein's *The Kids' Cartoon Bible*[29] present an image of God, since that is forbidden by Jewish tradition as well. But it would be a mistake to underestimate the power of cartoons, or to think of them solely as innocent fun for children. Cartoons have a long and important history as a medium of communication, from the biting political satire of the eighteenth century to modern cultural critiques of computer-animated cartoons. The recent controversy over the portrayal of Muhammad in a Danish cartoon in 2006 incited serious diplomatic sanctions, boycotts, and death threats, demonstrating the political force of religious cartoons.

That religion makes use of the latest communications technologies and marketing techniques is no surprise. Janice Peck, writing about televangelism in the 1990s, noted that "the appeal of contemporary evangelical programming resides in its form."[30] As forms change in the general culture, religions follow suit, depending on the tradition. Religious toys and games follow naturally from cultural trends in marketing and leisure at large. Cartoon religion, like religious games and other contemporary forms of religious promotion, variously exploits or succumbs to cultural trends, depending on your perspective.

We leave this section asking at what point blending fun and religion simply caters to the lowest common denominator. The promotional activities of cartoons, religious board games and dolls, Jesus rock concerts, and even large football stadium Team Jesus–styled events can all be fun. They can awaken enthusiasm and move the spirit. But like candy for the soul, they are not real nourishment. There is a limit to the spiritual efficacy of even the most formalized and controlled fun.

Prescribing Play

The cultural pressure to have fun, even while engaging in mundane tasks, extends to the concept of play as well. Play is strongly connected with children. Until Victorian times, children and their activities were not considered important enough to study, and play was not a subject of research until the twentieth century. We now accept without question that children should play, that it is good for them, that they need time to play, and that play in younger children is a learning experience. The attitude that play is necessary is not new; the proverb "All work and no play makes Jack a dull boy" dates back to the 1600s, with roots in ancient Egypt.[31] But combined with the contemporary orientation toward amusement and fun, the need for play takes on a new compulsory quality.

The need to play is taken to a dramatic extreme at the National Institute for Play Web site: play can prevent violence; if you do not let your children play, it can have disastrous results. Their page on play deprivation, titled "Play Deprived Life—Devastating Result: A Tortured Soul Explodes," states that an "expert international team," assembled by Texas Governor John Connally, determined that the reason that Charles Whitman killed seventeen and wounded forty-one[32] at the University of Texas at Austin on August 1, 1966, is that he did not play as a child.

> A lifelong lack of play deprived him of opportunities to view life with optimism, test alternatives, or learn the social skills that, as part of spontaneous play, prepare individuals to cope with life stress. The committee concluded that lack of play was a key factor in Whitman's homicidal actions—if he had experienced regular moments of spontaneous play during his

life, they believed he would have developed the skill, flexibility, and strength to cope with the stressful situations without violence.[33]

We may agree with them that "play is a powerful catalyst for positive socialization," and they claim only that the lack of play was a "key factor." But other causes, such as the report that Whitman had a brain tumor that may have increased his aggression,[34] are completely left out of this explanation. Instead, there is a heart-rending interview with a neighbor from the *Palm Beach Post*:

> As a kid, I'd wonder why Charles couldn't come over and play with us. Other kids and me, we'd climb the mulberry and mango trees in back of the house and in the woods, but not Charles. Charles never played with us. He wasn't allowed to have friends; he couldn't have friends over to his house.[35]

The implication is indisputable. Lack of play created a serial killer.

The fundamental belief that play is intrinsically both good and necessary for children underlies one motivation for the creation of religious games and toys. Games can be used to make religion attractive and fun and perhaps more easily instill proper religious values in children; play is frequently used in religious education. However, not everyone agrees with this reasoning. Play suffers from the same trivial connotations as do fun, dolls, and games, and the association of religion with play evokes a powerful sense of contradiction or dissonance for some people. Whenever we speak about and display religious games and dolls, there is usually someone in the audience who expresses profound discomfort with the juxtaposition of religion and toys, wondering whether the games somehow contradict the very nature of religion.

One campus minister who was introduced to some of the religious games shook her head and indicated that they went against her religious principles and did not correspond to what she felt young people needed to know about religion. The talking Jesus dolls are likewise controversial. Catherine Minkiewicz, director of adult faith formation for the Archdiocese of Boston, said they are "right up there with the Happy Meals from McDonald's restaurants," in terms of being just another new product and that marketing these dolls "trivializes important figures in church history." Steven Bonsey, a canon evangelist at the Cathedral of St. Paul (Boston), was concerned that "packaging the word of Jesus in a toy could circumvent the child's exploration of a relationship with God."[36]

This sort of discomfort with religious games and dolls seldom arises in people outside the Abrahamic religious traditions, where religion and play are not diametrically opposed to one another. For example, consider that many Native American sports, such as Apsáalooke Arrow Throwing, have their roots in sacred myth,[37] or recall the doll play in the Hindu Navratri ritual. As in the relationship between religion and commerce, the dichotomy between religion and play is rooted in the separation of sacred and ordinary so characteristic of nineteenth-century scholarship and the early compartmentalization of American life that accompanies it. This opposition is also rooted in colonialism, in the desire to distinguish the "good" religions—those of the colonizers—from those "others," those not-really-true religions of the colonized. The need to determine what is not proper religion, what is other,[38] continues today, and play is one marker of otherness that serves this purpose.

Yet even if we accept that religion and play are not antithetical, even if we understand that there is a cultural basis to this bias and leave it behind, there are still many places where the commingling of religion and games hits an odd note. We have already noted the problematic use of the term fun in marketing these games and dolls. Another example comes from the comment of a Muslim player regarding Race to the Kabah, which includes a Shaitan (Satan) square in its Danger Zone: "The concept of a Shaitan square is great—and hilarious."[39] Shaitan is taken very seriously in Islam, so it is difficult to see how a Shaitan square can be hilarious and still promote Muslim ethics and ideals. We end up with somewhat of a paradox. Even if we accept that religion and play, like religion and fun, can coexist, we might still want to acknowledge the existence of lines that probably should not be crossed in playing with religion.

There Is Some Play in These Definitions

As we saw in the case of fun, there is a general assumption that play is self-explanatory and needs no definition. We are convinced of the value of play, without a clear understanding of what it is. Before we can ask why play exists and determine how it functions, we need to define it. Roger Callois begins by outlining the major characteristics of play. Play is

- Free, or voluntary

- Unreal, separate from ordinary life, and thus set apart in space and time

- Uncertain: the outcome cannot be known in advance, and there is freedom to improvise

- Unproductive: not creating goods, wealth, or new elements of any kind

- Governed by rules

- Accompanied by a special awareness of a second reality or of a free unreality, as against real life.[40]

The significance of play in human life is clearly expressed by Johan Huizinga in the title of his seminal work, *Homo Ludens*. We are defined not merely as *homo sapiens*—rational beings—we are *homo ludens*—beings that play. And although the common understanding of play is that it is "not real," play does illuminate reality. Play is not only a mirror, reflecting and clarifying our understanding of current culture, it can also be seen as "one of the main bases of civilization."[41]

The view that play is not real is a widely shared assumption, found in most studies of play conducted by Western scholars. It is based on the understanding that play is separate from real life, and that once play matters it is no longer play. Callois, who, along with Huizinga, is one of the foremost scholars of play, states that play "is essentially a *side* activity . . . any contamination by ordinary life runs the risk of corrupting or destroying its very nature."[42] Yet clearly play can also be viewed as an integral element of real life for many people, a discussion to which we will return later.

Many scholars who have researched play have restricted their studies to games or organized play and have not included leisure activities or unorganized play. This inevitably affects their perspective and also limits their observations. There is a difference between the attitude of play that derives from an internal intention, and play that derives from games, which have an external direction.[43] Research on games will not necessarily bring to light material on internal states of play.

There are common areas, however, and one element attributed to both games and leisure activities is the player's own belief or attitude that a given activity is a fun activity.[44] There is a circularity in definition at work here between play and fun: playing means having fun, and having fun means playing. However, the inner attitude of play as a fun activity is not necessarily inherent in games, especially those in which one does not engage voluntarily, whether because a parent or employer forces participation, or because the game is a professional one, such as in sports. It is questionable whether sports even qualify as play, since they contradict so many of the characteristics listed, such as being unproductive or not serious. Sports are serious enough to earn players millions of dollars, not to mention that they sporadically give rise to mob behavior, such as the soccer riots in various European countries or Red Sox–related mob scenes in Boston.

Another inner characteristic of play is a different sense of self, sometimes understood to be a loss of self, or a change in the relation of self to objects or activities. Mihaly Csikszentmihalyi sees the inner experience as central to play, enabling him to see play not just in games, but in many activities, even in work. He is one of the few scholars who includes "real life" and unorganized play in his research; the characteristics he attributes to play extend into many spheres of life.

Besides defining play by its attributes, a method of analysis that looks at the structure of play, scholars have also analyzed it using other frameworks, taking a functional approach. This approach examines what play does and why it exists. Helen Schwartzman, for example, looks at play as an orientation and a means of cultural expression.[45] By this definition play is not limited to activities defined as games.

Psychologists have long been interested in the function of play in children. Jean Piaget views it as a developmental device.[46] He argues that through play infants and children develop physical, emotional, and social skills. One of the best-known scholars of play is Brian Sutton-Smith, also a psychologist. In *Toys as Culture*, he defines play as a form of communication, expression, and symbolization; like Piaget, he understands one of the functions of play to be socialization.[47] But socialization in this case does not necessarily mean a group orientation.

We think of play and toys as shared activity, although much of childhood play with toys is solitary. And while (logically enough) we understand socialization to be a process that enables children to become part of the social network, to function within society, the culture into which they are currently socialized through toys is one of autonomy and self-sufficiency. Sutton-Smith argues that this is in part because parents have little time for their children, but that it is also useful since so much adult time is now spent on solitary activities.

> The very family that gives toys as gifts on its Christmas celebration of togetherness, does not, paradoxically, expect to spend any great amount of time with the child to whom it has just given this toy. On the contrary, the toy is given so that the child can occupy itself without making any great demands on the parent's time. The parent who gets down on the floor to play with the child on Christmas Day is usually doing a most remarkable thing—something that may seldom be done again the rest of the year. These are, after all, busy parents who are committed to their own work or their own success in the larger society and who do not have much time left over to play with their children. Nor would they wish the children to expect them to. Success in the modern world is generally a relatively lonely pursuit.[48]

Dolls that quote Scripture are an interesting twist on this aspect of contemporary play. Rather than listening to or studying the Bible as a family activity, as in the past, it becomes a limited and individual pursuit without any necessary social context.

In a later work Sutton-Smith discusses the evolutional role of play in masking emotional vulnerability.[49] Most educators will recognize this protective function of play; it is easily observed not only in children but even in young adults in the college classroom, sometimes used as a way of maintaining distance or safeguarding a genuine interest or concern. Kathryn McClymond, a religious studies scholar, also finds play protective. In her response to a panel on play and religion presented at the American Academy of Religion, she states that she thinks of play "as a strategy of deferral. Play shifts the issue at hand (orthodoxy, power negotiations, gender issues) from the forefront to a more discreet position, and in so doing it seems to create room for maneuvering and movement and accommodation."[50]

How does the protective aspect of play function in regard to religious toys? Although playing with religious games or listening to dolls speaking scripture provides a repetitive familiarity, the play aspect of these games serves as a barrier by maintaining distance and defining the activity and play elements as not real. Play "retreats increasingly from the original objects of reference."[51] Play does not identify with its referents, it separates from them. The same function that protects vulnerabilities in other contexts here serves to limit the educative value of the games; learning remains at a superficial level. The aim of making religion more accessible through play may paradoxically be making it less accessible for spiritual growth.

Fun—A Work in Progress

Another interesting paradox is that although play and toys still carry the connotation of being trivial, toys have increasingly come to be seen as having educational value. Sutton-Smith observes, "A toy is seen both as a bauble and as an intellectual machine. In effect the parents are saying to the child, 'I give you this toy for you to play with and *not to take too seriously*, but now go away and play with it by yourself and *learn something serious from it*.'"[52] American parents take their children's educations very seriously; learning is anything but trivial. Yet toys and games are used increasingly in the classroom as well as in home learning environments.

That we learn through play is not a new idea. In fact, Plato argued that "we learn through playing, and only through playing."[53] There was a time when adults and children did the same work and played the same games. There was no sharp division between work and play. Children did not have toys or play separate from learning the skills needed to prepare for life. And in some non-Western cultures today, toys are still children's versions of adult tools, for example, bows and arrows for hunting, or miniature farm implements. In these situations, play and toys continue to prepare children for their roles as adults.

The contemporary value of play—and its frequent companion, fun—as an educational tool is now widely accepted, although play was not really seen in this light until the eighteenth century.[54] It is hard to imagine kindergarten without play, and play has become an educational tool for increasingly older students—used even at the college level. We use play ourselves, implementing religious games and toys as pedagogical tools in our religious studies classrooms, trying to determine what effects playing and studying religious board games have on teaching and learning about religion.

The educational value of play has transformed not only play; it has also transformed toys into educational tools. Some toys have become more specialized, with religious games and toys becoming a subset of educational games in general. The educational toy industry is designing materials for ever-younger consumers as well. But evidence for the efficacy of educational toys is scant. Although parents want to believe that buying educational toys will make their children smarter and give them a leg up in life, it may be mostly wishful thinking.[55] Worse, converting educational materials to TV may have the opposite effect from what is claimed. In *The Age of American Unreason* Jacoby avers that

> There is no large body of research indicating that it is a bad idea to turn on the television set for infants in the cradle because, until now, there has never been a large enough group of infant subjects. The first serious study on the subject, released in 2007 by researchers at the University of Washington and Seattle Children's Hospital, suggested that videos like Baby Einstein and Brainy Baby may actually impede language development in children between the ages of eight and sixteen months.[56]

Whether or not educational toys actually help children learn, play is widely understood as a learning experience, a kind of work for children. Following Piaget, many educators now commonly believe play teaches socialization skills, large and small muscle coordination, subjects such as math and social studies, and much more. According to some, it may even prevent violence, as we have seen in the story of mass murderer Charles Whitman.

On the other hand, play itself can be aggressive, or even violent. There is a sinister side to play that the romantic and idealistic view of play does not always consider. War-like play or war games are one example. And anyone who has watched middle-school-aged children play, participated in their play, or been a victim of their play can attest to the fact that there is a dark side involving power and opposition as well. Deep play,[57] which carries heavy risks such as gambling more than one can afford, also calls into question whether or not these activities still qualify as play.

There is a great temptation to draw lines here that divide "real" play from things that we are not quite certain really qualify as play. This gets tricky. As with fun, we may disagree with the person next to us about what, exactly, play is. Yet each of us is certain that we can differentiate playing from not playing, and we often define "play" and "game" according to what they are not. It seems that perspective figures largely in what counts as play, or fun, or even how something might be classified as a game. Middle-school bullies might think the games they play are great fun, while their victims disagree. Some of our religious games—such as *Karma Chakra* or *The Peacemaker Game*, both mentioned earlier—might be better described as teaching tools, rather than games or play or fun.

The study of play often focuses on activities such as games. But play is itself an experience or a relationship to action that is not dependent on engaging in any particular type of activity. This state may be referred to as *playfulness*, an attitude that "enables any activity to become play."[58] Unfortunately, playfulness has childish connotations that may limit its usefulness for our purposes and fails to capture a deeper sense of orientation that joyfully engages life. Perhaps a better term would be *ludicity*, a term derived from the Latin *ludere*, to play.[59]

We can experience ludicity in work as well as play. Some Americans feel that work is an obligation or a necessary evil—the less work the better. The idea of work being connected with play seems a contradiction. But there are some who find a deep satisfaction and enjoyment in their work, so much so that their experience mirrors the experience of those who are in play.

Csikszentmihalyi has written extensively on this experience, which he calls "flow."[60] He describes flow as "the holistic sensation that people feel when they act with total involvement . . . a unified flowing from one moment to the next, in which he is in control of his actions, and in which there is little distinction between self and environment, between stimulus and response, or between past, present, and future."[61] That people can experience flow at work as well as play calls into question "the deeply entrenched dichotomy between work and play."[62] What is more, the division between religion and play dissolves here as well, since the experience of flow is deeply related to transcendent and other higher religious states.

For some Americans, the idea that play or fun has a place in religion can be counterintuitive, if not truly problematic. But while play, fun, and games do not seem to have a natural place in Western ideas about religious thought and practice, it is difficult to find a religion that does not have *some* form of play. Take religious festivals and holiday celebrations. Purim (Jewish), Eid (Muslim), Christmas (Christian), Ganesh Chaturti (Hindu), and Beltane (Wiccan) are just a few examples that come to mind. Most of these are celebrations connected with the stories that form the mythical base of those religions, and many of them contain a great deal of play, playfulness, and fun.

In *Selling God*, R. Laurence Moore traces the efforts to find an acceptable relationship between religion and leisure in America, which resulted in fusions such as "the sight of young people roller-skating with arms around each other to a waltz version of 'Nearer, My God, to Thee'" or Bibles with "cartoon-like illustrations."[63] The challenge to find this relationship has a long history in the United States; it is the history of American leisure. Closely interwoven with Protestant culture, this history is the history of a deep struggle within the culture, and as Moore reports, at times a deep spiritual struggle as well.

Washington Gladden, whose career became synonymous
with the Social Gospel movement, recited an all-American
painful moment from his youth. When he was twelve and
considering the state of his immortal soul, he struggled with
his belief that salvation "involved the sacrifice of baseball."
This spiritual dilemma lacked something of the depths we
associate with the torments of Saint Augustine. Still, Gladden faced a crossroads. To him it was a sweet vision indeed
that convinced him of the moral probity of holding a ball and
bat in his hands.[64]

Religious toys and games seem a far cry, indeed, from the wrench-
ing dilemma of choosing between baseball and spirituality.

The division in and uneasiness about the relationship between
work and play, like that between religion and play, is deeply embedded in the American psyche. Not that there was ever a time that
Americans did not find time to enjoy themselves—even Puritans,
who are generally thought to have originated joyless attitudes
toward leisure (hence the term "puritanical"), enjoyed themselves.[65] In the struggle to find a way to make leisure activities
morally acceptable, one of the approaches was to make them sound
more like work. Fun for its own sake was unacceptable to many:
"Amusements had to have a purpose."[66] This attitude is echoed
even today in the religious games and toys that use children's play
as an opportunity to inculcate religious values. And as we have
seen, just as fun is now required to have a practical value, in effect
making it a type of work, work must also be more like fun and
play, but a controlled and organized form of fun and play.

On closer inspection this uneasy division between play and
work comes into question; the boundaries are not clear after all.
If work is defined as serious, in contrast to play, then how do we
define games in which the play is quite serious, such as sports or
education? Some scholars, such as Huizinga, are not certain that
high-stakes sports should be called play. In a classroom the teacher
and students might differently classify an activity as play or work.
For example, students may define an activity as play if they like it
and as work if the teacher assigns it.[67] For them, work and play are
not defined in relation to whether they are productive, but from the
perspective of whether the activity is voluntary or mandated, an

element we have seen in definitions of play. Teachers, in contrast, may define activities as work if they are productive; this occurs in scholars' definitions of play as well.

Religious games are meant to be productive—to reinforce religious education—but at the same time they are meant to be a form of play. According to these shifting definitions, religious games straddle an indefinite area between work and play. They are designed to be fun, but if parents insist that children play *these* games rather than secular ones, then that game play is not voluntary, and perhaps it is not really fun as well.

Whether or not an activity is productive is a common guideline for whether it is work or play. By this definition having fun at work does not make it play, since the aim is still productivity. Furthermore, if participation in work fun is required, then it does not correspond to the voluntary nature of play. And it is doubtful that those who are forced to have fun at work will want to spend more time there. In fact they may want to spend less time, since now their ability to choose when, where, how, and with whom they play, usually outside the control of work superiors, is being compromised.

The way we define work, rather than the experience of work, may be part of the reason we feel that the less time we spend at work the better. Our experience and attitudes toward work are filled with contradiction: "Work . . . provides some of the most intense and satisfying moments, it gives a sense of pride and identity, yet it is something most of us are glad to avoid."[68] Of course it is true that not everyone has an enjoyable job, yet much of this antiwork attitude derives from the history of work in Western civilization, for example from Greece and Rome, where "idleness was considered a virtue" and "only a man who did not have to work could be happy."[69] Later developments such as industrialization, while bringing terrible work conditions to many, also opened the door for new skills and creativity, making it possible for work to provide a deep sense of enjoyment and satisfaction.

The contradiction between our attitudes toward work and our experiences is learned early.[70] Yet in spite of the attitude that we would rather not be at work, being out of work can cause a real crisis of identity, especially for men who have been brought up to define themselves through their work, or who feel a strong cultural expectation to provide for their family. Work, not just money, provides a satisfaction and self-esteem that goes deeper than fun or pleasure.

Work and participation in the economy may also provide a more profound meaning than simply satisfaction and self-esteem. If, as Dell DeChant proposes in *The Sacred Santa*, the economy is our new religion, then acquiring, consuming, and disposing are the new rituals. Through participating in these activities "one gains significance in the cosmic scheme of existence by engaging in a sacred activity and actually penetrating the sacred realm itself."[71] There is a sacred obligation to consume. According to this view, being out of work involuntarily and thus not being able to consume affects not only one's self-esteem but also one's place in the social or even the cosmic order.

That work can be deeply satisfying and even pleasurable, or more surprising still, an encounter with the sacred, is a vexing contradiction; it conflicts with the often-posited dualism between work and play. This dichotomy is so entrenched that we even use this phrase to convey the totality of our daily lives: a whole made of two parts, work and play.

What is it about play that invites contradiction? Paradox appears frequently in the study of play: toys are trivial, but they educate. They socialize, but they socialize us to solitude. Although we are accustomed to the "distinction of (mere) play from (real) seriousness,"[72] play can be serious. Play is not necessarily fun; conversely, work *can* be fun. Religion is serious business, but here we are writing about religious games and toys.

Paradox comes by holding contradictory ideas at the same time. These contradictions are often culturally based and not necessarily inherent in the topics at hand. The dichotomy between play and other cultural expressions, religion or work, for example, is absent from the Hindu worldview, in which the concept of *lila* (*leela*), or sacred play, is an "essential part of the cosmology."[73] In the next chapter we will examine *lila* and other ways in which play interweaves with religion and life through ritual.

RITUALIZING PLAYFULNESS

Religion as "magic"? Of course; and why not?

William Dever, *Did God Have a Wife?* 249

Sacred Play

Throughout the book, we have been using religious games and dolls to examine the complex and often thorny relationship between religions and play. We have found that, far from being able to draw neat and clearly defined compartments labeled fun or work or play or religion, experience reveals a wealth of sometimes unexpected connections between them, making boundaries suspect. In this chapter, we explore one of the strongest connections between religion and play—the ritualized nature of play itself.

Earlier chapters have focused largely, although not exclusively, on Christianity. But in order to explore ways that ritual and play interconnect, we need to look more closely at concepts and practices from religions other than Christianity or the other Abrahamic traditions. The dualistic view of religion, which separates high from low religion, religion from everyday activities, and religion from play, is not a dominant perspective outside Western or Abrahamic traditions; examples from a wider variety of religious traditions can show us other ways of being religious and conceiving of religion-in-the-world. One of the clearest examples is in the way that other cultures view play.

Traditionally, many Western scholars have isolated religion, including religious ritual, from the "contaminating influences of play." Ritual was serious religious business—formalized actions or enactments that dealt with the most sacred and solemn occasions of human life. Play was, well, play—trivial, mundane, frivolous, and unimportant. Performance and ritual studies scholar Richard Schechner suggests that "in the West, play is a rotten category, an activity tainted by unreality, inauthenticity, duplicity, make believe, looseness, fooling around, and inconsequentiality."[1] Its reputation is only partially redeemed by being "associated with ritual and game theory"—to which we would add educational games and dolls and the sorts of controlled and monitored play allowed at work as an organized funtivity, discussed at length in the previous chapter.[2] Schechner attributes this devaluing of play to its position in a "hierarchy of increasing reality"[3] ranging from make-believe to science and medicine—or "just the facts, Ma'am."

However, play is not everywhere seen as inconsequential, and may even be understood as a sacred state or activity, as in the Indian model of reality, *maya-lila*. This concept is a combination of *maya* and *lila*, Sanskrit words for illusion and play. *Lila* means play and is etymologically related to the Latin *ludus* and the English ludic. *Maya* is trickier to define, with the English word *illusion* not quite covering its full "play" of meaning.[4] Religious studies scholar Wendy Doniger O'Flaherty tells us *maya* originally meant *only* what was "real" and described an ability to create, divide, and even find the universe by "bringing it out of chaos." "Magicians do this; artists do this; gods do it. But according to certain Indian philosophies, every one of us does it every minute of our lives."[5]

The *really* real—what some scholars have attempted to call the sacred—is *maya-lila*, the play of the gods themselves. In such play, the potential of multiple worlds opens up to our experience: "creative, slippery, and ongoing. . . . The cosmos itself from the highest heaven . . . to the most ordinary of daily activities—is an immense playground.[6] *Maya-lila* generates a host of "interpenetrating, transformable, nonexclusive, porous realities . . . from the Indian perspective, playing is what the universe consists of."[7]

When we engage in play we are engaging in sacred activity, reflecting the actions of the gods: "living the stories of Krishna's play . . . opens up a new perspective, namely, that all life is *lila*, or purposeless play. The subjective experience of this realization . . . is *ananda*, or limitless joy."[8] Mahayana Buddhism conveys a similar idea with the concept of enlightened beings, bodhisattvas, who choose to stay in the cycle of reincarnation in order to help other beings and do so joyfully; for them, to stay in the world is to be "playing there."[9]

Lila is understood not as mere ego-satisfying or pleasure-seeking games, but as a higher form of play. Neither is *lila* a disinterest in life, but rather a fully engaged detachment, if such a paradoxical phrase may be permitted. It is being self-consciously aware of living life from another level, yet still "playing the game." The highest of paths, *lila* is play as the "best and most God-like way of living."[10]

In some respects, *lila* complicates Western definitions of play, usually understood as being separate from ordinary life, as well as voluntary. But can you simply say "I don't want to play anymore" if the game is life itself?

Lila is not exclusively a Hindu concept. Ananda Coomaraswamy makes reference to Meister Eckhart in his discussion of *lila*;[11] and Plato's ideas of "the world . . . as God's playmate" and humans as the playthings of the Gods arise within the context of Western philosophy as well.[12] Huizinga is well aware of the transcendence of play:

> The more we try to mark off the form we call "play" from other forms apparently related to it, the more the absolute independence of the play-concept stands out. . . . Play lies outside the antithesis of wisdom and folly, and equally outside those of truth and falsehood, good and evil.[13]

Reality beyond dichotomy is ultimate reality, whether it is understood as God, Buddha-nature, Allah, or Brahman. Play is sacred and resists all attempts to confine it neatly within any container in which it is placed.

The recognition of a higher reality is imperative to understanding *lila*. While not taking our lives seriously in an ordinary sense, we must play well. "Play implies order"[14]—the rules are set for us, and the outcome is not ours to determine. We may not serve only our personal ambitions if we are truly to play this game. This way of being, Coomaraswamy notes, mirrors the divine, and if we play it fully it encompasses the whole of our lives.

> The activity of God is called a "game" precisely because it is assumed that he has no ends of his own to serve; it is in the same sense that our life can be "played," and that insofar as the best part of us is in it, but not of it, our life becomes a game. At this point we no longer distinguish play from work.[15]

This is a deeply disturbing statement for those who are firmly ensconced within a philosophical worldview that celebrates clear boundaries. Sometimes called logical positivism, this Western rational framework is dependent on the ability to discern what appear to be fundamental dualities: body/mind, true/false, real/not real, sacred/secular, play/work, me/not me—the list of possible binaries is endless.

This is not just a problem for scholars, however. Many of us like and perhaps even need to be able clearly to distinguish and separate domains of our lives. Our sense of identity, individual or collective, is based in part on this process. The tendency to reduce complex and more nuanced interconnected realities to simple distinctions like right and wrong is obvious in some forms of religion and often in politics, but many boundaries and divisions shift more subtly through our lives; a lack of clarity or order may be experienced as problematical, or even chaotic.

The desire to create order from chaos is one characteristic of some forms of religion, but not of all. One central role of ritual is sometimes to ensure safe outcomes for journeys through in-between states, protecting us from the potential dangers found within the liminal state. Liminality, coming from the Latin *limen*, threshold, is perilous simply *because* it is not clearly defined; it is neither here nor there, but on the way, in between. Ritual also performs the magic of transformation, making use of the power of play to metamorphose one state of being into another. While *maya-lila* threatens an identity and sense of purpose that is tied to a rationalist worldview, it opens up many alternate ways of defining and transforming our selves and our realities through the sacred magic of ritual play.

Duck Soup

Increasing numbers of scholars have come to speak of the ritualized aspects of play and—more rarely—of the playful aspects of ritual. Ritual and play are intimately interconnected, each lying at the center of overlapping and sometimes interlocking webs of meaning. Consider the scene in the classic Marx brothers' movie *Duck Soup* in which Harpo, dressed as Groucho, portrays his brother's image in a mirror that is no longer there. He matches Groucho's every move perfectly—when Groucho is watching. But when Groucho's back is turned, Harpo does something else. After each character walks through the mirror and emerges on the other side, Groucho knows something is up, but nevertheless continues the play. The charade of the mirror is totally broken when Chico comes in dressed as a third Groucho and collides with both of them, finally causing Groucho to break the pretense and chase them out of the room.

Like the brothers in the mirror that isn't there, play and ritual reflect one another, sharing enough of the same characteristics to resemble each other but not to be quite the same. Both are thoroughly studied today, to the point where there are whole subgenres of scholarship devoted to theories of play and theories of ritual, neither of which successfully captures all of the ways of understanding either one. In fact, rather than studying the various *acts* of play, scholars such as Victor Turner, Richard Schechner, and Brian Sutton-Smith suggest it might be more productive to study *playfulness*, what it is people *do* and *experience* when they are at play. A similar move from ritual to ritualizing is suggested by Ron Grimes.

Ritual and play often share ways of setting themselves apart from everyday activities, often through narrative or behavior that suggests a special event is about to occur.[16] Much like the words "once upon a time" signal the beginning of a particular kind of story, usually a fairy tale, the donning of special robes, lighting of incense, or the assumption of a particular posture may signal the beginning of a ritual. There are a variety of other familiar markers for both play and ritual—"did you hear the one about . . ." signaling a joke, and "dearly beloved, we are gathered here today . . ." marking the start of a wedding.

Playing a game may likewise involve its own set of special actions that frames the activity of play: getting out the board game and setting up the pieces, shuffling the deck of cards, or even moving to a special play space such as a doll house can all be frames for play. Johan Huizinga asserts that such communicative frames establish activities as a world apart, like ritual, separating play from the ordinary environment.

> Just as there is no formal difference between play and ritual, so the "consecrated spot" cannot be formally distinguished from the play-ground. The arena, the card-table, the magic circle, the temple, the stage, the screen, the tennis court, the court of justice, etc., are all in form and function play-grounds, i.e., forbidden spots, isolated, hedged round, hallowed, within which special rules obtain. All are temporary worlds, within the ordinary world, dedicated to the performance of an act apart.[17]

But contrary to the expectations of both students and scholars such as Huizinga, ritual and play do not necessarily need to be marked off as entirely separate areas of life, either spatially or in terms of activity. Csikszentmihalyi's idea of flow, for example, discussed in the last chapter, allows him to see play in all activities. According to *maya-lila* and similar ways of thinking, the whole world is the ground of play, and ritual space occurs through the performed acts of participants, what people do.[18] Schechner rejects entirely the notion of frame as a

> rationalist attempt to stabilize and localize playing, to contain it safely within definable borders . . . if one needs a metaphor to localize and (temporarily) stabilize playing, "frame" is the wrong one—it's too stiff, too impermeable, too "on/off," "inside/outside." "Net" is better: a porous, flexible gatherer, a three-dimensional, dynamic, flow-through container.[19]

Certainly porous net might be a better description of the spatial activities of some kinds of religious rituals. Students watching religious rituals on DVDs in our classes are often astonished to see ordinary events and activities bleed through into ritual space. For example, monkeys play in Hindu temples; dogs walk across Balinese ritual space. Both play and ritual may have long periods where people are just waiting around. Perhaps they are waiting for their turn to play or waiting for the ritual to progress to the next part. Sometimes people are indifferent to the ritual activities taking place, and it is quite possible that they may even be unaware of play or ritual going on around them, as is the case with certain forms of what Schechner calls dark play—"playing in the dark when some or even all of the players don't know they are playing," as in "being the butt of a practical joke or scam" or being the victim of the "double cross, spying, or con games."[20]

Often ritual is interspersed with people going about their daily activities: children playing near ritual spaces, people coming and going, making food, momentarily stopping at the temple to light a stick of incense and bow before running to catch the train on the way to work. Even the most significant ritual displays of a religion, such as the Christian Nativity, may contain rather crude and humorous reminders of the ordinariness of daily life, as in the little defecating figure of the crèche—*el caganer*, literally "the crapper"—so popular in parts of Spain.[21]

If there are borders here between play and not-play or ordinary and nonordinary reality, exactly where they are is often unclear. The students' confusion likely reveals more about their own expectations of ritual and play than anything else. Both ritual and play simultaneously create and then transgress boundaries and expectations, undermining our modern predilection toward separating activities into tidy compartments. The students' expectations of ritual propriety often belie a certain Protestant sensibility in particular: religious rituals should take place at a certain time and place—perhaps on Sunday, in church, and away from both the home and the secular world—a restriction even other Christians such as Catholics and Eastern Orthodox may find too limiting.

According to a way of thinking that places play and ritual at opposite ends of a spectrum, religious rites should be serious and formal affairs, in part perhaps because they can be seen as spiritually productive—a form of labor. The thought of a playful ritual seemingly violates the wall of separation that divides play from religion as readily as play from work. As we have seen with Hinduism and the sacred play of *lila*, this wall can be quite permeable, and even nonexistent, in some religious cultures.

This permeability is seen in the intimate intertwining of play and ritual during solemn occasions, which strikes many Westerners as odd or out of place, an improper crossing of the line between sacred and ordinary worlds. Anthropologist Margaret Drewal investigates the playful aspects of ritual by illustrating the intimate connection between ritual and play for the Yoruba people of West Africa in her book *Yoruba Ritual: Performers, Play, Agency*. For the Yoruba, play lies at the heart of some of the community's most serious rites—funerals, birth, divination—transforming important ceremonies with playful ritual improvisation and theatrical gestures, even sexual innuendo.

In addition to Yoruba religions, excellent studies of the playful nature of ritual performance can be found among religions as varied as African religions in the diaspora, Hinduism, and Wicca. Following folklorist Bill Ellis' study of ritualized mock camp ordeals, Bado-Fralick provides a glimpse into the playful ritual teasing expected during initiation ceremonies for a particular Wiccan lineage.[22] In the same group, sexual innuendo and joking are also routine parts of ritual playfulness—especially in the erection of the maypole at the Beltane festival—and sexuality is considered a sacred and healthy part of life symbolically performed in ritual. Similarly, in Makunduchi, Zanzibar, obscene songs play a part in the New Year's festival rites.[23]

Of course play in ritual need not be sexually oriented. Laughter in a syncretic Brazilian Catholic women's ritual serves the purpose of releasing tension.[24] Shingon Buddhism provides a particularly transparent example of playfulness in the mixing of seriousness and humor during the ritual celebration of founder Kūkai's (Kōbō Daishi) birthday at Kōyasan in Japan on June 15.

> A procession of illuminated floats is slowly moving up the street through the twilight, a swaying tree of glowing lanterns leading the way. The first float in the parade carries an

internally lit upright mandala pushed by a team of Kōyasan
Boy Scouts. On one side of the display is a simplified version of
the Diamond Realm, on the other side a version of the Womb
Realm. But notice, scattered among the painted mandala
images are the cartooned faces of children. And more than
that, Shākyamuni is wearing a Cub Scout cap and Dainichi
sports a handlebar moustache and an Indiana Jones fedora.
What should we make of such playfulness? The float answers
with its cheering slogan, Itsu-mo-genki. "Always healthy."[25]

Within the Abrahamic traditions, however, explorations of
the playful aspects of ritual are likely to be somewhat rare in the
scholarship due to the ways in which religion and play are characterized within Western culture. It's not that ludic rites don't exist
in these traditions, but we often don't think to look for them, or we
leave their collection and discussion marginalized as oddities for
folklorists, rather than religious studies scholars, to study.

One exception is the Jewish celebration of Purim, which has
a tradition of theatrical parody and a carnival-like atmosphere.
Storytelling and plays abound; when the story of Esther, her good
uncle Mordecai, and the evil Haman is retold, "everyone present yells, hoots, and rattles a noisemaker each time the name of
Haman is mentioned."[26] Many of the narratives are "parodies
of sacred texts."[27] As with *holi* and other rituals, theater studies
scholar Eli Rozik notes that what would normally be considered
wild, irreverent behavior is

> officially authorised indulgence . . . not meant to undermine
> well established religious beliefs, but, according to a widely
> accepted approach, to reinforce their validity by the very
> release of strain produced by religious practice itself. This was
> achieved by the establishment of a day of culturally controlled
> folly, resembling in several respects Christian carnival.[28]

Studies of Purim demonstrate that scholars will investigate fun
in ritual when it is seen as having more serious underpinnings.
For example, Rozik makes the case that Purim opened the door
for Jews to accept theatre, while in other articles the organized
chaos of Purim is related to themes of violence.

If playful rites are a bit more difficult to uncover within some
traditions, ritualized aspects of play are fairly easy to find, both in

history and in the contemporary world. Consider the grand ritual elements of the Olympics, beginning with the international journey of the torch bearer, the regal march of costumed athletes, and the display of flags.

Less grand, perhaps, but equally ritualized is the boisterous emergence of high-school warriors cheered loudly onto the football field for Friday-night battle. And after Roland Barthes' brilliant and humorous essay on wrestling in his book *Mythologies*,[29] no one could possibly miss the mythic and ritual elements of the battle between good and evil performed in the ring. This epic and religious ritual battle is thoroughly exploited by World Wrestling Entertainment (formerly the World Wrestling Federation) in their televised ads for "Armageddon: The Battle between Good and Evil." Japanese Sumo wrestling, which includes purification rites with clear historical connections to Shinto, is another example.

Elements of ritual performance are just as important to the board games, cards, and dice we discussed in chapter 1. Perhaps the simplest example is game rules, the written or oral regulations that ritualize play. Normally, one does not play *Monopoly* according to the rules of *Snakes and Ladders*, or tag according to the rules of Simon Says. Formalized games of skill and chance also have rather obvious rituals connected with them.

The Powers of Play

As performance activities, both play and ritual share in the power of transformation, that ability to imagine and act "as if," creatively to hold multiple meanings and multiple identities at the same time. Sometimes ritual reveals the double grounding of an extraordinary world opened up within the ordinary—a place where magic and transformation routinely occur, as when the morning's fresh-baked bread becomes the holy body of Christ at the Serbian Orthodox Church or the High Priestess becomes the Goddess and speaks with Her voice in the Wiccan Circle.

No less a work of magic, the game board itself transforms into a sacred space, a mythic landscape conjured through play and performed ritually, becoming the seemingly endless *BuddhaWheel* of life, death, and rebirth. Or the convoluted and perilous political path toward the *Vatican* and winning the Holy See. Or the rich and fruitful trade routes between Mecca and Medina. Or the wild and dangerous lands of the yet unconverted, ripe for the planting of new missions. The design of the board may itself function as a kind of mandala, whose very sight awakens enlightenment, or may function as a kind of *darṣan*—seeing and being seen by the sacred—which invites enlightened understanding.

The players ritualistically move their stylized selves, in one game a Bible or a dove, in another a kosher hotdog, or even a chic cardboard cardinal with a terrific pair of shades—each player reflexively choosing the game identity that fits him best. The roll of a die moves the player inexorably over mythic landscape to conduct the sacred quest. Dice tumble and play in a game of divination revealing your fate. It names you martyr, or transforms you from hungry ghost to human to bodhisattva, or wins you final entry into heaven.

Dolls have a long history of magic and transformation—tiny plastic beings who, through ritualized play, become the Mother of God, or defeat evil giants by throwing small stones. Dolls are plastic here in more than one sense, as their own identities and roles shift and twist in ritualized play. They are in some sense ontologically empty, wanting only the spark of creative play in order to fill magically with whatever meaning the heart desires, or the psyche needs.

Religious board games and dolls become microcosms of imagined experience reflecting all aspects of life, from daily activities that are mimicked in play to sacred roles and rituals of the utmost importance. They become the instruments of *maya-lila* in the West, their ritualized play undermining rigid categories. Multiple and interpenetrating meanings and aspects of self are not only *reflected* but also *created* through ritualized play, markers of the power of agency bestowed on participants through the magic of performance.

These transformative and creative powers of play and ritual are frequently trivialized and overlooked by both modern society and scholarship. Academic disciplines such as folklore and popular culture are often denigrated for their serious treatment of play. And psychologist and folklorist Brian Sutton-Smith notes the "absence of the key term *play* from the index of almost every book" written about human behavior. Considering how universal play is to humanity, this is odd indeed. He also points out that significant groups of people are trivialized by the rejection of play, including "children, women, minority groups, mass-media devotees, couch potatoes, and the folk wherever you find them"—all groups thought to spend an inordinate amount of time at play, and therefore worthy of marginalization.[30]

Suggesting that we overlook these groups of people at our peril, Sutton-Smith notes that all of them are as deadly serious about their own play as are those who denigrate them. "They are not frivolous in their own eyes; they are seriously at play."[31] They are engaged in the creation of worlds of meaning.

Similarly, ritual studies scholar Tom Driver points out that many people in Western society are as skeptical and dismissive of the transformative powers of ritual as they are of play—"except perhaps the inducement of changes that can be taken as primarily subjective or psychological in nature,"[32] from meditation, for example. Confronting the "m-word"—magic—head on, Driver points to a possible reason for this skepticism, noting that it is "strongest in those sectors of society that would have the most to lose were any major social transformation to occur. . . . One way of guarding the status quo against change is to deny the rationality of any expectation that rituals can do much to alter it."[33]

In other words, Driver is asking us to consider the consequences of viewing acts of play and ritual—the acting "as if"—as though it had the power to become real, to produce tangible change in the "real world." In the case of religious games and dolls, ritualized play may produce perceptible change by instilling values and beliefs that go beyond memorizing a prayer or accepting a creed. Play invites in the worlds of symbol and myth and summons the transformative power of ritual—and yet we would never think of this simple play as magic.

Resistance to the creative and transformative power of ritual is rooted in the modern culture of disbelief and its stance of methodological atheism that still permeate areas of religious studies.

Pretending to be a neutral, or even objective, position that needs no reflexivity, this attitude goes beyond withholding judgment about assertions of transformation to a fixed belief that all such claims are examples of misrecognition, either patently false or simply self-delusional.[34] The magic in the transformative power of both play and ritual is often dismissed as either wishful thinking or bad science. Like play, magic can be a way of demarcating high and low religion, separating the idealized religion of elites from the "folk practices" of the masses. Magic is almost always something *they* do; what *we* do is prayer, or liturgy, or even science. Our skepticism demonstrates our superiority.

Countering those moves of superiority, ritual-studies scholar Ron Grimes points out the multiple forms of magic hiding in plain sight within contemporary Western culture, including meditation and visualization techniques widely recommended for patients with serious medical diseases such as heart disease or cancer. Additionally,

> modern therapy and modern sexuality are as laden with magical thinking as healing and fertility rites ever were . . . advertising is full of it. People deny that they believe in magic, but ingest this pill and use that shampoo expecting "somehow" (the cue for magical transcendence) to become what they desire.[35]

Indeed, we have observed that late-night television is full of examples of magical pills that increase sexual satisfaction as well as help men obtain vastly younger and quite attractive female partners, and sleep aids that transform haggard, overstressed adults into patient, smiling parents. Magic made over as marketing.

Mythical themes are often seen in advertising—purity and cleanliness vs. the evils of dirt or germs, with rescuers in the form of magic pills or cleaning potions that magically appear, and fables of other products with enchanted powers as well. Magical scrubbing bubbles to get your bathroom sparkling clean are a distant cousin to the tiny beings who come to the aid of the shoemaker. Numerous fairy tales from diverse cultures tell tales of purses or animals that provide never-ending quantities of gold or gems, as in the story of the golden goose. Other never-ending supplies include the mill that cranks out salt in the ocean or soup pots that never empty. In their place, we are given toilet paper rolls that seem to go on forever. The appeal to deeply symbolic, archetypal themes is there in advertising and marketing.

More to our point, however, is the advertising of magical dolls that will transform a potentially wayward child into a model of modestly dressed, morally pure Christian/Jewish/Muslim womanhood, or religious games that promise to instill religious values in a climate of fun. The magical properties of games and dolls intended to produce metamorphoses abound in both their marketing and in the rules of their play. For instance, reading aloud from the *Termatext* in the game *Karma Chakra* is a reflection of listening to sutras in Buddhism—a transformative practice that accumulates merit, whether you "believe" it or not. Playing the game is *somehow*—using Grimes' cue for magical transcendence—intended to fundamentally change the player. Playing with a grandmother-approved Gali Girl will magically ensure that the Jewish granddaughter will *somehow* dress modestly and want to learn Jewish religious behavior and history, becoming an exemplary model of young Jewish womanhood.

Risking Playfulness

Returning to *Duck Soup*, let's take a closer look at the role of Chico, the bumbling third brother who breaks the by then barely contained farce into total chaos. Chico seems to personify the very nature of playfulness, stumbling into the game and marking the mirror as an invisible border, highlighted, made present through its absence, and waiting to be crossed. Chico's actions illustrate the usefulness of moving our attention away from the labeling and categorization of discreet acts to the acting itself. Without Chico, we might be tempted to settle into a long argument about where play ends and ritual begins. Which is Groucho and which is Harpo? As playfulness, Chico breaks not only the dance in the mirror but the restriction of our need to draw borders.

In the previous chapter, the slippery boundaries between play and religion and also between play and work preoccupied us, and in the end we concluded that we could not, in reality, clearly distinguish the two. While quite funny, there is nevertheless something unnerving about the dance of these brothers in the mirror—religion, play, and work—from the perspective of Western philosophical rationalism.

Chico's actions point us to significant connections between playfulness and ritualizing. Both deal with the negotiation of boundaries, holding in tension not only their creation but also the very promise of their transgression. Both play and ritual are processes that unlock multiple worlds of magic and transformation, worlds of meaning and performed identity. And both are at work in the world of religious games and dolls.

Schechner points out that both play and playfulness—and here we would include ritual and ritualizing as well—have properties that allude to inherent dangers lurking behind the masks of both play and ritual, dangers that point to the ambiguities of play/playfulness, and ritual/ritualizing.

> [P]lay creates its own (permeable) boundaries and realms: multiple realities that are slippery, porous, and full of creative lying and deceit; . . . play is dangerous and, because it is, players need to feel secure in order to begin playing; . . . the perils of playing are often masked or disguised by saying that play is "fun," "voluntary," a "leisure activity," or "ephemeral"— when in fact the fun of playing, when there is fun, is in playing with fire, going in over one's head, inverting accepted procedures and hierarchies; that play is performative . . . and frequently at cross-purposes.[36]

While Schechner is speaking above of play, similar points might be made for ritual. Ritual creates permeable boundaries and realms; its multiple realities are slippery, porous, and—if not full of creative lying and deceit—at least capable of mere pretense or impersonation. Ritual is dangerous because it *can* work, and because it can, ritualists need to know what they are doing in order to begin ritualizing. While the perils are seldom masked by saying that ritual is fun, ritual is often enrobed or shrouded with the words "serious," "traditional," and "eternal."

But a truly effective ritual also frequently plays with fire, goes over one's head, inverts accepted procedures and hierarchies, and perhaps causes mischief or flirts with whimsy. Ritual at least occasionally or potentially produces the unexpected and perhaps even works at cross-purposes to all serious intentions. At the heart of ritual is the power of raw, untamed play.

Many rituals engage danger directly—in altered states such as trance that are not completely controllable, for example, or in the attempt to negotiate other situations of liminality. Religious studies scholar Sam Gill gives examples of the perils of ritual initiations in which the shock of disenchantment forms the basis for spiritual growth. In one, Hopi children are introduced into the world of kachinas. The children "watch them move about the village; they may be whipped by them; they are told special stories about them; and they are given special gifts, which they are told are brought from the kachinas' home in the San Francisco Peaks."[37] For the children, kachinas are special beings, totally different from themselves, and the children are promised that they may one day become a kachina after death. Gill continues:

> The nurturing of a perspective from which reality is viewed naïvely appears to lay the basis for the shock experienced at the conclusion of the initiation rite. This naïveté is shattered in the instant of realization that the kachinas are masked figures, impersonations perpetrated by members of their own village, even their own relatives. The loss of naïveté is always irreversible. The result . . . is that the reality of kachinas, one's destiny, and the whole basis for reality are called into serious question.[38]

The outcome of a ritual is never guaranteed. A Hopi child may bear "not the joys of conversion and revelation but rather feelings of betrayal and disenchantment."[39] In Chinese funeral rituals, the dead spirit may become a hungry ghost instead of a revered ancestor if the funeral is not performed properly. The boy who goes on a vision quest may not receive the vision he needs to become a medicine man if the spirits do not offer it. The Wiccan High Priestess may fail in her ritual invocation of the Goddess. And even the most earnest ritual to St. Joseph may fail to sell the house in times of extraordinarily tight markets.

When we ritualize, we risk the dangers of playfulness; the agency is never solely ours but rests in the hands of the gods—and in the imaginations of children playing at their dolls. Risk is inherent in these undertakings and produces unintended consequences, as we have seen with the discussion of doll play in chapter 2. The stately ritual dance choreographed for the talking Bible dolls, in which the children learn Scripture and modesty, may break out into a playful jumble of doll bodies, pieces of clothing, and mangled headless Mary-Esther-Barbies, with Samson and David presiding over doll funerals.

Strategies of playfulness break through the mirror that isn't there and set ritual and play free to chase one another, ripping off ritual's mask of seriousness, tradition, and eternity in the process. For example, playfulness decorates a statue of the Buddha with a Cub Scout cap, or gives him a handlebar mustache and Indiana Jones fedora at the celebration of Kūkai's birthday, or adorns the corpse with a jaunty baseball cap at a Toraja funeral ritual in Indonesia.

Playfulness or ludicity—the willingness to indulge in levity, frivolity, sauciness, whimsy, impertinence, mischief, and creative sleight-of-hand—is inherent in ritual; it peers out from behind ritual's shroud of sober tradition; it scampers throughout the ritual process, first creating and then breaking through boundaries at their weakest points like some mad court jester, invoking the magic that sets ritual free. Ritualized playfulness engages us in a dance of continuous creation and destruction, invoking the alchemical power of *maya-lila* to transmute multiple and sometimes contradictory realities into one another. For every person worried that the art of storytelling—or orality, or literature, or literacy, or religion, for that matter—is dead, new stories, literature, and religious forms arise from the remnants and ashes of the old.[40]

The role of the fool or trickster, an embodiment of play seen in myths the world over, is almost always a terribly serious one, breaking much more than mirrors—breaking the very boundaries and expectations of self and revealing the sacred behind the mask. This is a central meaning for play: through play the mask dissolves and the true self can emerge.

Ritual playing can create complex, multiple realities or identities that play and interact with each other and with other selves in a complex ritual and somatic dance. Describing the ritual festivities of Raslila in Brindaven, India, Schechner notes that the Brahmin boys who play Krishna, Radha, and the *gopis*, or cowherd girls, don't stop being little boys. Rather, their multiple roles are "mutually porous." "The boys/gods swat at flies, doze, giggle, or look longingly for their mothers; but they acquire sudden dignity while dancing or when reciting the lines whispered into their ears by ever-attentive priests/directors."[41]

Another example of ritually holding multiple identities can be found in the Nepalese Kumari Devi, the prepubescent virgin girl chosen as the living representative of the Goddess Durga. After tests that include spending a night alone in a room filled with severed heads of ritually slaughtered goats and buffalo, her life is severely restricted and isolated as the living Goddess until she reaches menarche. At this point the Goddess abruptly leaves her body, and she theoretically becomes a normal woman—if anyone could be considered normal after such a childhood.

Ludicity requires the acquisition of new skills. Wiccan ritual invocations of God and Goddess demand the acquisition of what anthropologist Thomas Csordas calls "somatic modes of attention" that enable the priest or priestess to hold *consciousness with* deity, to be aware of and engaged with multiple and complex realities at the same time. Zen Buddhism also uses embodied practices to cultivate a particular form of mindfulness that does not require letting go of reality, but the ability to be fully engaged in washing dishes and also aware of the living Buddha-nature at the same time. The active participation of the body as the doer of religious practices is required in all traditions, in different ways. The potential for transformation is here, grounded in experiences of diverse selves and meanings, depths and levels.

The transformation of breaking down traditional ways of being or seeing requires acts of intentional vulnerability and self-conscious exposure. It demands courage and skill—a willingness to explore, to engage, to reveal that mixture of play and seriousness that intertwines in our perspectives on the multiple worlds within which we live. It also demands openness—a willingness to be engaged, to both play with and consider seriously the multitude of perspectives that are revealed.[42] In short, it demands playfulness, a willingness both to create and transgress boundaries, to engage in multiple and partial identities, and to simultaneously challenge and transcend limitations.

Subversive Play

Playfulness is therefore not without its risks, to both self and community. It may challenge boundaries and undermine traditional religious structures of authority and practice in favor of the creation of new ones. This can cause problems for both institutions and individuals, as change and improvisation threaten familiar patterns. Traditional forms of religious practice—what scholars such as folklorist and religious studies scholar Leonard Primiano have called Religion with a "big R"—can be protective of their own institutional authority or power, as discussed in chapter 3, but they are also at least occasionally or ostensibly protective of the individuals who make up the community of their worshippers. The potential breakdown or disruption of existing practices, institutional structures, or personal boundaries and identities becomes a dual problem for religious institutions that want to continue to exist and exert power over the individuals they shelter.

Challenges to institutional power and authority may also pose problems for individuals who feel a loss of faith or loss of personal meaning from the breakdown of tradition. People can be personally threatened by playfulness, by a changing of the rules, or by a change in religious forms or practices. It is difficult for some to be open to religious change or innovation, to allow others to practice differently without feeling threatened or challenged. This is especially true in religious traditions that assert there is only one correct way to interpret text, one way to believe, one way to practice, and one path to the divine. Ritual play can create totally new forms of religious practice that subvert traditional religious structures.

Scholars note the tendency for cultures and religions to surround ritual play with protective devices that prevent the subversion of expected roles and the transgression of boundaries or the escape of unintended consequences. This is especially true in the category of *ilinx*, a combination of giddy play and ecstatic religion taken from Callois' four types of play. Ritual-studies scholar Adam Seligman observes,

> The utter freedom at the extreme of this kind of experience opens up a world of new possibilities, but we should recall that "anything can happen" is a recipe for horror as much as delight. This is why most social worlds in which ilinx-like ritual is important place great barriers around it, trying to keep it under control. Thus Victor Turner writes about communitas—the variant of ilinx created in the liminal periods of rites of passage or pilgrimages—that when it becomes normatively recognized "its religious expressions become closely hedged about by rules and interdictions—which act like the lead container of a dangerous radioactive isotope."[43]

Other manifestations of ilinx in culture, such as spirit mediums, are "either carefully trained in advance (as in many African cases) or subjected to interpretation by unpossessed intermediaries."[44]

Traces of "mystical transcendence, ecstatic rapture, and inspired vision" are carefully controlled and regulated by institutional hierarchy. For instance, claims or use of healing powers outside of accepted ritual practice are frowned on by the Catholic Church, which is also the ultimate authority that authenticates or denies miracles for Catholics. While authorities may attempt to prescribe and narrow the manifestations of religion, the need for ritual experiences that reveal a dimension of consciousness beyond the world of everyday life ensures that the transcendent will nevertheless break through.

This is evident even within secular culture, from the exhilaration felt at sports events or rock concerts to the rush to see where a miraculous image has occurred—these are ways in which the need to participate in something larger than the individual self, something out of the ordinary, maybe even something we might call the sacred, breaks through. And in these examples, as with religious ones, authority seeks to control them. Security stands watch at public events; miracles undergo institutional scrutiny.

Likewise, in the previous chapter we saw similar attempts to control play by corporations—and religious institutions—that want to harness the power of play while keeping its more challenging, subversive, and explosive elements under control. Within the context of corporations, control takes the shape of ritualized funtivities—formalized play activities designed by funsultants and summarily imposed on workers. In the context of religions, control takes the form of interpretation of text, limited authority over rites, and perhaps scripted play with religious games and dolls as well, which often carries the advertised intention of teaching about the religion or instilling the values of the religion.

Another way in which those in power reinforce and protect the status quo is through the marketing of "safe toys," an advertising motif that apparently extends beyond religious games and toys. The need to manage play's risk is evident in a Macy's advertisement[45] announcing the introduction of FAO Schwartz toys in its stores, categorizing them as "fun play" (remote-controlled vehicles), "safe play" (dolls), and "good play" (wooden toys). Here the tendency to classify and partition is a form of control; it prevents raw play from breaking through the surface. This is tame play, play that does not challenge or raise uncomfortable questions.

That good play is illustrated by wooden toys also references contemporary confidence in the educational potential of toys; for many this especially applies to simpler toys, those that are believed to provide more creative room for children's imaginations. But sociologist Joel Best argues that this sentimental view not only disregards the "commercial apparatus that supplies toys," it also has a limited memory.

> Nostalgic critics recall a day when toys were simpler and bet-ter than their modern counterparts, when children had fewer toys—and were richer for it. In the past, they insist, children had to make their playthings, and this fostered creativity, imagination, and other valued qualities. . . . Such nostalgia idealizes the play of the past, emphasizing its innocence and ignoring the idleness, violence, vandalism, and other dangers that inspired generations of reformers to devise programs for structuring and supervising children's play.[46]

The dangers of unstructured play were brought to heel through imposing order, using more formalized games and regulated toys, but as a result toy producers have acquired strong influence over children's play. Does this also mean that manufacturers are shap-ing children's development? One question raised by religious toys is how much effect they have on children's social and emotional growth, or on their learning.

There are strong suggestions that ritualized play with religious games and toys can indeed perform a formative role in the development of children—but quite possibly not in the manner intended. Sugarman argues that "the play of children has been seen to have particular significance for the developing individual. Play, in this view, supports growth. However it may do so more by its subversive and ritualistic nature than by serving as a preparation for life through adult-approved activities and role models."[47] A logical consequence of this is that the more toys are developed and produced for educational ends by adults, the less they might actually serve children as a means for development.

Luckily subversion is innate to children, so they will always find ways to use toys and games to their own ends anyway: "kids constantly manipulate playthings as they uniquely see fit."[48] Although we stated above that games are played according to their own rules, sometimes, to make the games their own, to challenge authority, or to overcome boredom, children reinvent games, as taken to an extreme by the comic strip character Calvin of *Calvin and Hobbes* and his ever-changing rules for *Calvinball*.

While children may change or adapt the rules of board games to suit themselves (a phenomenon also observed among students in some of our classes), the subversive elements of ritualized play are most readily seen with dolls, perhaps in part because of the power that comes from their resemblance to humans. The tension between intended meanings of the games and dolls and the intrinsically subversive nature of play and playfulness appears in creative doll play. Children are not simply *tabula rasa*, passive consumers, but have agency. They are capable of producing meanings of their own—meanings that may surprise, challenge, and even undermine the goals of both marketing and parents.

As you recall from chapter 2, the imagined doll play suggested by one2believe in their advertising was a narrow, highly restricted, and ritualized form of play. Almost everything about the scenario was romanticized, from the protective and concerned religious parents to the compliant children, eagerly waiting instruction. Perhaps the most important feature of the scenario, however, is that the play occurs under parental supervision, a clear and unequivocal expression of the desire to control play with the dolls. Writer Erica Jong comments on the necessity of banishing parental supervision for childhood play:

> I have always felt that childhood requires more benign neglect than it usually gets. In the favorite books of our childhood— Mary Poppins, Winnie-the-Pooh, Alice in Wonderland—all the magic happens when the adults aren't looking. In fact, the adults have to be banished for the childhood magic to occur. Alice can only travel to Wonderland alone.[49]

In earlier centuries, research on children's play relied in part on coming across children playing, free of adult oversight, or on adults' memories of play in their youth. American children's free time is currently highly regulated, partly in an effort to make sure they participate in all the "right" activities, but also because the world is regarded as being less safe. If you let your young child play freely in the yard they might be kidnapped; older children are in danger from drugs, alcohol, and sex. Children playing freely without supervision in the United States today is a rarer and rarer occurrence.

The idea that children *need* to play is a common reaction to what is seen as the overorganization of children's free time, as noted in the last chapter. This need is usually understood to refer to unstructured play. But there are conflicting goals here. The need for children to have free play is seen as a developmental necessity; children require relaxation, leisure, and freedom. But that freedom can be dangerous or subversive; play needs to be controlled. The magic of ritualized play in childhood happens free of control and supervision. The script for the religious dolls prevents this, surrounding the danger of free expression with a barrier of closely monitored behaviors, rules, and interdictions.

The success of this kind of closely monitored doll play is challenged by Linda Scott, who reminds us in her book *Fresh Lipstick* that attempts to limit what children do with their dolls underestimate the challenge and rebelliousness of children's creativity. Folklorist Jeannie Banks Thomas observes these qualities in once-popular doll funerals, an adult ritual that children recreated with dolls during the latter half of the nineteenth century. In a time period when death was colored by romanticism, and grieving and mourning were considered proper feminine roles, the doll players staged their funerals as expressions of aggressive feelings and hostile fantasies, changing the emphasis of the play from ritualized funerals to cathartic executions.[50] Lest the reader think that such morbid doll play has long passed, Thomas writes about a woman whose granddaughter "keeps a bag of 'dead Barbie' parts. The adults around her are not attuned to which Barbies are dead and which are alive, but the child knows, and she carefully keeps, stores, and sometimes buries the parts of the dead Barbies."[51]

Even a quick sampling of Barbie literature comes up with scores of cases in which doll play is morbid or sexualized: baked Barbies, drowned Barbies, decapitated Barbies, Barbie body parts, or Barbie sexual play. It is easy to imagine that this play would seem scandalous to religious people desiring a clean, moral, upstanding doll for their little girls. Religious doll makers are betting that talking Mary and Esther, the Muslim Razanne or Fulla, or the Gali Girls will change all this, or at least offset it. The problem, however, lies not with Barbie but with play.

Doll play constructs an imaginative world, much in the same way as ritual. It is an invitation to power, a key that unlocks human agency and creativity. Doll play is interactive and multivalent. Dolls may provide a socially unacceptable personality, an outlet for unsanctioned feelings, an act of rebellion, and a means of stepping outside the approved societal model. A doll can be a projection of who you are not supposed to be, a testing of opposites, a juggling of dual and contradictory roles.

A literal expression of this in American history is the "topsy-turvy" doll. The highly problematic and racially charged Topsy-Eva version of this was mentioned in chapter 2. Other examples of dolls with opposing heads exist in world folklore—Little Miss Muffet and The Spider, Little Red Riding Hood and The Wolf—eloquently articulating the paradoxical nature of play. These dolls evoke the mythical self and other. Like the fool, they show us that we are not what we believe ourselves to be, while at the same time demonstrating that the other and the self are one. The most effective subversion occurs on a deep inner level—the self reflected in the mirror that is not there.

There is something almost intrinsically liberating and subversive about the rituals of doll play in particular because they so directly open a channel to the imagination. Thomas writes of the scores of interviews she collected on Barbie:

> In the diverse stories of play that follow, Barbie appears as a wife and mother, she cross-dresses in Ken's clothes, or she lies around naked on the bedroom floor all day. She is an equestrienne; she is also Godzilla and mother to G.I. Joe. She packs a toothbrush gun in games of cowboys and Indians and plays hide-and-seek. She is a fashion model, a soap opera star, a hostage, and a member of the Cleaver family. She consoles a child about the dysfunction in his family. She shops, goes to college, makes sushi, has sex with aliens, gets pregnant, and works at jobs ranging from babysitter to dentist to stewardess to architect. She participates in race-car driving, camping, dating, swimming, mountain climbing, and movie watching.[52]

While the somewhat limited and scripted roles of Virgin Mary and Esther might curtail the imagination a bit, it is not difficult at all to visualize little girls playing—out of sight of watchful eyes—with Mary and Esther exactly as they would with Barbie or any other plastic doll. The lack of ready-made accessories may slow them down, but children can be inventive about creating things out of whatever materials are at hand. And Fulla provides as many accessories as Barbie. The possibilities of play with religious dolls, as with any other doll, are limited only by the imagination—and the controlled supervision of parents.

What makes doll play so powerful? Perhaps because play/playfulness is so much like ritual/ritualizing. As Victor Turner notes,

> Playfulness is a volatile, sometimes dangerously explosive essence, which cultural institutions seek to bottle or contain in the vials of games of competition, chance, and strength, in modes of simulation such as theater, and in controlled distortion, from roller coasters to dervish dancing.[53]

Both play and ritual are forms of metacommunication.[54] They contain multiple and paradoxical meanings that twist and slide and fold in on themselves in a wonderful dance of subversion. Play and ritual are complementary, their perils masked by fun.[55] The stylized nature of doll play, their rituals and games, parallel fairy tales and myths and embody fantasies, whether enlightenment, heaven, happiness, or goods. The throw of dice evokes the rituals of divination, the progress of pieces around the board a sacred journey conducted in ritual time.[56] And with dolls, the power of play simultaneously to entertain, to educate, to heal, to establish, and to undermine is, once again, easily concealed by "it's only a doll."

Making Sense of Play

The power of play derives in part from our embodied state. Unlike text, sensory information can transmit multiple meanings simultaneously; contradictions and paradoxes do not exist in bodily experience, at least not in the same way they do in verbal, rational reasoning. Body knowledge transcends the verbal. Enculturation itself is an embodied process,[57] which is part of the reason that ritual and religious play are not inconsequential. Religious understanding and experience are conveyed through the body and are culturally specific. To say that something is "only play" is to trivialize this process.

A few of the games and dolls we have studied advertise something called "kinesthetic learning," a particular feature of one2believe's Messengers of Faith series. The implication of this phrase is that the body is engaged in a learning process through play, an indication of at least a cursory understanding of the role of the body in religious education. But the scripted scenarios of Messengers of Faith dolls raise questions about how this bodily engagement is imagined and what the body is supposed to be learning.

Think for a moment about the body's role in ritual. In some religions, the body does not seem to do much. In fact, in some traditions, the body seems to be more of a nuisance—if not worse—leading us into temptation, refusing to sit still during meditation, requiring things like food, sex, and sleep to be happy, and above all, being mortal. Even in those religions where the body is more involved in religious practices—standing up, sitting down, kneeling, praying, lighting candles—there still does not seem to be much learning about religion going on. Or is there?

Think for a moment how a child learns what religion is. Take the example of an American Serbian Orthodox child, to whom religion meant getting dressed up in her uncomfortable clothing and being told by her mother to "stay clean." Her earliest memories of church are a swirl of images, sounds, and smells: larger-than-life paintings of all the holy people—God, Jesus, the Virgin Mary, and saints of whom non-Orthodox folk have never heard. Candles burning in every corner, flames flickering through the sweet, heavy smoke of the incense. Long periods of ritual spent standing and singing—"stop swaying"—interspersed with the relief of sitting on hard wooden pews—"stop squirming." The walls of the old church ringing with the call and response of priest and cantor, and the voices of the choir in the loft upstairs. The line formed to kiss the icon of Mary and baby Jesus. The taste of wine and bread.

For her, religion means experiences mediated through the body: a kaleidoscope of smells and sweat and taste and heat. We learn religion through our bodies first, and possibly best, as our experiences shape our expectations about what it *means* to do religion. Exposure to the rich sensual and tactile dimensions of religious ritual counteracts the idea that religion is only about beliefs, abstract concepts, or scriptural texts. It opens up a theological world within which religion emerges as a practice that centrally includes the physical body as the doer of spiritual learning.

Given this rich and sensual kinesthetic engagement with religion through ritual practice, it is hard to see how pressing a button on the back of a doll and listening to a minute of Scripture constitutes kinesthetic learning. If anything, it seems to reinforce the idea that religious doll and toy makers are perhaps inadvertently limiting and hampering the experience of ritual and kinesthetic play, not engaging it.

While dolls are moveable objects and so engage the tactile senses, their simplified and narrow ritualistic play is no substitute for the richness of bodily engagement suggested by the phrase kinesthetic learning. In the case of board games, embodied and sensual ritual practices are reduced to the ritual toss of dice, draw of cards, and movement of game pieces around the sacred space of the game board. The body, in terms of full sensory engagement, seems to be erased, not highlighted, in the ritualizing that accompanies game and doll playing, as a result de-embodying religion even further.

And yet, part of the impetus behind religious toys is precisely their materiality. They are colorful and attract us through our senses. They are sensory—visual, auditory, tactile. A few toys even bring taste into play. One is a box of kosher chocolate plagues for Passover.[58] Another product is the Salvation Candy Tube, a plastic tube with divisions labeled Heaven, Sin, Jesus' Blood, Clean Heart, and Growth. The tube comes with squeeze bottles chosen from forty-two different flavored sugars—flavors like wild cherry, fruit punch, or chocolate, each a different color.[59] Children fill the different sections with whichever flavors they prefer. For example, the " 'green growth' of Jesse's shoot has the flavor of little green apples. 'Jesus' blood' is sweet as cherries. And 'heaven' tastes exactly like it sounds—cool lemonade on a hot, hot day. Leftovers? How about sprinkles for sanctified cupcakes?"[60]

Once again we are faced with apparent contradiction. Religious toys both embrace and detach from the body, or perhaps it is more accurate to say that they engage the body in different ways. In highly scripted and limited play with game and toys, the body is highlighted to some extent as a natural body, a physical presence that engages and absorbs information about the world in which it is placed. But in the act of ritualizing playfulness, the body may be engaged more fully as an active participant in the religious process.

Playing with board games, our students lie on the floor, propped up on their elbows, and lean against each other. These are hardly traditional postures for the classroom, but this is part of the effectiveness of game play as a teaching tool. By taking the postures of play, the students relax, and learning engages different parts of the brain. Some game designers, for example Chodak Tashi Ghartsang, the creator of *Karma Chakra*, utilize this relaxation intentionally, in order to increase understanding.

But knowledge imparted through game play depends on more than simply relaxing. Playing games can be an active form of ritualizing, as noted earlier, and as such utilizes symbols as well as states of deep absorption, both of which also shape ritual experience. In play as in ritual, players enter mythical time and participate in a symbolic world.

The state of play, of flow, of concentration is necessary to many rituals. The transformation at the heart of the ritual depends on entering another state of awareness, whether it is a profound state of prayer, meditation, or trance. In these states impressions come in more deeply, the mental filters that protect us in everyday life temporarily dismantled. Impressions that come in during these states of awareness shape our experience, and do so within a specific historical and cultural context. Thus while prayer, meditation, and trance are all altered states of consciousness, they can be very different states, on both cultural and personal levels.

Game playing mimics these states. In the case of religious games, the impressions taken in during play may shape religious consciousness for years to come. Think of favorite stories, toys, or treasured objects from childhood. At least one of them will stand out, perhaps the touch of a leather Bible received during First Communion, or the pictures in a favorite book—the impression seemingly still as strong now as it was then. Memories are formed more intensely during altered states of consciousness or when in open states of awareness—states that are more accessible to children, and to people at play or in ritual. Twenty years later, some adults' strongest memories of play might prove to be the time spent with an Esther doll or *Exodus* game.

Playing with religious games and toys also corresponds to ritual in the use of symbols. For C. G. Jung, the founder of analytical psychology, symbols are the language of the subconscious. Used in ritual, they allow the conscious and subconscious to become more integrated, necessary in becoming a whole and healthy human being. For Jung, symbols are not purely personal representations or signs. Many symbols, which he calls archetypes, are universal to all people and speak powerfully to us through ritual, calling on deeply shared meanings arising from the depths of human consciousness.

Religious games display and use many of the same kinds of symbols as rituals. Celestial Weapons and Eternal Treasures attract us because they are mythological and deeply symbolic. According to Jung, "The symbolic process is an experience *in images and of images*."[61] Archetypal symbols appeal directly to our senses and emotions and speak to the most profound levels of our subconscious. So do the graphics and television pictures addressed in chapter 4. Their ability to affect us even at the level of the subconscious is another reason to be concerned about the power of imagery on television and in other media.

Playfulness makes use of symbols in a manner similar to ritualizing, engaging our attention and shaping our consciousness. On the surface, playing with games may not seem as strong a religious force as ritual—this is partly because play is often not as organized, and may not be carried out regularly with a group of people who engage in it with the intention of attaining specific religious aims. Nonetheless, both play and ritual are primary ways in which humans create multiple worlds and their meanings, absorbing both values and beliefs through manipulating symbols.[62]

The free range of both ritualizing and playfulness challenge us to rethink our understanding of religion. All too often, students in our classrooms think of religion merely as a label—usually something that indicates a community into which they are born and which gives them an identity. They tend to allow only one label per forehead; anything more complicated than that makes them nervous. These same students understand religions as discrete entities or distinct categories, bounded by tidy lines, neatly labeled and placed in a box on a shelf. Students tend to see ritual as a static and repetitive ordeal formalized by authority and/or tradition and performed for us or on us. Rituals must therefore be followed; occasionally they must even be endured. Religious rituals are often seen as prescriptive and boring, rather than as creative and adaptive.

All of this changes when we explore the playful dynamic of ritual practices. As processes, play and ritual illuminate religion as an activity, a *doing*, and they reveal our bodies as active learners in the ritual process. Ritual play enables us to let go of rigid definitions, to acknowledge the sacred as permeating all aspects of life, to see that the religious realm is not separate from the world, and to understand that to be playful is perhaps to be the most serious of all. It also shows us that being serious is not necessarily the same as being solemn. It can be light and meaningful at the same time. To be profound is not necessarily to be ponderous.

Through the exploration of ritualizing playfulness we also learn that there are many ways of being religious, and that utilizing humor or play within a religious context does not mean that the result will be superficial or disrespectful. However, there is still some question of whether play is still play when it is imposed by adults with didactic, edifying, or moralistic aims. Religion can embrace fun, but can fun withstand control? Raph Koster, a video-game designer, clearly presents this dilemma. "This is an important insight for game designers: *the more formally constructed your game is, the more limited it will be.*"[63] We find a similar dualism as well in the world of play therapy, where it is understood that the more structured a game, the less likely it is to release information from the subconscious.[64] According to these views, play needs to be unrestricted both for the sake of play and to enable the free participation of the subconscious.

At the end we are once again being tempted by a simple division—that controlled or structured play is not play. But as we have seen over and over, there are no firm boundaries in the worlds of playfulness and ritualizing. Borders are permeable, porous, and mutually interpenetrating. Regulation and control cannot stop the sacred dance of *maya-lila*. The symbols of the subconscious still call out to us, subversion shows its teeth in the mischievous smile of playfulness, and children make play their own.

Conclusion

GAME OVER

All play means something.

Huizinga, *Homo Ludens*, 1

Fun Matters

Games and dolls have long been a part of religious expression, so it should not surprise us that they continue to be so today. As material manifestations of both religion and popular culture, religious games and dolls are subjects for serious scholarship. They reveal the complex and often paradoxical relationships among religion, fun, play, ritual, commerce, and work. Each of these subjects is engaged in a tense and complex dance of contested meaning and shifting boundaries not only with the subject of religion but also with one another.

The power of games and dolls to display the complexity of these connections has been obscured by religious studies scholarship that focuses on the religion of the elite, high church ritual, and scriptural exegesis, while ignoring the religion of the everyday, the level of "individuals-practicing." Religious games and toys have flown under the radar, marginalized as the trivial playthings of children. Today an increasing number of scholars are paying attention to religions as they are lived, and material manifestations of religious expression such as toys and games have become proper subjects of study.

That we may not readily associate games and dolls with religion says more about the artificial lines drawn around religion than the intrinsic nature of games or play. These lines are partially due to the nature of traditional Western scholarship, which has divided the world into sacred and secular, holy and mundane. It is also partially due to the nature of the Abrahamic religions, in which the connections between play and religion are often overlooked if not hidden outright or even shunned. The compartmentalism that developed to establish the separation of Church and State so valued in American history also instigated the separation of religion from more secular activities such as leisure, entertainment, and play.

To some extent this curtain of separation is moving, if it has not come down altogether, and the worlds of entertainment and religion are enthusiastically overlapping, to the dismay of some. We could, in fact, argue that this lively mingling of entertainment and religion in America goes back to the tent revivals of the First Great Awakening, thrived in the religious performances of the 1920s Chautauqua Circuit, and continues in today's megachurch extravaganzas. And in the early 1900s, fiery Iowa evangelist-outfielder Billy Sunday forever united baseball and God. Today, religious games and dolls join religious rock concerts, Holy Land theme parks, vacation Bible camps, and even Christian nudist camps as places where entertainment and religion frolic hand in hand.

Religious games and dolls matter. They are not simply the trivial playthings of children, nor are they mere entertainment. Games and dolls express a multitude of competing purposes, and their roles and meanings are diverse. They amuse or appall us, depending on who we are and how offensive or outrageous we deem them. Some of the toys are clearly meant as satire or parody, which itself expresses a critique of culture or religion or both. Even a toy meant to be a playful parody can nevertheless remind us of an important religious point, as is the case with a squeaky toy of a Buddha seated at a laptop: we should not take things so seriously, including religion. Games and toys reflect our culture. They are at varying times droll, satirical, competitive, cooperative, educational, persuasive, coercive, militant, violent, nonaggressive, and—of course—fun.

Some of the games and dolls are grounded in a genuine effort either to educate about a religion or to instill particular religious ethics and ideals. Whether or not they succeed, and whether or not children are attracted to them and find them fun to play with, many of these toys are born out of a sincere regard for the religious and spiritual lives of others.

We must take that intention seriously. But we also reserve the right to analyze and critique how effectively this aim translates into reality, and whether there are hidden costs and implications associated with it. Just because a religious game or toy maker is sincere does not mean the product will be successful or desirable. And indeed, in the course of conducting our research, we have encountered a number of serious issues in the world of religious games and dolls.

How religious aims are carried through is one problematic area. The spiritual intention of some of the toys may range from gentle persuasion—a plush Torah toy—on the one end, to militant coercion—a pitched "Battle for the Toybox"—on the other. The latter is hardly conducive to promoting interreligious understanding or cooperation, in fact quite the opposite.

Another issue is embedded in the forms themselves, the worry that the medium overshadows the message and that religious principles are eclipsed by the need to make the games exciting, visually attractive, fun to play, or profitable. A greater emphasis on the product than the religion would suggest that religion is itself "being played" by the games, replacing the message of God with one of fun and money. This is the fear that popular culture and commerce have the upper hand, and that religions are losing their core identities and sense of purpose as they adapt ever more to the changing whims and fads of culture and the modern ethos.

Even at their best, religious games and toys necessarily present limited and sometimes distorted perspectives, the restrictions inherent in their medium preventing anything like full transmission of a religious tradition. There is only so much information that can be included in one game, and the act of game playing does not usually present an opportunity for reflection or in-depth discussion. Those few games that do present this opportunity include it at the risk of being neither fun nor profitable.

Sometimes the nature of different elements of game play such as competition, setting punishments or rules for losing players, or the construction of game identity through role-playing may conflict with the religious principles being conveyed, obscuring or even distorting their meanings. For example, competition is so overvalued in contemporary American culture and so much an expectation of game playing that the desire to win or to beat other players can overshadow more pedagogical aspects of the game. The act of winning also typically provides an ego boost that seems counterproductive to lessons about humility and cooperation. Winning becomes an even bigger identity issue in *Bibleland*. In Christianity death is the entry to everlasting life through Christ, and in this game winning means entering heaven. Playing this game in class, one student declared "Wait a minute! I don't want to win, that means I'll be the first one to die!" While the essential points of the religious teachings that are portrayed may be correct, their meanings mutate through game design and play.

All elements of the games communicate. Not only the components that are designed to intentionally instill values or knowledge, such as cards or board design, but every element of the game, from the box to the directions, can be read as cultural text. For example, games that have long or complicated directions are usually those from hierarchical or highly regulated religions. This makes sense, since the designers have included what they consider to be important, and in these religions rules and principles are fundamental and crucial constituents. Unlike the intentional symbols and meanings embedded in religious games, directions are more subliminally illustrative, yet nonetheless teach important aspects of religious life.

During the course of our research, we encountered troubling board games that express a darker side to play. These games might attempt to be humorous or accessible and fun to play, but what they present are undignified portraits of a religion, or—at worst—an arrogant and demeaning attitude toward people and religions of other cultures. *Missionary Conquest* is one example earlier discussed; its attitude toward Muslim countries is especially troubling, not only because these are sensitive and explosive political times, but also because the twenty-first-century global community has different ideas about missionary work than in past centuries. And the *Vatican*'s portrayals of the political trials and tribulations in the process of becoming pope—game questions and scenarios about kidnapping, pedophilia among priests, racism, whether to placate the more liberal or conservative factions of the Church—while they may be to some extent an accurate reflection, are hardly flattering.

If games present a mixed message of morality and consumerism, what about dolls? Dolls also aim to convey religious principles through body image and clothing or by way of Scripture and stories. Fulla, created as a role model for Muslim girls, has the same accessorized lifestyle as Barbie, in spite of being designed to contrast with her consumeristic approach to life; the makers of Razanne have the same eventual aim for her. The differences between these dolls are only skin deep.

But perhaps this is an accurate reflection of consumer culture in the twenty-first century. Stores in Jordan carry much of the same merchandise as in the United States. Without the Arabic writing on some items, one would be hard-pressed to know that one was not in a Western store.

What do we do, as parents, scholars, and possibly as religious people ourselves, when we encounter games and toys that portray religious manifestations that we find troubling or with which we strongly disagree? One course of action is to ignore them. But this strikes us as uncomfortably close to ignoring the importance of the games, viewing them as mere child's play—something against which we argue throughout this book. Religious games and dolls can be accurate reflections of meanings in both religion and culture, and if we take them seriously as cultural and religious artifacts, then we must deal with their messages seriously as well.

In the religious studies classroom, we have used these encounters with the more problematic aspects of religion as teaching moments. Students who are concerned about the ways in which religions and countries are framed in *Missionary Conquest* engage in conversation with those who see no problems. The same is true of those students who object to the overwhelming heterosexuality of the Latter Day Saints game *Mortality*. It is interesting to listen to the arguments and the justifications or rationales flying back and forth. Some students argue from the standpoint of "It's only a game—how could you take this stuff seriously?" Others launch into attack/defense mode as their religions and worldviews are challenged.

Pedagogically, the trick is to turn these challenges into meaningful dialogue. Students do not always agree, but if they can glimpse for a moment another person's religious perspective, or gain some fleeting insight into why someone reacts as they do, perhaps the ground has been laid for more productive communication. While it is overly optimistic to expect that such discussions will end religious conflict or international strife, they are nevertheless a beginning.

Different but equally serious challenges emerge with religious talking dolls, beginning with their accuracy. Some offer such inaccurate quotes that it is difficult to understand how the designers can imagine that they are providing any religious content at all. Given the toys' educational purpose, their reduced and slanted scriptural bias should be a concern, as it raises the possibility that children will develop partial or skewed religious views. This apprehension is partially alleviated by the likelihood that the talking dolls are not going to be used in a vacuum. Parents, religious institutions, and other forms of religious influence will provide a larger and more complete context of religious education to supplement the partial views of religious games and the narrow or even inaccurate range of the dolls' scriptural expressions.

Another issue is whether the way in which children are supposed to play with the dolls will hamper their abilities eventually to develop their own mature religious views. Recall the stilted play scenario of the David and Goliath dolls, which compliant children were supposed to enact ritually with their approving parents. In this tightly controlled setting, play appears to be a coercion, an artificial frame of activity into which children are forced to fit in order to absorb proper religious values. On the other hand, perhaps that scenario is just an idealized promotion; advertising always portrays an idealized world.

The artificial framing of play applies as well to the attempts to use dolls to control and guide young women's sexuality and instill proper religious values, usually in the form of the oft-repeated advertising of "modest dress." While attire may seem a minor point, especially since doll clothes can be removed or changed, it is one of the main emphases in promotional material for religious dolls. Modest dress and body image are significant because religions are lived through the body, and religions control what people do with their bodies: food, clothing, sex, etc. These dolls reflect body regulation meant to be mirrored by children's bodies, if not now, then later.

But neither parents nor children are limited to a required or pre-ordained structure, and Gali Girls, Goddess dolls, Fulla, Razanne, and others provide the opportunity for role-play that instills world-views and makes them part of the inner world of children. At their best they present the possibility for constructive, religiously guided play, play that may include working out contradictory expectations and balancing religious and worldly influences.

Religiotainment

If, as McDannell has proposed, in the contemporary United States these games and toys are expressions of religiosity growing out of contemporary modes of communication and exchange, it becomes necessary to understand the layers of culture, relationship, and identity embedded in them. Parents' love for children, nieces, nephews, or other family members combined with a strong externalized religious identity could make these toys ideal as gifts. As such they might convey overt messages of religious identity, affection, or persuasion, as well as provide opportunities for religious dialogue.

For example, on the one hand, if I feel a strong dedication to Jesus and I love you and care about your salvation, the gift of an ethical Christian toy or game can readily communicate these feelings. If I am Jewish and love you and wish you to grow up to be an integrated and fulfilled member of the Jewish community, a Jewish doll or game can convey these aims, and so on. As gifts of love, religious toys and games convey the message that the abbreviated and partial representation of beliefs and practices embodied in the games are appropriate, are positive and valuable renderings of the tradition shared by giver and recipient. Such gifts are also a validation that we can play with religion, that it can be fun and can more freely become part of our everyday lives.

On the other hand, such gifts may be experienced as a form of persuasion, imposition, or even intimidation. Depending on the game or toy, the gift may also convey messages the recipient may feel are off-topic or even antithetical to appropriate religious expression, especially if the game or toy expresses a disdain or disrespect for other cultures.

But children are not merely passive receptors of either the information presented by the games or the way the games are played. They change the rules and turn play and games into activities that satisfy their wishes and needs, which often means discarding adult directives. Play and ritual can be wonderfully subversive, resisting all attempts to make them conform to a narrow pattern of expression. In other words, religious dolls and games matter as playthings, but maybe not in the way they are intended, resulting in unforeseen consequences and perhaps unpleasant surprises for those who think that fun and play can be controlled. Subversion is the nature of play itself, *paidia*, the outpouring of a vital force, untamed, expressing itself in the moment, without need of or use for structure and regulation. Play with religious toys may alter intended meanings, reverse parental or institutional aims, and upend the wished-for orderly world.

Another apprehension over the mixture of religion with games and dolls is the increasing commodification of religion that the sale of these items implies. The fear is that religions have sold out, their spiritual foundations crumbling, their ethical principles contaminated, and the power and influence of their doctrines and practices diminished due to consumerism, a preoccupation with money and commerce. Are these fears well grounded? Religion and commerce have been closely linked with American religious life for centuries, partly because of the separation of Church and State and the need to promote religions to gain members. However, the increase in and varieties of the commodification of religion are relatively new. Religions are not immune from market forces and the influence of popular culture. As trends and movements progress through the culture at large, many religious institutions follow suit, fueled by the dual concerns of keeping younger generations interested and doing well economically. Religious games and toys are a means through which religious traditions are forced into compromised, contracted, and partial representation, limiting religious expression through the confines of both manufacturing and marketing strategies.

As with the issue of religion and commerce, we have frequently noted the temptation to categorize, to separate religion from other aspects of ordinary life, such as fun; or similarly to divide play from work or attempt to define play in such a way that it inhabits its own sphere. This tendency is so deep-rooted that even some of the best scholars can fall into it. Robert Wuthnow, in *God and Mammon in America*, titles his first chapter "Serving Two Masters"—presenting God and material wealth in opposition, even while addressing relevant complexities.[1] Postman bemoans the decline of religious man, degenerating because he is no longer separate from commercial man.[2]

We have become extremely aware of this temptation in the process of writing this book, seeming ourselves to discover at one moment clear boundaries between fun and work or play and religion, only to find that those boundaries are a mirage that fades or slips away in the next sentence or paragraph—meanings shift, relationships change, and categories and divisions elude easy definition. Commercial Man and Religious Man (and Woman!) are indeed intertwined. This is not new; only the forms and the means have changed.

Religious games and toys reflect and transmit culture; their form, design, and marketing strategies mirror the world around them. And what we see in that mirror are sometimes not the best aspects of culture. Most religious board games are simply religious versions of familiar games like *Monopoly* or *Risk*, with churches and missions replacing railroads and hotels. And Fulla and Razanne, Muslim dolls who wear the *hijab*, look a lot like Barbie. As noted throughout the book, however, these toys are not always merely innocuous imitations. Cartoon-like pharaohs and other biblical characters might grin or sneer from the board, and Christ the Savior smiles, chubby-cheeked, happily resurrected, in *Bibleland*. To what extent is the medium the message? Like the infotainment that now passes for televised news, this is entertainment religion—*religiotainment*—brought to you by playing boards and plastic dolls. Spin the wheel of plagues. It's fun! Right?

The call for "fun, fun, fun!" is a call to be externally related, to be immersed in the quick and easy search for superficial entertainment. The creation and marketing of Heritage USA, Holy Land theme parks, megachurches, Jewish rap, Team Jesus events, Islamic musical YouTube videos, TV evangelism, religious rock concerts, and religious games and toys blend a high degree of entertainment with religious messages. Activities such as these are not new; festivals and entertainment have long been associated with religion. What is new is the imbalance between entertainment and inner reflection.

The impulse toward diversion, both in the sense of amusement and as distraction from our inner state of being, is insidious, forceful, and pervasive, not just in religion but in culture as a whole. Some of our students cannot sit still for thirty seconds to try meditation—one even reported finding it terrifying to consider who she was if she was not her thoughts. And the pervasiveness of diversion is not limited to the United States or to Abrahamic traditions. The Temple at Karnak? There is no opportunity to sit in stillness taking in the scale—of both size and time—that one breathes in there. Instead, come to the Temple of Karnak Light and Sound show—a dramatization that is loud and mellifluously intoned. This show, taking place in the temple at night, is an attempt to *insert* feeling, insistent on evoking superficial responses—automatic sentiments—to grandeur and the passage of time, since people do not have the opportunity to reflect and take in deep impressions of the temple atmosphere for themselves, or no longer know how to. The lack of opportunity for or valuation of quiet internal reflection produces atrophied being, stilted from constantly turning outwards toward movement, action, religiotainment.

Scholars have pointed to many possible reasons for this. Postman blames television—if not other electronic media as well—and the commercialism of the mass media. Others, such as Jacoby,[3] add to this mix a triumphalist religious fundamentalist agenda, a lazy and credulous public, and mediocre public education. Certainly no other institution compartmentalizes time as much as education does, which structures time into increasingly shorter spans that cannot help but produce equally short attention spans. Add to this corporate and religious institutional systems that attempt to control the creativity of play and constrain the raising of uncomfortable questions—and the mix becomes extremely disquieting.

Religious dolls and games generally do not seek to raise uncomfortable questions but rather to promote the prevalent friendly, accessible, and cozy religion of twenty-first-century America, what historian Robert McElvaine calls "Christianity Lite,"[4] although this trend is not limited to the Christian tradition. Huggable Jesus is a tangible manifestation of the "warm and fuzzy Jesus" image, a representation that has little relation to the Christ who brought not "peace, but a sword."[5] Theologian and ethicist Mark Allman, in *Who Would Jesus Kill*, his book on war and peace in the Christian tradition, refers to this view as "caricature," a form of religion that cossets rather than challenges,[6] a therapeutic Christianity that, according to H. Richard Niebuhr, believes that "a God without wrath brought men without sin into a kingdom without judgment through the ministrations of a Christ without a cross."[7] The transition from a "God-fearing to a Jesus-loving" religious outlook and the development of a sweet and sentimental Jesus occurred over a number of centuries,[8] however stable and enduring this portrayal may appear now.

Images of Jesus in a chubby angelic style, as seen in *Bibleland*, promote the same "warm and fuzzy" outlook. These dolls and games place children in an idealized and safe world, where the role of religion is to comfort, as Wuthnow avers. "We pray for comfort but do not expect to be challenged. We have domesticated the sacred by stripping it of authoritative wisdom and by looking to it only to make us happy."[9] But the deepest aims of religious traditions are for profound and lasting transformation; comfort can never transform.

The Messengers of Faith dolls, in contrast, are not soft and cuddly; even their hair is made of hard plastic. These dolls tell stories as well as offer quotations; when they quote Scripture they are relatively accurate, unlike the Holy Huggables versions of the dolls. Accuracy is not a selling point, however, and most people either do not know whether the dolls' Scripture quotes are accurate or do not care: "This talking Jesus doll is so encouraging, like a real friend. He says things that reassure us of what Jesus says to us in Scripture, like 'I love you and I have an exciting plan for your life' and 'I am the Way, the Truth and the Life. No one can come to the Father except through Me.' "[10] Theological doctrine is not the point of the dolls; of seven "uplifting" messages, only one comes from Scripture. Instead, comfort and reassurance are their essential functions: "Very neat doll. Scriptures are nice and clear. I bought it for my 5 year old daughter since she is sometimes scared to sleep on her own. It really helps."[11]

Feel-good religion is also evident in Eastern traditions as they have been transposed to the United States. Buddhism, especially, stands out in this regard, with meditation included in spa treatments or touted as stress-relieving and replenishing. While acknowledging that meditation can be difficult at first, descriptions often clearly aim for an unproblematic state of being. This being the twenty-first century, the beneficial effects of meditation are validated through backing from various scientific sources, including brain imaging and other neurobiological and physiological reports.

Is a braver Jesus able to provide a more balanced path for children than the warm and fuzzy one? Promotional material on the box that contains the Messengers of Faith Jesus doll conveys the message of Christ the Adventurer.

> A long time ago, God sent His only Son, Jesus, from Heaven to Earth. He was born to a woman named Mary and a man named Joseph. His earthly parents raised Jesus until He became a man. Then, He left them to travel all around the

land. He helped lots of people by teaching them, healing them and performing many miracles! (New Testament Gospels)

To find out more about this exciting Tale of Glory, read the enclosed "Story of Jesus." Follow along while Jesus recalls some of His great adventures! Designed for young readers, this is a fun and exciting way to teach children about one of the Bible's fascinating Tales of Glory.

In this description, Jesus sounds like he is poised to become another Indiana Jones. The enclosed "Story of Jesus," however, is a small 3x5 pamphlet in a huge font (for young readers) that tells the story of Christ feeding the multitudes, the same story that the doll relates. The come-on of "great adventures" is not reflected in the pamphlet or the story. And though he is here an adventurer, he is a friendly adventurer—there is still no conflict, no struggle.

Play Paradoxes

But the possibility for engagement is there. Religious games and dolls evoke the transformative power of ritual, and a number of them embody it to one degree or another. The colors, symbols, and actions associated with religious toys not only reflect religious ideals and practices but construct them as well. While not as significant a shaping force as frequent participation in ritual practice or community worship, they should not be underestimated. We are trained to the inner experience of religion through the body; religious toys are sensory objects that transmit religious culture through their physicality. As Norris has argued elsewhere, our inner possibilities, religious and spiritual experiences of all levels, are shaped through embodied, encultured practices.[12]

Yet while toys certainly have some effect, concern over their shaping power is often overstated and undersupported. The apprehension over occult toys, for example, mentioned in chapter 4, extends to Smurfs and Care Bears—hardly toys that spring to mind as paragons of subversion. More importantly, promotional hyperbole attributes unrealistic abilities to games. The claims that *Prayer Path* can teach children the mysteries of the Rosary, or that *Inheritance* can reveal "the secrets of the seven pillars of Wisdom as revealed by God to King Solomon" are meaningless.

Those deep understandings are realizable only through profound inner effort.

As with other goals, people would like spiritual achievements to be easily gained. We desire simple, clear answers. If we are ill, we want the doctor to give us a clear diagnosis and an unambiguous treatment plan. Likewise in the classroom, students expect clear-cut answers from the instructor, something that is not always possible when teaching or studying religion.

Throughout this book we have discussed the lack of simple categories and divisions among religion and various other cultural articulations such as play and commerce. Some readers may not be comfortable with this deduction, a point that indeed corroborates what we are saying. The natural movement toward tidy differentiation in our thinking expresses the inherent uneasiness we experience in the face of ambiguity or uncertainty. The state of uncertainty, of in-betweenness, the liminal state, is uncomfortable. In this state we are literally unidentifiable—we have no clear identity. It is a state awaiting resolution.

Religion provides ways to ameliorate the discomfort of liminality, to remove us from a state of ambiguity and return us to the security of certainty. Ritual is one way of resolving liminality, especially when help is needed or the passage is dangerous, especially during universal transitions such as birth, death, and other significant life changes. Many traditions attempt to shut out the discomfort of incertitude by providing definite and absolute answers.

Despite, or perhaps because of, its discomfort, liminality possesses transformative power, and religions throughout history have made use of this, employing physical and mental discipline or even pain to achieve spiritual growth.[13] And there are a few teachings, such as Zen Buddhism or Gurdjieff, that engage the potential of uncertainty through questioning, through *not* providing answers.

Play is another way of engaging liminality; certainly it is intrinsic to religious toys. Toys cross categories of religion and fun, and embody the blurring of other divisions, such as religion and commerce, or play and ritual. The discomfort many feel when reflecting on religious games and toys is the discomfort of equivocal meaning. We want to be able to place them, to make a determination as to what they are and where they belong.

Contradictions and paradox abound throughout the world of religious games and toys. One aim of these items is to instill religious morals and concepts, which raises the question of whether these games are play or work. According to some scholars, one of the essential qualities of play is that it has no utilitarian end. Callois states that play must be unproductive, "creating neither goods, nor wealth, nor new elements of any kind."[14] Likewise, Huizinga says that play is "connected with no material interest, and no profit can be gained from it."[15] Yet religious education is a form of profit; learning is a new element.[16] Given these contradictory aims, is playing with religious games and dolls somehow not really play? Or in asking this are we falling back into the easy path of dualism, of trying to define these toys as one thing or another, when really they can be and are both play and work.

A more profound paradox is that religious games have a sacred or nonordinary reality built into them. By their very nature they reference heaven or Allah or nirvana. But as structured play they do not immerse the player in that reality; in fact, they may diminish the taste of the sacred and the ability to feel and distinguish its presence by referencing it through mundane materials and actions. Trials of faith, blessings, and eternal treasures become everyday terms, no different from *Monopoly* money or hotels. Religious games and dolls are immersed in a secular world, and while they may transmit religious ideals or customs, they cannot convey a sense of the sacred. While the sacred is typically understood as relating to that which is most real, it is now being communicated through the materials of play, defined by many as that which is not real.

But here again we approach the danger of trying to separate religion and play, and the dichotomies between religion and fun, and religion and play, cannot stand up to scrutiny. Indeed, trying to understand play leads directly to the nature of religion.

It may not be possible to pin play down through a definition, whether it is a set of characteristics, developmental functions, or something else entirely. Like the sacred reality at the heart of all religions, play stands outside of rational categorization: "Any thinking person can see at a glance that play is a thing on its own, even if his language possesses no general concept to express it." Maybe, as Huizinga states, about the only thing of which we can be sure with play is that "whatever else play is, it is not matter."[17]

Perhaps it is in the nature of play to be paradoxical, to break down boundaries and dualistic ways of perceiving the world. It is doubtful that those who are designing and marketing religious games and toys are thinking along these lines; nonetheless, play may be the most natural way to transform rigid attitudes about religion and how it "should" be practiced.

Nontraditional and innovative forms of religious practice are currently heated topics of discussion. On one side there are traditionalists who think that it can only be true religion if it stays the way it was. This has never been possible and never will be, nor has there ever been agreement on what was correct in the first place. On the other hand, there are those who think that religion should be as accessible as possible, and that using contemporary cultural material such as rock music or tattoos is perfectly acceptable. Others fall in between, and even those who have little personal interest in religion find themselves alternately horrified and amused by some of these innovations, such as Christian training camps or talking Bible dolls, sports-themed Bibles or religious games.

The changes in interpersonal and global communication as well as access to cultural information and goods are not simply shifts in content, but catalysts for a transformation in conceptualization processes, as Postman points out. This transformation means that religion may need to be defined outside of the institutions that traditionally shaped and transmitted religious knowledge and practice. While religion is alive and well,[18] the simple dichotomies that seemed to define religion no longer work.

Religious games and toys are evidence of the ways in which religious institutions and practitioners use cultural trends to breathe life back into their traditions. Fun and play have become cultural imperatives; religious practices follow suit. This is a new form but an ancient relationship; after all, "the gods are often represented as playing."[19] Rather than mocking or insulting religion, this new form asks that we step outside a rigid framework, step outside of dualistic thinking, and enter a world of flexible and changing relationships, a world that is open and vivifying.

The study of religious toys is the study of embodied, lived religion. We express, transmit, and experience religion with our bodies not only by means of music, dance, posture, gesture, and ritual actions but also through material culture. We communicate with each other through material culture—a more direct medium than words. By more direct we mean that impressions are immediate; they enter as sense experience, not through verbal explanation. Yet at the same time the material expression of religion is subtler and can carry multiple meanings at one and the same time; it is polysemic.

This, indeed, is one of the truths about religious toys—they convey many layers of meaning. Even the simplest toys express multiple aims, wishes, and subtexts: a parent's wish to instill values, a designer's selection of color or text, a manufacturer's need to control costs, a marketer's program choices. Each of these in turn is connected with another series of relationships and scripts: the Internet economy, parents' needs to keep their children entertained and their need to be seen as upright members of their religious institutions . . . the list goes on.

Many of the games and dolls we have described can be wonderful props for those who are religious. Parents can play them with their children, children can play them together, and cousins, aunts and uncles, and children of different ages can all enter into the spirit of these playthings and learn from them and each other. These toys can facilitate conversation. But as we have shown, they are by no means harmless, and perhaps those who use them should consider their limitations and the many contexts and dimensions that motivate these toys. Understanding religious games and toys more deeply brings depth and vitality to the table. Children and adults who explore and question keep their traditions alive through making them their own, and make dialogue across traditions more possible.

What we have taken from our work with these enigmatic objects is the potential of perplexity and the delight of the unexpected. We entered this wonderland drawn in by the magic of play and fun; we leave it knowing there are no simple answers. The power of play, like the sacred, moves through the world, in and out, at one moment appearing, in the next, gone. Play intertwines with our lives; it engages the sacred. The play of the gods is embodied in our very lives.

Let the games begin.

NOTES

CHAPTER 1

1 It is difficult to trace the movement of games; some scholars trace this game back to Buddhist origins in Tibet. See Mark Tatz and Jody Kent, *Rebirth: The Tibetan Game of Liberation* (Garden City, N.Y.: Anchor Books, 1977), 15.

2 R. C. Bell, *Board and Table Games from Many Civilizations* (New York: Dover, 1979), 1:54–55.

3 Chodak Tashi Ghartsang, interview by Rebecca Sachs Norris, March 16, 2007.

4 Resurrection Eggs, CBD stock number WW297220, *Christianbook. com*, http://www.christianbook.com.

5 Plush Plagues Bag, JDC number 88177, http://www.judaism.com/ display.asp?nt=bCbDEk&etn=IIBHH.

6 *Divine Interventions*, http://www.divine-interventions.com.

7 Holy Toast Bread Stamp, *Perpetual Kid*, http://www.perpetualkid .com/index.asp?PageAction=VIEWPROD&ProdID=1585.

8 Lookin' Good for Jesus collection, *Blue Q*, http://www.blueq.com/ shop/114-catId.117440633_114-productId.0.html.

9 Seven Deadly Sins Wristbands, item M6133, *Archie McPhee*, http:// www.mcphee.com/items/M6133.html.

10 Nunzilla, item 10354, *Archie McPhee*, http://www.mcphee.com/ items/10354.html.

11 While *Look at the Schmuck on that Camel* sounds like another game in this category, it was an educational game that taught Yiddish.

12 Dashboard Monk, product 15/58, *Daddy Zero*, http://www.daddyzero .com/dashboard-monk-p-1760.html.

13 Sally Sugarman, "Children on Board: Images from Candy Lands," in *Images of the Child*, ed. Harry Eiss, 323–34 (Bowling Green, Ohio: Bowling Green State University Popular Press, 1994), 323.

14 Leonard Primiano, "Vernacular Religion and the Search for Method in Religious Folklife," in *Reflexivity and the Study of Belief*, ed. David Hufford, special issue, *Western Folklore* 54, no. 1 (1995): 37–56.

15 Nikki Bado-Fralick, *Coming to the Edge of the Circle: A Wiccan Initiation Ritual* (Oxford: Oxford University Press, 2005).

16 Mihaly Csikszentmihalyi and Stith Bennett, "An Exploratory Model of Play," *American Anthropologist* 73, no. 1 (1971): 46.

17 Réal Breton, *Kingdom of Heaven* game (Evangeli-Vision Canada, Montréal, P.Q., Canada, 1984) (emphasis in original).

18 Csikszentmihalyi and Bennett, "An Exploratory Model of Play," 47.

19 Alice Gomme, *The Traditional Games of England, Scotland and Ireland* (London: Thames & Hudson, 1984), 460.

20 That a game must have a winner or loser is not a given in non-Western cultures, and the Navaho traditionally defined play activities as anything upon which one could bet, rather than as resulting in a winner or loser. See Janet M. Cliff, "Ludicity: A Model for Understanding Play and Game" (Ph.D. diss., University of California, 1990), 30, 82.

21 Bell, *Board and Table Games*, 1:v; H. J. R. Murray, *A History of Board Games Other Than Chess* (Oxford: Clarendon, 1951), 4–5. *Mancala* games are games of strategy, with two or more rows of holes or depressions holding pebbles or similar playing pieces. This game type applies to other games with lines and cells as well.

22 See onlineislamicstore.com.

23 Associated Press, "Stick Joins Lineup in Toy Hall of Fame," *Boston Globe*, November 7, 2008, http://www.boston.com/news/nation/articles/2008/11/07/stick_joins_lineup_in_toy_hall_of_fame/.

24 Murray, *History of Board Games*, 18–19.

25 Gary Rollefson, "A Neolithic Game Board from 'Ain Ghazal, Jordan," *Bulletin of the American Schools of Oriental Research* 286 (1992): 1.

26 Murray, *History of Board Games*, 12.

27 Murray, *History of Board Games*, 229.

28 Csikszentmihalyi and Bennett, "An Exploratory Model of Play," 47.

29 William Hallo, "The First Purim," *Biblical Archaeologist* 46, no. 1 (1983): 20–23.

30 Murray, *History of Board Games*, 235.

31 Bell, *Board and Table Games*, 1:6.

32 Bell, *Board and Table Games*, 1:6; Stewart Culin, *Games of the North American Indians* (New York: Dover 1975), 792.

33 John Fox, "Students of the Game," *The Smithsonian*, April 2006, 110–17.

34 Steve Craig, *Sports and Games of the Ancients* (Westport, Conn.: Greenwood, 2002), 127–28.

35 Lewis Spence, *Myth and Ritual in Dance, Game and Rhyme* (London: Watts, 1947), 12.

36 Csikszentmihalyi and Bennett, "An Exploratory Model of Play," 52.

37 Stewart Culin, "American Indian Games," *American Anthropologist* 5, no. 1 (1903): 61–62.

38 Murray, *History of Board Games*, 235.

39 Gomme, *Traditional Games*, 472.

40 J. W. Crombie, "History of the Game of Hop-Scotch," *Journal of the Anthropological Institute of Great Britain and Ireland* 15 (1886): 403–8.

41 Tatz and Kent, *Rebirth*, 1.

42 Steven Slater, "Game of Rebirth," http://www.chebucto.ns.ca/~s-slater/Dharma.

43 Spence, *Myth and Ritual*, 16, 19, 22; Murray, *History of Board Games*, 34.

44 Murray, *History of Board Games*, 14.

45 Edward Falkener, *Games Ancient and Oriental and How to Play Them* (New York: Dover, 1961), 99.

46 Murray, *History of Board Games*, 235; Rachel Corr, "Death, Dice, and Divination: Rethinking Religion and Play in South America," *Journal of Latin American and Caribbean Anthropology* 13, no. 1 (2008): 3.

47 Elliott M. Avedon and Brian Sutton-Smith, *The Study of Games* (New York: John Wiley & Sons, 1971), 22; Andrew Lo, "The Game of Leaves: An Inquiry into the Origin of Chinese Playing Cards," *Bulletin of the School of Oriental and African Studies* 63, no. 3 (2000): 389–406.

48 Avedon and Sutton-Smith, *Study of Games*, 23.

49 Edmond Bordeaux, *The Art of Asha* (Tierra del Sol, Calif.: Mille Meditations, 1966), 27, 29.

50 Murray, *History of Board Games*, 230.

51 Mara Leveritt, "School Prayer and Football Games: Don't Sideline the U.S. Constitution," *Church & State* 53, no. 1 (2000): 20; Perry A. Zirkel, "The Games, They Are a-Changin'," *Phi Delta Kappan* 82, no. 2 (2000): 175.

52 L. Gregory Jones, "The Games We Play," *Christian Century* 121, no. 7 (2004): 32.

53 Chen Chiung Hwang, "'Molympics'? Journalistic Discourse of Mormons in Relation to the 2002 Winter Olympic Games," *Journal of Media and Religion* 2, no. 1 (2003): 29.

54 Catherine Perry Hargrave, *A History of Playing Cards and a Bibliography of Cards and Gaming* (New York: Dover, 1966), 161.

55 Hargrave, *History of Playing Cards*, 9, 20.

56 Hargrave, *History of Playing Cards*, 324.

57 Hargrave, *History of Playing Cards*, 162.

58 Hargrave, *History of Playing Cards*, 191, 193.

59 Hargrave, *History of Playing Cards*, 171.

60 J. H. Plumb, "The Great Change in Children," *Horizon* 13, no. 1 (1971): 7. See also Philippe Aries, *Centuries of Childhood: A Social History of Family Life*, trans. Robert Baldick (New York: Vintage Books, 1962), 71.

61 Aries, *Centuries of Childhood*, 81.

62 Aries, *Centuries of Childhood*, 82.

63 Charles Cotton, *Games and Gamesters of the Restoration* (Port Washington, N.Y.: Kennikat Press, 1971), 1.

64 Aries, *Centuries of Childhood*, 71, 84.

65 Neil Postman, *The Disappearance of Childhood* (New York: Vintage Books, 1994), 18.

CHAPTER 2

1   Max von Boehn, *Dolls and Puppets*, trans. Josephine Nicoll (New York: Cooper Square Publishers, 1966), 24.

2   For a glimpse into the controversies, see, e.g., Marija Gimbutas, *The Goddesses and Gods of Old Europe 6500–3500 BC: Myths and Cult Images* (1974; repr., Berkeley: University of California Press, 1982); idem, *The Living Goddesses* (Berkeley: University of California Press, 1999); Lotte Motz, *Faces of the Goddess* (Oxford: Oxford University Press, 1997); Lucy Goodison and Christine Morris, eds., *Ancient Goddesses: The Myths and the Evidence* (London: British Museum Press, 1998); and Cynthia Eller, *The Myth of Matriarchal Prehistory: Why an Invented Past Won't Give Women a Future* (Boston: Beacon Press, 2000).

3   Janet Pagter Johl, *The Fascinating Story of Dolls* (New York: H. L. Lindquist, 1941), 5; Von Boehn, *Dolls and Puppets*, 107–9.

4   Von Boehn, *Dolls and Puppets*, 49.

5   Von Boehn, *Dolls and Puppets*, 59–61.

6   Von Boehn, *Dolls and Puppets*, 61.

7   Richard Dorson, *Folk Legends of Japan*, illus. Yoshi Noguchi (Rutland, Vt.: C.E. Tuttle, 1962), 49–50 ("The Shrine Built by Straw Dolls").

8   Contemporary Western versions of this doll include the large clown punching doll that rights itself after being knocked over. Other current varieties include large blow-up Anubis and Boy-King (Tutankhamen) dolls.

9   There are many online descriptions and photographs of Bommai Kolu doll displays, including the discussion "Bommai Kolu—Arrangement of Dolls during Navratri and Dusshera" on the *Hindu Blog* (http://www.hindu-blog.com/2007/10/bommai-kolu-arrangement-of-

dolls-during.html), Sharath Bhat's article "Navratri Bommai Kollu Festival" on *Metblogs* (October 24, 2007, http://bangalore.metblogs .com/2007/10/24/navratri-bommai-kollu-festival/), Sri Ganesha Temple's online explanation of Kolu (http://www.ganeshatemple.org/ Articles/Article_2(pdf)/Navarathri.pdf), and pictures from Professor Vasudha Narayanan's online Bommai Kolu site at http://bangalore .metblogs.com/2007/10/24/navratri-bommai-kollu-festival/.

10 Von Boehn, *Dolls and Puppets*, 50.

11 *Gali Girls* Web site, http://www.galigirls.com/index.php.

12 *Ghee Happy* (http://www.gheehappy.com) and *Sepia Mutiny* (http:// www.sepiamutiny.com/sepia) Web sites.

13 See Kelli Lincoln's Web site *Dancing Goddess Dolls*, http://www .dancinggoddessdolls.com.

14 See the *Dancing Goddess Dolls* Web site.

15 *Timboucher.com*, journal entry for July 11, 2006, http://www .timboucher.com/journal/2006/07/11/goddess-barbie-dolls/.

16 Amma Dolls, *The Amma Shop*, http://www.theammashop.org/ aadolls.html.

17 Erik Davis, "Amma's Cosmic Squeeze," *Salon*, July 19, 2007, http:// www.salon.com/mwt/feature/2007/07/19/amma/index.html.

18 Mike Brooker, posting on the *Audarya Fellowship* Web site, December 23, 2001, http://www.indiadivine.org/audarya/ammachi/214996-my-amma-doll.html.

19 Shamita Dasgupta, "Activists Call for a Protest of 'Asia Goddess' Barbie," November 25, 1998, www.hartford-hwp.com/archives/50/094 .html.

20 Lisa Tsering, "Barbie Goes Indian with Diwali-themed Doll," *India West*, news feature, October 21, 2006.

21 Robert MacGregor, "The Eva and Topsy Dichotomy in Advertising," in *Images of the Child*, ed. Harry Eiss, 287–306 (Bowling Green, Ohio: Bowling Green State University Popular Press, 1994), 289–90.

22 MacGregor, "Eva and Topsy Dichotomy," 292.

23 MacGregor, "Eva and Topsy Dichotomy," 290.

24 MacGregor, "Eva and Topsy Dichotomy," 287.

25 Eric Clark, *The Real Toy Story: Inside the Ruthless Battle for America's Youngest Consumers* (New York: Free Press, 2007), 101. See especially the chapter "Barbie Goes to War: Battle of the Dolls," 76–108.

26 Laura Smith-Spark, "Faith-Based Toys to Hit US Stores," *BBC News*, July 30, 2007, http://news.bbc.co.uk/2/hi/americas/6916287.stm.

27 Smith-Spark, "Faith-Based Toys to Hit US Stores."

28 Joyce Pellino Crane, "Talking Dolls Designed to Teach Children Scripture," *Boston Globe*, March 17, 2005.

29 *Holy Huggables*, www.talkingbibledolls.com/faq.htm.

30   Sally Cunneen, *In Search of Mary: The Woman and the Symbol* (New York: Ballantine Books, 1996).

31   Diane Long, David Elkind, and Bernard Spilka, "The Child's Conception of Prayer," *Journal for the Scientific Study of Religion* 6, no. 1 (1967): 106.

32   *Christianbook.com*, customer review of the Huggable Jesus Doll, CBD stock number WW817005, http://www.christianbook.com/ Christian/Books/product?item_no=817005&kw=817005&en=froogl e&p=1013824.

33   Nancy Carlsson-Paige and Diane E. Levin, "The War-Toy Connection," *Christian Science Monitor*, October 5, 1999, http://www .csmonitor.com/1999/1005/p9s2.html.

34   See the press release for Levine's book *G.I. Joe: The Story behind the Legend* at http://www.mr1964.com/headquarters_quarterly/don_ levine.html.

35   One2believe's more martial preoccupation seems to have come about at the same time that their Web site reflected ties with Focus on the Family and FamilyLife, a family-oriented division of Campus Crusade for Christ.

36   Clark, *Real Toy Story*, 166.

37   Clark, *Real Toy Story*, 186.

38   "Middle East: Islamic Doll Kicks Barbie's Ass," *Western Resistance*, September 22, 2005, http://www.westernresistance.com/blog/ archives/000179.html; "Egypt: Fulla the Muslim Doll Conquers Land of the Nile," *Western Resistance*, January 17, 2006, http://www .westernresistance.com/blog/archives/001467.html.

39   Terri Simmons, Guest Bio, "Don Levine: Noah, Moses and G.I. Joe," *The 700 Club*, http://www.cbn.com/700club/guests/bios/don_ levine081808.aspx. See also Kevin Jackson, "G.I. Joe Creator Launches Biblical Action Figures Line," *Christian Post*, May 13, 2007, http:// www.christianpost.com/Entertainment/General/2007/05/g-i-joe-creator-launches-biblical-action-figures-line-13/index.html.

40   "Chris Waters: Waging 'Angel Wars,'" *The 700 Club*, http://www .cbn.com/700club/Guests/Bios/chris_waters121305.aspx (emphasis added).

41   "Chris Waters: Waging 'Angel Wars'" (emphasis added).

42   Kendall Lyons, interview with Chris Waters, *Animation Insider*, January 18, 2007, http://www.animationinsider.net/article.php? articleID=1253.

43   Chris Hedges, *American Fascists: The Christian Right and the War on America* (New York: Free Press, 2006), 29.

44   Richard Allen Greene, "Christian Video Game Draws Anger," *BBC News*, December 14, 2006, http://news.bbc.co.uk/2/hi/technology/ 6178055.stm.

45 Jonathan Hutson, "The Purpose Driven Life Takers," part 1, *Talk to Action*, May 29, 2006, http://www.talk2action.org/story/2006/5/29/195855/959.

46 Zach Whalen, "Left Behind: Eternal Forces—First Impressions, Finally," *Gameology*, September 7, 2006, http://www.gameology.org/node/1233/print.

47 Hutson, "Purpose Driven Life Takers."

48 Hutson, "Purpose Driven Life Takers."

49 Carlsson-Paige and Levin, "War-Toy Connection."

50 From their Web site www.one2believe.com.

51 From their Web site www.one2believe.com.

52 Clark, *Real Toy Story*, 100–101.

53 "Dara and Sara—Iran's Islamic alternative to Ken and Barbie," *Islam for Today*, http://www.islamfortoday.com/iran02.htm.

54 Rebekah Zes, "A Special Word for Proverbs 31 Tomboys," speech given at the Vision Forum Ministries 2003 Father and Daughter Retreat in San Antonio, Texas, October 21, 2003, http://www.visionforumministries.org/issues/family/a_special_word_for_proverbs_31.aspx (emphasis added).

55 The word *lesbian* lurks beneath the surface, and the gender stereotypes are fierce: feminists and tomboys are the same thing; women who dress as "girly girls" in feminine outfits cannot be feminists; feminists/tomboys cannot really be Christians.

56 CNN, "Muslim Doll Offers Modest Alternative to Barbie," October 8, 2003, http://www.cnn.com/2003/EDUCATION/10/08/muslim.barbie.ap/index.html. This article is no longer available online.

57 Malak Labib, "Veiled Fulla Is Arab Answer to Barbie: Sartorial Evolution of Little Muslim Girls' Toy Doll Mirrors Broader Phenomenon of Islamisation in Arab Society," *Middle East Online*, January 11, 2006, http://www.middle-east-online.com/english/?id=15449.

58 Mark MacKinnon, "Bye-Bye Barbie: Muslim Families Pick Modest Fulla Doll," *Chicago Sun-Times*, October 30, 2005.

59 Mary Rogers, *Barbie Culture* (London: Sage Publications, 1999), 2.

60 Rogers, *Barbie Culture*, 3

61 Rogers, *Barbie Culture*, 80.

62 Ruth Handler with Jacqueline Shannon, *Dream Doll: The Ruth Handler Story* (Stamford, Conn.: Longmeadow, 1994), 3.

63 Quoted in Rogers, *Barbie Culture*, 80.

64 Linda M. Scott, *Fresh Lipstick: Redressing Fashion and Feminism* (New York: Palgrave Macmillan, 2005), 255.

65 Brian Sutton-Smith, *Toys as Culture* (New York: Garden Press, 1986), 8–9.

66 M. G. Lord, *Forever Barbie* (New York: Walker, 2004), 244.

67 CNN, "Muslim Doll Offers Modest Alternative to Barbie."

68   Ed O'Loughlin, "Fulla Has the Mid-East Doll Market Covered," *Sydney Morning Herald*, December 23, 2005.

69   Katherine Zoepf, "Bestseller in the Mideast: Barbie with a Prayer Mat," *The New York Times*, September 22, 2005.

70   Craig Nelson, "Modest Fulla Doll Displaces Barbie in Mideast Toy Stores," *Cox News Service*, November 20, 2005.

71   MacKinnon, "Bye-Bye Barbie."

72   Scott, *Fresh Lipstick*, 255.

73   Nelson, "Modest Fulla Doll Displaces Barbie."

74   Clark, *Real Toy Story*, 84.

75   Tom Parry, "Girls Burn Barbie in Hate Ritual," in *Daily Mirror*, online edition, December 19, 2005, http://www.mirror.co.uk/news/top-stories/2005/12/19/girls-burn-barbie-in-hate-ritual-115875-16499826/.

76   Zoepf, "Bestseller in the Mideast."

77   Jason Grubbs, "Updated: Does Doll Deliver Islamic Message?" Scripps TV Station Group, October 9, 2008, http://www.kjrh.com/news/local/story/UPDATED-Does-doll-deliver-Islamic-message/yjo4XNLDPUu0pVqBCLpJcQ.cspx. What is truly baffling is that not only is the first message almost impossible to decipher, but this site also claims that some people hear a second message: "Satan is King." Even if the doll were promoting Islam it would not say this—Satan (*Shaitan*) is regarded much the same way in Islam as in Christianity and would not be praised in this way.

78   "Little Mommie Doll Says Islam Is the Light, Instead of Mama," WDEF, http://www.youtube.com/watch?v=bE4kifrUxDE&NR=1.

79   "Doll Says 'Islam,' Baffles Many," WBAL-TV, http://www.youtube.com/watch?v=Lao8STY45xo.

80   "Doll Says 'Islam,' Baffles Many."

81   Clark, *Real Toy Story*, 101.

82   Mohammad Al-Hamroni and Ukba Al-Humaidy, "Hijab-Clad Fulla 'Wanted' in Tunisia," *Islam Online.net*, September 22, 2006, http://www.islamonline.net/English/News/2006-09/22/05.shtml.

83   *Halalco Supermarket*, www.halalco.com.

Chapter 3

1   See, e.g., Douglas Carl Abrams, *Selling the Old-Time Religion: American Fundamentalists and Mass Culture, 1920–1940* (Athens: University of Georgia Press, 2001); Jeremy Carrette and Richard King, *Selling Spirituality: The Silent Takeover of Religion* (London: Routledge, 2007); Dell DeChant, *The Sacred Santa: Religious Dimensions of Consumer Culture* (Cleveland: Pilgrim Press, 2002); Stewart Hoover and Lynn Schofield Clark, eds., *Practicing Religion in the Age of the Media: Explorations in Media, Religion and*

Culture (New York: Columbia University Press, 2002); David Lyon, *Jesus in Disneyland: Religion in Postmodern Times* (Cambridge: Polity Press, 2000); Vincent Miller, *Consuming Religion: Christian Faith and Practice in a Consumer Culture* (London: Continuum, 2003); R. Laurence Moore, *Selling God: American Religion in the Marketplace of Culture* (Oxford: Oxford University Press, 1994); C. K. Robertson, ed., *Religion as Entertainment* (New York: Peter Lang Publishing, 2002); William Romanowski, *Pop Culture Wars: Religion and the Role of Entertainment in American Life* (Downers Grove, Ill.: InterVarsity, 1996); Leigh Schmidt, *Consumer Rites: The Buying and Selling of American Holidays* (Princeton: Princeton University Press, 1995); James Twitchell, "Two Cheers for Materialism," in *The Consumer Society Reader*, ed. Juliet Schor and Douglas Holt, 281–90 (New York: The New Press, 2000).

2   Carrette and King, *Selling Spirituality*, ix.

3   Twitchell, "Two Cheers for Materialism," 290.

4   Xinhua News Agency, "Dispute over Sports Car for China's Most Famous Monk," China View, August 22, 2006, http://news3 .xinhuanet.com/english/2006-08/22/content_4993996.htm.

5   Matthew 19:21-24, NIV.

6   Moore, *Selling God*, 67.

7   Moore, *Selling God*, 274.

8   Moore, *Selling God*, 274.

9   Abrams, *Selling the Old-Time Religion*, 124.

10 Max Weber, *The Protestant Ethic and the Spirit of Capitalism*, trans. Stephen Kalberg (Los Angeles: Roxbury, 2002).

11 "Several essential features of today's capitalism were either unimaginable or positively condemned throughout most of Christian history. We no longer question the legitimacy of making money with money. But throughout Church history, up through the Reformation, the charging of interest was proscribed. In earlier eras, the church would have regarded stock market speculation as nothing more than profligate gambling . . . in the Christian-influenced West in which capitalism originated, for capitalism to succeed it required a theological foundation and legitimation. Capitalism had to be learned" (Rodney Clapp, "Why the Devil Takes Visa: A Christian Response to the Triumph of Consumerism," *Christianity Today*, October 7, 1996, 21).

12 *CBA: The Association for Christian Retail*, http://www.cbaonline .org/nm/RR.htm.

13 Frances Fitzgerald, "Come One, Come All," *The New Yorker*, December 3, 2007, 46.

14 Moore, *Selling God*, 275.

15 Breton, *Kingdom of Heaven* game. Please note that grammatical errors are in the original translation.

16 "In the 1920s and 1930s, fundamentalists energetically embraced the business ethos with its secular values of organization, efficiency, consumerism, promotionalism, and emphasis on size and numbers. To evangelize and build institutions, they tapped innovative modern strategies and technologies, such as advertising, magazines, and radio . . . When President Coolidge in a famous dictum of the 1920s compared a factory to a temple and its workers to worshippers, he reflected an affinity between business and religion that fundamentalists also celebrated, sometimes to embarrassing extremes" (Abrams, *Selling the Old-Time Religion*, 11–12).

17 Abrams, *Selling the Old-Time Religion*, 26.

18 Abrams, *Selling the Old-Time Religion*, 124.

19 Moore, *Selling God*, 10.

20 *Armor of God* card. To win this game, children must collect all the pieces of the Armor of God: "Finally, be strong in the Lord and in his mighty power. Put on the full armor of God so that you can take your stand against the devil's schemes. For our struggle is not against flesh and blood, but against the rulers, against the authorities, against the powers of this dark world and against the spiritual forces of evil in the heavenly realms. Therefore put on the full armor of God, so that when the day of evil comes, you may be able to stand your ground, and after you have done everything, to stand. Stand firm then, with the belt of truth buckled around your waist, with the breastplate of righteousness in place, and with your feet fitted with the readiness that comes from the gospel of peace. In addition to all this, take up the shield of faith, with which you can extinguish all the flaming arrows of the evil one. Take the helmet of salvation and the sword of the Spirit, which is the word of God" (Eph 6:10-17).

21 *The Christian Fitness Game* playing card.

22 Heather Hendershot, *Shaking the World for Jesus: Media and Conservative Evangelical Culture* (Chicago: University of Chicago Press, 2004), 20–21.

23 Hendershot, *Shaking the World for Jesus*, 29.

24 Hendershot, *Shaking the World for Jesus*, 34.

25 Pastor Guy Uong, *Kingdom of Heaven* game (emphasis in original).

26 *Buddhawheel*, "Players' Page," http://www.buddhawheel.co.uk/Players.html.

27 Handler, *Dream Doll*, 4–5.

28 John Michlig, *G.I. Joe: The Complete Story of America's Favorite Man of Action* (San Francisco: Chronicle Books, 1998), 17, quoted in Jeannie Banks Thomas, *Naked Barbies, Warrior Joes, and Other Forms of Visible Gender* (Urbana: University of Illinois Press, 2003), 130.

29 Zoepf, "Bestseller in the Mideast."

30 O'Loughlin, "Fulla Has the Mid-East Doll Market Covered."

31 Zoepf, "Bestseller in the Mideast."

32 Clapp, "Why the Devil Takes Visa," 23.

33 Schmidt, *Consumer Rites*, 166.

34 Moore, *Selling God*, 205.

35 *The Christmas Resistance Movement*, http://www.xmasresistance
    .org.

36 *Redefine Christmas*, http://www.redefine-christmas.org.

37 *Redefine Christmas.*

38 *Redefine Christmas.*

39 *Buy Nothing Christmas*, http://www.buynothingchristmas.org.

40 Primiano, "Vernacular Religion and the Search for Method," 54.

41 William Dever, *Did God Have a Wife?: Archaeology and Folk Religion
    in Ancient Israel* (Grand Rapids: Eerdmans, 2005), 251 (emphasis in
    original).

42 Moore, *Selling God*, 14.

43 One example is the case of goat sacrifice during a Catholic mass
    in South Africa, referred to as "liturgical abuse" by the national
    liturgical coordinator. See John Donnelly, "In Africa, a Vibrant yet
    Conflicted Faith: Some Catholics Defy Rome, Shaping Church to
    Continent's Needs, Customs," *Boston Globe*, April 11, 2005.

44 *Missionary Conquest* Afghanistan card. This statement also appears
    on the Cuba card.

45 Moore, *Selling God*, 13.

46 Colleen McDannell, *Material Christianity: Religion and Popular
    Culture in America* (New Haven: Yale University Press, 1995),
    23–24.

47 McDannell, *Material Christianity*, 180.

48 McDannell, *Material Christianity*, 38.

49 McDannell, *Material Christianity*, 62.

50 "Body Piercing Saved My Life" T-shirt, www.trenzshirts.com. Note
    that the placement of the nail in the palm rather than the wrist is
    controversial.

51 Faithfulness, Gentleness, Goodness, Joy, Kindness, Patience, Love,
    Peace, Temperance.

52 *InheritanceGame*,http://www.myinheritanceonline.com/resources/
    mechanics.php. This page is no longer available online.

53 McDannell, *Material Christianity*, 272.

54 Rajesh Priyadarshi, "Harrods Apology over Hindu Bikinis," *BBC
    News*, April 22, 2009, http://news.bbc.co.uk/1/hi/world/south_
    asia/3790315.stm. There is a critical difference between these exam-
    ples. Harrods' carrying of Hindu underwear is an appropriation of
    symbols from another culture, whereas the Christian items are pro-
    duced and marketed from within.

55 McDannell, *Material Christianity*, 261.

56 The promotional material for the Bank AmeriKid ATM states, "This fun, interactive bank works just like a real ATM! Children learn how to save money and bank like grownups using Bank AmeriKid's multifunction electronic keypad and programmable ATM card. Kids will love making deposits, withdrawals, and building a savings account while they learn to reach savings goals. Even includes security alarm, locking cash drawer and built-in calculator! Works with both real and play money. Next stop, Wall Street!" Bank AmeriKid ATM, UPC 086002030603, *Christianbook.com*, http://www.christianbook.com/ Christian/Books/customer_review?sku=343060.

57 *Little Spender Game*, CBD stock number WW04365, *Christian book.com*, http://www.christianbook.com/Christian/Books/ product?item_no=04365&netp_id=104607&event=ESRCN&item_ code=WW&view=covers.

58 In contrast, a shopping game found on numerous Jewish Web sites, *Let's Go Schlepping*, which teaches children how to identify kosher foods at the grocery store, has an identifiable link to Jewish life and practice.

59 *Indian Bindi*, http://www.indianbindi.com.

60 Miller, *Consuming Religion*, 84.

61 *Atlantis Resort, Paradise Island, Bahamas*, Mayan Temple description, www.atlantis.com/water/aquaventure/mayantemple.aspx.

62 Miller, *Consuming Religion*, 37–38, 65.

63 See xmasresistance.org.

64 Jacqueline Bodnar, "Religious-Themed Products Become Mainstream," *PR Newswire Association*, February 28, 2006.

65 Miller, *Consuming Religion*, 76.

66 McDannell, personal communication, 2008.

67 And if, as Dell DeChant has argued in *Sacred Santa*, the economy is our new religion, then all of these things around us, marketed to us, desired and bought by us, are conveyances of the sacred.

68 Miller, *Consuming Religion*, 140.

69 Lyon, *Jesus in Disneyland*, 77.

70 Miller, *Consuming Religion*, 25.

71 Moore, *Selling God*, 272.

72 Moore, *Selling God*, 145.

73 "consumer culture, while it may be pervasive and influential, resembles in only some discrete and specific ways older sign systems or means of orientation that could (however mistakenly) be thought of as dominant ideologies" (Lyon, *Jesus in Disneyland*, 77).

CHAPTER 4

1 The world's Muslim population is now too large for the annual *hajj* to accommodate all Muslims who want to participate in any given

year, so the Saudi government determines by lottery who can come. Approximately one of every hundred Muslims per country can participate.

2 *Missionary Conquest* game, CBD stock number WW71000, *Christian book.com*, http://www.christianbook.com/Christian/Books/ product?item_no=71000&netp_id=184234&event=ESRCN&item_ code=WW&view=covers.

3 Ivor Morgan and Jay Rao, "Making Routine Customer Experiences Fun," *MIT Sloan Management Review* 45, no. 1 (2003): 93–94.

4 Rebecca Sachs Norris, "The Paradox of Healing Pain," *Religion* 39, no. 1 (2009): 22–33.

5 Johan Huizinga, *Homo Ludens: A Study of the Play Element in Culture* (Boston: Beacon Press, 1950), 3.

6 Asef Bayat, "Islamism and the Politics of Fun," *Public Culture: Bulletin of the Project for Transnational Cultural Studies* 19, no. 3 (2007): 435. See also Brian Sutton-Smith, "Evolving a Consilience of Play Definitions: Playfully," in *Play Contexts Revisited*, ed. Stuart Reifel, 239–56 (Stamford, Conn.: Ablex, 1999), 244 on religious fear of play because it promotes diversity.

7 Cliff, "Ludicity," 24.

8 Matt Labash, "Are We Having Fun Yet? The Infantilization of Corporate America," *Weekly Standard*, September 17, 2007.

9 Neil Postman, *Amusing Ourselves to Death: Public Discourse in the Age of Show Business* (New York: Penguin Books, 2006). Unlike most conversations about the problem of TV, which focus on the information conveyed by TV and the question of whether TV is harmful, Postman examines the changes in our thinking and perceptions caused by the medium of TV and other electronic forms of communication.

10 Postman, *Amusing Ourselves to Death*, 105. Postman's MacNeil quotations are from Robert MacNeil, "Is Television Shortening Our Attention Span?" *New York University Education Quarterly* 14, no. 2 (1983): 2, 4.

11 Amy Goodman and David Goodman list them in their article "Why Media Ownership Matters," *Seattle Times*, April 3, 2005. http:// seattletimes.nwsource.com/cgi-bin/PrintStory.pl?document_ id=2002228040&zsection_id=268883724&slug=sundaygoodman03 &date=20050403/.

(1) Rupert Murdoch's News Corporation: FOX, HarperCollins, *New York Post*, *Weekly Standard*, *TV Guide*, DirecTV, and 35 TV stations

(2) General Electric: NBC, CNBC, MSNBC, Telemundo, Bravo, Universal Pictures, and 28 TV stations

(3) Time Warner: AOL, CNN, Warner Brothers, *Time*, and 130+ magazines

(4) Disney: ABC, Disney Channel, ESPN, 10 TV and 72 radio stations

(5) Viacom: CBS, MTV, Nickelodeon, Paramount Pictures, Simon & Schuster and 183 U.S. radio stations

(6) Bertelsmann: Random House and its more than 120 imprints worldwide, and Gruner + Jahr and its more than 110 magazines in ten countries.

12 "The defining characteristics of junk thought, which manifests itself in the humanities and social sciences as well as the physical sciences, are anti-rationalism and contempt for countervailing facts and expert opinion" (Susan Jacoby, *The Age of American Unreason* [New York: Pantheon, 2008], 211).

13 Jacoby, *Age of American Unreason*, 241.

14 Goodman and Goodman, "Why Media Ownership Matters."

15 Barbara Ehrenreich, "Guys Just Want to Have Fun," *Time*, July 31, 2006, 72.

16 Leslie Yerkes, "How to Create a Place Where People Love to Work," *Journal for Quality and Participation* 26, no. 4 (2003): 48.

17 Martha Wolfenstein, "The Emergence of Fun Morality," *Journal of Social Issues* 7, no. 4 (1951): 15–25.

18 Barbara Smaller, "Fun Is Work Cartoon," *The New Yorker*, January 8, 2007, 60.

19 Howard Chudacoff, *Children at Play* (New York: New York University Press, 2007), 165–66.

20 David Elkind, "The Hidden Power of Play," *Boston Globe*, October 9, 2006.

21 In fact, a knowledgeable friend with teenaged children remarks that one does not get as drunk using these games since the timing of taking a drink is controlled by the rules, rather than having another drink as soon as one has emptied one's glass.

22 Bob Geiger, "St. Paul's Metro Lofts Using Fun and Location to Market Condos," *Finance and Commerce*, February 10, 2005.

23 Andrew Walmsley, "No One Wants to Shop in a Vacuum," *Marketing Magazine*, November 22, 2006, 13.

24 Emily Rayson, "Capturing the Joy of Online Experiences," *Marketing Magazine*, March 1, 2004, 17.

25 The same issue arises in Yerkes' article; she lists a number of results from integrating fun in the workplace: mending conflicts, stimulating activity, fostering commitment, positive impact on productivity, and stronger customer relationships. The few that are employee centered still have increasing business as an underlying agenda (Yerkes, "How to Create a Place," 50).

26 The article goes on to give examples of how these invigorating online experiences can be developed by savvy online marketers. The first

example is of a major paint brand whose Web site was "vague" and "ordinary." After researching how decorators kept a scrapbook of colors, the marketers added an online scrapbook to the Web site (Rayson, "Capturing the Joy"). This was a good idea, except that every monitor shows color differently; it is not possible to see color accurately on a computer screen.

27   There is already a backlash to super-emotive marketing techniques, usually talked about in terms of "minimalist marketing" strategies. These strategies seem to reflect a desire to trim advertising costs as well as appeal to the eye by presenting something different.

28   E.g., "Hanuman," http://www.youtube.com/watch?v=d74zxZAslm8; "Ramayana," http://www.youtube.com/watch?v=TjUzxTpVqSo&feature=related, no longer available online; "The Story of ZamZam," http://www.youtube.com/watch?v=AzHX8SlJkoM.

29   Chaya Burstein, *The Kids' Cartoon Bible* (Philadelphia: Jewish Publication Society, 2002).

30   Janice Peck, *The Gods of Televangelism* (Cresskill, N.J.: Hampton Press, 1993), 10.

31   Stuart Flexner and Doris Flexner, *Wise Words and Wives' Tales: The Origins, Meanings and Time-Honored Wisdom of Proverbs and Folk Sayings, Olde and New* (New York: Avon Books, 1993), 8.

32   The exact figures are unclear, as sources vary on the number injured.

33   *The National Institute for Play*, "Play Deprived Life—Devastating Results," http://nifplay.org/whitman.html.

34   Stephen King, "The Role of the Amygdala in Aggression," http://www.wiu.edu/users/smk102/psy452.html, 2002. See also Nicole Rafter, *Criminal Brain: Understanding Biological Theories of Crime* (New York: New York University Press, 2008), 204, and Allan Siegel, *The Neurobiology of Aggression and Rage* (Boca Raton, Fla.: CRC Press, 2005), 96–98.

35   *The National Institute for Play*, "Play Deprived Life."

36   Crane, "Talking Dolls."

37   Nathan Bender and Richard Singer, "The Sacred Sport of Apsáalooke Arrow Throwing," paper presented at the American Folklore Society, Milwaukee, Wisc., October 20, 2006.

38   Robert Orsi, *Between Heaven and Earth: The Religious Worlds People Make and the Scholars Who Study Them* (Princeton: Princeton University Press, 2005), 198.

39   "Shaitan Square," http://www.onlineislamicstore.com/a3492.html. Quotation is no longer available online.

40   Roger Callois, *Man, Play and Games*, trans. Meyer Barash (Urbana: University of Illinois Press, 2001), 6, 9–10. See also Huizinga, *Homo Ludens*, 13. "Summing up the formal characteristics of play we might

call it a free activity standing quite consciously outside 'ordinary' life as being 'not serious,' but at the same time absorbing the player intensely and utterly. It is an activity connected with no material interest, and no profit can be gained by it. It proceeds within its own proper boundaries of time and space according to fixed rules and in an orderly manner."

41 Huizinga, *Homo Ludens*, 5.

42 Callois, *Man, Play and Games*, 43 (emphasis in original).

43 Cliff, "Ludicity," 163.

44 Cliff, "Ludicity," 37.

45 "Play is an orientation or framing and defining *context* that players adopt toward something (an object, a person, a role, an activity, an event, etc.) . . . play gives shape as well as expression to individual and societal affective and cognitive systems" (Helen Schwartzman, *Transformations: The Anthropology of Children's Play* [New York: Plenum Press, 1978], 330 [emphasis in original]).

46 Jean Piaget, *Play, Dreams and Imitation in Childhood* (New York: Norton, 1962).

47 Sutton-Smith, *Toys as Culture*; see also Sutton-Smith, "Evolving a Consilience."

48 Sutton-Smith, *Toys as Culture*, 23.

49 "The emotional vulnerabilities, which are the essence of play, are masked from the players by the rules, the play ethic, and their own inversive masteries. Thus, play is meant not only to represent these vulnerabilities but also to bring protection against them by masking their relevance" (Brian Sutton-Smith, "Play as a Parody of Emotional Vulnerability," in *Play and Educational Theory and Practice*, ed. Donald Lytle, 3–17 [Westport, Conn.: Praeger, 2003], 13).

50 Kathryn McClymond, "That Can't Be Religion—They're Having Fun!" American Academy of Religion panel response, Washington, D.C., November 19, 2006.

51 Sutton-Smith, *Toys as Culture*, 138.

52 Sutton-Smith, *Toys as Culture*, 127 (emphasis in original).

53 Gavin Ardley, "The Role of Play in the Philosophy of Plato," *Philosophy* 42, no. 161 (1967): 234.

54 Sutton-Smith, *Toys as Culture*, 119.

55 Sutton-Smith, *Toys as Culture*, 124–25.

56 Jacoby, *Age of American Unreason*, 250.

57 Clifford Geertz, "Deep Play: Notes on the Balinese Cockfight," 412–53 in his *The Interpretation of Cultures* (New York: Basic Books, 1973); Sutton-Smith, "Evolving a Consilience," 244.

58 Gwen Gordon and Sean Esbjörn-Hargens, "Are We Having Fun Yet? An Exploration of the Transformative Power of Play," *Journal of Humanistic Psychology* 47, no. 2 (2007): 201.

59 Cliff, "Ludicity," 21.

60 Mihaly Csikszentmihalyi, *Beyond Boredom and Anxiety: The Experience of Play in Work and Games* (San Francisco: Jossey-Bass, 1975); *Flow and the Psychology of Discovery and Invention* (New York: HarperCollins, 1996); idem, *Finding Flow: The Psychology of Engagement with Everyday Life* (New York: Basic Books, 1997).

61 Csikszentmihalyi, *Beyond Boredom and Anxiety*, 36.

62 Csikszentmihalyi, *Beyond Boredom and Anxiety*, 185.

63 Moore, *Selling God*, 105, 254.

64 Moore, *Selling God*, 153.

65 Bruce Daniels, *Puritans at Play: Leisure and Recreation in Colonial New England* (New York: St. Martin's Griffin, 1995).

66 Moore, *Selling God*, 153.

67 Robyn Holmes, "Kindergarten and College Students' Views of Play and Work at Home and at School," in *Play Contexts Revisited*, ed. Stuart Reifel, 59–72 (Stamford, Conn.: Ablex, 1999), 61.

68 Csikszentmihalyi, *Finding Flow*, 49.

69 Csikszentmihalyi, *Finding Flow*, 50.

70 "By age ten or eleven, they have internalized the pattern that is typical of society at large. When they are asked to say whether what they are doing is more like 'work' or more like 'play' (or like 'both' or 'neither') sixth graders almost invariably say that academic classes in school are work, and doing sports is play. The interesting thing is that whenever adolescents are doing something they label as work, they typically say that what they do is important for their future, requires high concentration, and induces high self-esteem. Yet they are also less happy and motivated than average when what they do is like work. On the other hand, when they are doing something they label as play, they see it as having low importance and requiring little concentration, but they are happy and motivated. In other words, the split between work that is necessary but unpleasant, and pleasant but useless play, is well established by late childhood" (Csikszentmihalyi, *Finding Flow*, 54–55).

71 DeChant, *Sacred Santa*, 36.

72 Ananda Coomaraswamy, "Play and Seriousness," in *Coomaraswamy*, ed. Roger Lipsey, 156–58 (Princeton: Princeton University Press, 1977), 156.

73 Gordon and Esbjörn-Hargens, "Are We Having Fun Yet?" 200.

Chapter 5

1 Richard Schechner, *The Future of Ritual: Writings on Culture and Performance* (London: Routledge, 1993), 27.

2 Schechner, *Future of Ritual*, 27.

3 Schechner, *Future of Ritual*, 27.

4   This is further complicated by the fact that the word *illusion* is also related to *ludus*.

5   Wendy Doniger O'Flaherty, *Dreams, Illusions, and Other Realities* (Chicago: University of Chicago Press, 1984), 117–19, quoted in Schechner, *Future of Ritual*, 28.

6   Schechner, *Future of Ritual*, 31.

7   Schechner, *Future of Ritual*, 34.

8   David L. Haberman, *Journey through the Twelve Forests: An Encounter with Krishna* (Oxford: Oxford University Press, 1994), viii.

9   William LaFleur, *Buddhism: A Cultural Perspective* (Englewood Cliffs, N.J.: Prentice Hall, 1988), 25.

10 Ananda Coomaraswamy, "Līlā," in *Coomaraswamy*, ed. Roger Lipsey, 148–55 (Princeton: Princeton University Press, 1977), 151.

11 Coomaraswamy, "Līlā," 148.

12 Ardley, "Role of Play," 234, 235.

13 Huizinga, *Homo Ludens*, 6.

14 Coomaraswamy, "Play and Seriousness," 157.

15 Coomaraswamy, "Play and Seriousness," 158.

16 Many scholars have contributed to the discussion on framing and metacommunicative or metanarrative strategies, including Erving Goffman, Mary Douglas, Mary Hufford, Barbara Babcock, Bert Wilson, and Nikki Bado-Fralick.

17 Huizinga, *Homo Ludens*, 10.

18 See e.g., Schechner, *Future of Ritual*, on ritual space and Bado-Fralick's 2002 discussion of the creation of the Witches' magic circle ("Mapping the Wiccan Ritual Landscape: Circles of Transformation," *Folklore Forum* 33, no. 1/2 [2002]: 45–65).

19 Schechner, *Future of Ritual*, 41.

20 Schechner, *Future of Ritual*, 26, 36.

21 From *cagar*, a vulgar term, not for polite company.

22 See Bill Ellis' 1981 discussion of mock ordeals during camp and Bado-Fralick's 2002 discussion of ritual teasing during initiation. Bill Ellis, "The Camp Mock-Ordeal: Theater as Life," *Journal of American Folklore* 94, no. 374 (1981): 486–505; Bado-Fralick, "Mapping the Wiccan Ritual Landscape."

23 Magnus Echtler, "'The Clitoris Is Indeed Your Sweet': Negotiating Gender Roles in the Ritual Setting of the Swahili New Year's Festival," in *Negotiating Rites*, ed. Uta Hüsken and Frank Neubert (Oxford: Oxford University Press, forthcoming).

24 Steven Engler, "Playing at Syncretism: New Rituals in a Brazilian Catholic Women's Group," *American Academy of Religion*, Washington, D.C., November 19, 2006.

25 Philip L. Nicoloff, *Sacred Kōyasan: A Pilgrimage to the Mountain Temple of Saint Kōbō Daishi and the Great Sun Buddha* (Albany: State University of New York Press, 2008), 242.

26 Alicia Ostriker, "Esther, or the World Turned Upside Down," *Kenyon Review* 13 (1991): 18.

27 Eli Rozik, "The Adoption of Theatre by Judaism Despite Ritual: A Study in the Purim-Shpil," *European Legacy* 4, no. 2 (1999): 78.

28 Rozik, "Adoption of Theatre by Judaism," 78.

29 Roland Barthes, *Mythologies*, trans. Annette Lavers (New York: Hill & Wang, 1972).

30 Brian Sutton-Smith, *The Ambiguity of Play* (Cambridge, Mass.: Harvard University Press, 1997), 208.

31 Sutton-Smith, *Ambiguity of Play*, 208

32 Tom F. Driver, *The Magic of Ritual: Our Need for Liberating Rites that Transform Our Lives and Our Communities* (New York: HarperCollins, 1991), 166–67.

33 Driver, *Magic of Ritual*, 166–67.

34 Bado-Fralick, *Coming to the Edge of the Circle*, 7.

35 Ronald L. Grimes, *Beginnings in Ritual Studies*, Revised Edition (Columbia: University of South Carolina Press, 1995), 50.

36 Schechner, *Future of Ritual*, 26–27.

37 Sam D. Gill, "Disenchantment: A Religious Abduction," in *Readings in Ritual Studies*, ed. Ronald L. Grimes, 230–39 (Upper Saddle River, N.J.: Prentice Hall, 1996), 234.

38 Gill, "Disenchantment," 234.

39 Gill, "Disenchantment," 234.

40 This point comes from Eric Waite, a graduate student at Iowa State, who works on the "new orality" within video games.

41 Schechner, *Future of Ritual*, 30.

42 Bado-Fralick, *Coming to the Edge of the Circle*, 14.

43 Adam B. Seligman, Robert P. Weller, Michael J. Puett, and Bennett Simon, *Ritual and Its Consequences* (Oxford: Oxford University Press, 2008), 83.

44 Seligman et al., *Ritual and Its Consequences*, 83.

45 *Boston Globe*, November 16, 2008, page A12.

46 Joel Best, "Too Much Fun: Toys as Social Problems and the Interpretation of Culture," *Symbolic Interaction* 21, no. 2 (1998): 199.

47 Sally Sugarman, "Playing the Game: Rituals in Children's Games," in *Rituals and Patterns in Children's Lives*, ed. Kathy Merlock Jackson, 124–38 (Madison: University of Wisconsin Press, 2005), 124.

48 Steven Dubin, "Who's That Girl?" in *The Barbie Chronicles*, ed. Yonda Zeldis McDonough, 19–38 (New York: Touchstone, 1999), 27.

49   Erica Jong, "Twelve Dancing Barbies," in *The Barbie Chronicles: A Living Doll Turns Forty*, ed. Y. Z. McDonough, 201–3 (New York: Touchstone, 1999), 202 (emphasis in original).

50   Thomas, *Naked Barbies*, 127–28.

51   Thomas, *Naked Barbies*, 128.

52   Thomas, *Naked Barbies*, 134.

53   Victor Turner, "Body, Brain, and Culture," *Zygon* 18, no. 3 (1983): 233.

54   Don Handelman, "Play and Ritual: Complementary Frames of Meta-Communication," in *It's a Funny Thing, Humor*, ed. Antony J. Chapman and Hugh C. Foot, 185–92 (Oxford: Pergamon, 1977), 185.

55   Schechner, *Future of Ritual*, 26.

56   Sugarman, "Playing the Game."

57   Rebecca Sachs Norris, "Examining the Structure and Role of Emotion: Contributions of Neurobiology to the Study of Embodied Religious Experience," *Zygon: Journal of Religion and Science* 40, no. 1 (2005): 181–99.

58   Ten Plagues in Chocolate, *The Sweet Tooth*, http://www.thesweet tooth.com/search.php?searchText=plagues&x=0&y=0.

59   Salvation Candy Tube, *Bible Candy*, http://www.biblecandy.com/salvation.htm.

60   Rose Marie Berger and Jonathan Mendez, "Sweet Salvation," *Sojourners*, June 2007.

61   C. G. Jung, *The Archetypes and the Collective Unconscious*, trans. R. F. C. Hull (Princeton: Princeton University Press, 1977), 38 (emphasis in original).

62   "The effectiveness of play for personal transformation can also be seen in the use of play in children's therapy, though there are questions about its effectiveness" (Abigail Matorin and John McNamara, "Using Board Games in Therapy with Children," *International Journal of Play Therapy* 2 [1996]: 6).

63   Raph Koster, *A Theory of Fun for Game Design* (Scottsdale, Ariz.: Paraglyph, 2005), 38 (emphasis in original).

64   Alberto Meschiany and Sharon Krontal, "Toys and Games in Play Therapy," *Israel Journal of Psychiatry and Related Sciences* 35, no. 1 (1998): 36.

CONCLUSION

1   Robert Wuthnow, *God and Mammon in America* (New York: Free Press, 1994).

2   Neil Postman, *The Disappearance of Childhood* (New York: Vintage, 1994), 107.

3   Jacoby, *Age of American Unreason*.

4   Robert McElvaine, *Grand Theft Jesus: The Hijacking of Religion in America* (New York: Crown, 2008), 2.

5   Matthew 10:34.

6   "*Caricature*: This refers to reducing the image of God, Jesus, or the entire biblical ethic to a facile commandment, most usually of love. I've encountered many who believe the popular misconception that 'Jesus preached a message of unconditional love.' Nowhere does Jesus endorse unconditional love; in fact, Jesus attaches several conditions to discipleship. . . . This belief in a 'warm and fuzzy Jesus' represents a therapeutic Christianity, one that affirms without challenging and that tends to endorse the American, middle-class, suburban status quo. The danger in this image is that it is profoundly unbiblical and bears little semblance to the radical first-century Jewish prophet from Nazareth whose preaching ultimately cost him his life" (Mark Allman, *Who Would Jesus Kill? War, Peace, and the Christian Tradition* [Winona, Minn.: Saint Mary's Press, 2008], 26).

7   H. Richard Niebuhr, *The Kingdom of God in America* (New York: Harper & Row, 1959), 193.

8   Stephen Prothero, *American Jesus: How the Son of God Became a National Icon* (New York: Farrar, Straus & Giroux, 2003).

9   Wuthnow, *God and Mammon in America*, 6.

10 Holy Huggables Jesus Doll, *Holy Huggables*, http://www.talking bibledolls.com/talkingjesus.htm.

11 Holy Huggables Jesus Doll.

12 Norris, "Examining the Structure and Role of Emotion."

13 Norris, "Paradox of Healing Pain."

14 Callois, *Man, Play and Games*, 10.

15 Huizinga, *Homo Ludens*, 13.

16 Further, if one of the defining characteristics of play is that it cannot have results, how can there be functional definitions? By its very nature a functional definition states that there is a result. Similarly, Cliff's view is that anything not done out of necessity is play, and anything done out of necessity is not play, yet Piaget's developmental analysis presents us with children's play as an innate drive—an evolutional necessity. If Piaget is correct, then according to Cliff play is not play.

17 Huizinga, *Homo Ludens*, 3.

18 While "[c]onventional, mainline religious groups may have fallen on hard times," this does not mean that religion is on its way out, since "the curtain has yet to fall on faith, spirituality, and the quest for transcendence" (Lyon, *Jesus in Disneyland*, 137).

19 Huizinga, *Homo Ludens*, 29.

BIBLIOGRAPHY

700 Club. "Chris Waters: Waging 'Angel Wars.'" *The 700 Club*, http://www.cbn.com/700club/Guests/Bios/chris_waters121305.aspx.

Abrams, Douglas Carl. *Selling the Old-Time Religion: American Fundamentalists and Mass Culture, 1920–1940*. Athens: University of Georgia Press, 2001.

Adamson, Rondi. "Can Fulla Save Muslim Girls from Barbie?" *Christian Science Monitor*, November 25, 2005.

Al-Hamroni, Mohammad, and Ukba Al-Humaidy. "Hijab-Clad Fulla 'Wanted' in Tunisia." *Islam Online.net*, September 22, 2006, http://www.islamonline.net/English/News/2006-09/22/05.shtml.

Allman, Mark. *Who Would Jesus Kill? War, Peace, and the Christian Tradition*. Winona, Minn.: Saint Mary's Press, 2008.

Ardley, Gavin. "The Role of Play in the Philosophy of Plato." *Philosophy* 42, no. 161 (1967): 226–44.

Aries, Philippe. *Centuries of Childhood: A Social History of Family Life*. Translated by Robert Baldick. New York: Vintage Books, 1962.

Avedon, Elliott M., and Brian Sutton-Smith. *The Study of Games*. New York: John Wiley & Sons, 1971.

Bado-Fralick, Nikki. *Coming to the Edge of the Circle: A Wiccan Initiation Ritual*. Oxford: Oxford University Press, 2005.

———. "Mapping the Wiccan Ritual Landscape: Circles of Transformation." *Folklore Forum* 33, no. 1/2 (2002): 45–65.

Barthes, Roland. *Mythologies*. Translated by Annette Lavers. New York: Hill & Wang, 1972.

Baumeister, Roy, and Pamela Senders. "Identity Development and the Role Structure of Children's Games." *Journal of Genetic Psychology* 150, no. 1 (1989): 19–37.

Baxter, Jane Eva. *The Archaeology of Childhood: Children, Gender, and Material Culture.* Walnut Creek, Calif.: AltaMira Press, 2005.

Bayat, Asef. "Islamism and the Politics of Fun." *Public Culture: Bulletin of the Project for Transnational Cultural Studies* 19, no. 3 (2007): 433–59.

Belk, Russell W. *Collecting in a Consumer Society.* London: Routledge, 1995.

Bell, R. C. *Board and Table Games from Many Civilizations.* 2 vols. New York: Dover, 1979.

Bender, Nathan, and Richard Singer. "The Sacred Sport of Apsáalooke Arrow Throwing." Paper presented at the American Folklore Society, Milwaukee, Wisc., October 20, 2006.

Berger, Rose Marie, and Jonathan Mendez. "Sweet Salvation." *Sojourners,* June 2007.

Best, Joel. "Too Much Fun: Toys as Social Problems and the Interpretation of Culture." *Symbolic Interaction* 21, no. 2 (1998): 197–212.

Bodnar, Jacqueline. "Religious-Themed Products Become Mainstream." *PR Newswire Association,* February 28, 2006.

Bordeaux, Edmond. *The Art of Asha.* Tierra del Sol, Calif.: Mille Meditations, 1966.

Brumbaugh, Robert. "The Knossos Game Board." *American Journal of Archaeology* 79 no. 2 (1975): 135–37.

Bryman, Alan. *The Disneyization of Society.* London: Sage Publications, 2004.

Buckingham, David, and Margaret Scanlon. "Parental Pedagogies: An Analysis of British 'Edutainment' Magazines for Young Children." *Journal of Early Childhood Literacy* 1 no. 3 (2001): 281–99.

Burstein, Chaya. *The Kids' Cartoon Bible.* Philadelphia: Jewish Publication Society, 2002.

Butsch, Richard, ed. *For Fun and Profit: The Transformation of Leisure into Consumption.* Philadelphia: Temple University Press, 1990.

Byassee, Jason. "My 'Jesus Camp.'" *Christian Century* 123 no. 24 (2006): 11.

Callois, Roger. *Man, Play and Games.* Translated by Meyer Barash. Urbana: University of Illinois Press, 2001.

Carlsson-Paige, Nancy, and Diane E. Levin. "The War-Toy Connection." *Christian Science Monitor*, October 5, 1999, http://www.csmonitor.com/1999/1005/p9s2.html.

Carrette, Jeremy, and Richard King. *Selling Spirituality: The Silent Takeover of Religion.* London: Routledge, 2007.

Chiung Hwang, Chen. "'Molympics'? Journalistic Discourse of Mormons in Relation to the 2002 Winter Olympic Games." *Journal of Media and Religion* 2, no. 1 (2003): 29.

Chudacoff, Howard. *Children at Play.* New York: New York University Press, 2007.

Clapp, Rodney. "Why the Devil Takes Visa: A Christian Response to the Triumph of Consumerism." *Christianity Today*, October 7, 1996.

Clark, Eric. *The Real Toy Story: Inside the Ruthless Battle for America's Youngest Consumers.* New York: Free Press, 2007.

Cliff, Janet M. "Ludicity: A Model for Understanding Play and Game." Ph.D. diss., University of California, 1990.

CNN. "Muslim Doll Offers Modest Alternative to Barbie." October 8, 2003, http://www.cnn.com/2003/EDUCATION/10/08/muslim.barbie.ap/index.html.

Coomaraswamy, Ananda. "Līlā." In *Coomaraswamy*, edited by Roger Lipsey, 148–55. Princeton: Princeton University Press, 1977.

———. "Play and Seriousness." In *Coomaraswamy*, edited by Roger Lipsey, 156–58. Princeton: Princeton University Press, 1977.

Corr, Rachel. "Death, Dice, and Divination: Rethinking Religion and Play in South America." *Journal of Latin American and Caribbean Anthropology* 13, no. 1 (2008): 2–21.

Cotton, Charles. *Games and Gamesters of the Restoration.* Port Washington, N.Y.: Kennikat Press, 1971.

Cowan, Douglas E. *Sacred Terror: Religion and Horror on the Silver Screen.* Waco, Tex.: Baylor University Press, 2008.

Craig, Steve. *Sports and Games of the Ancients.* Westport, Conn.: Greenwood, 2002.

Crane, Joyce Pellino. "Talking Dolls Designed to Teach Children Scripture." *Boston Globe*, March 17, 2005.

Crombie, J. W. "History of the Game of Hop-Scotch." *Journal of the Anthropological Institute of Great Britain and Ireland* 15 (1886): 403–8.

Cross, Gary. *A Social History of Leisure Since 1600.* State College, Penn.: Venture Publishing, 1990.

Csikszentmihalyi, Mihaly. *Beyond Boredom and Anxiety: The Experience of Play in Work and Games*. San Francisco: Jossey-Bass, 1975.

———. *Finding Flow: The Psychology of Engagement with Everyday Life*. New York: Basic Books, 1997.

———. *Flow and the Psychology of Discovery and Invention*. New York: HarperCollins, 1996.

Csikszentmihalyi, Mihaly, and Stith Bennett. "An Exploratory Model of Play." *American Anthropologist* 73, no. 1 (1971): 45–58.

Culin, Stewart. "American Indian Games." *American Anthropologist* 5, no. 1 (1903): 58–64.

———. *Games of the North American Indians*. New York: Dover, 1975.

Cunneen, Sally. *In Search of Mary: The Woman and the Symbol*. New York: Ballantine Books, 1996.

Daniels, Bruce. *Puritans at Play: Leisure and Recreation in Colonial New England*. New York: St. Martin's Griffin, 1995.

Dasgupta, Shamita. "Activists Call for a Protest of 'Asia Goddess' Barbie." November 25, 1998, www.hartford-hwp.com/archives/50/094.html.

Davis, Erik. "Amma's Cosmic Squeeze." *Salon*, July 19, 2007, http://www.salon.com/mwt/feature/2007/07/19/amma/index.html.

DeChant, Dell. *The Sacred Santa: Religious Dimensions of Consumer Culture*. Cleveland: Pilgrim Press, 2002.

Dever, William. *Did God Have a Wife? Archaeology and Folk Religion in Ancient Israel*. Grand Rapids: Eerdmans, 2005.

Donnelly, John. "In Africa, a Vibrant yet Conflicted Faith: Some Catholics Defy Rome, Shaping Church to Continent's Needs, Customs." *Boston Globe*, April 11, 2005.

Dorson, Richard. *Folk Legends of Japan*. Illustrated by Yoshi Noguchi. Rutland, Vt.: C. E. Tuttle, 1962.

Drake, Tim. "Toy Box Battle." *National Catholic Register*, July 31, 2007. http://www.ncregister.com/site/article/3306

Drewal, Margaret Thompson. *Yoruba Ritual: Performance, Play, Agency*. Bloomington: Indiana University Press, 1992.

Driver, Tom F. *The Magic of Ritual: Our Need for Liberating Rites that Transform Our Lives and Our Communities*. New York: HarperCollins, 1991.

Dubin, Steven. "Who's That Girl?" In *The Barbie Chronicles*, edited by Yona Zeldis McDonough, 19–38. New York: Touchstone, 1999.

Echtler, Magnus. "'The Clitoris Is Indeed Your Sweet': Negotiating Gender Roles in the Ritual Setting of the Swahili New Year's Festival." In *Negotiating Rites*, edited by Uta Hüsken and Frank Neubert. Oxford: Oxford University Press, forthcoming.

Ehrenreich, Barbara. "Guys Just Want to Have Fun." *Time*, July 31, 2006, 72.

Elkind, David. "The Hidden Power of Play." *Boston Globe*, October 9, 2006.

Eller, Cynthia. *The Myth of Matriarchal Prehistory: Why an Invented Past Won't Give Women a Future*. Boston: Beacon Press, 2000.

Ellis, Bill. "The Camp Mock-Ordeal: Theater as Life." *Journal of American Folklore* 94, no. 374 (1981): 486–505.

Engler, Steven. "Playing at Syncretism: New Rituals in a Brazilian Catholic Women's Group." American Academy of Religion, Washington, D.C., November 19, 2006.

Erikson, Erik H. *Toys and Reasons: Stages in the Ritualization of Experience*. New York: Norton, 1977.

Everett, A., and S. C. Watkins. "The Power of Play: The Portrayal and Performance of Race in Video Games." In *The Ecology of Games: Connecting Youth, Games, and Learning*, edited by K. Salen, 141–64. Cambridge, Mass: MIT Press, 2008.

Falkener, Edward. *Games Ancient and Oriental and How to Play Them*. New York: Dover, 1961.

Fitzgerald, Frances. "Come One, Come All." *The New Yorker*, December 3, 2007, 46–56.

Flexner, Stuart, and Doris Flexner. *Wise Words and Wives' Tales: The Origins, Meanings and Time-Honored Wisdom of Proverbs and Folk Sayings, Olde and New*. New York: Avon Books, 1993.

Formanek-Brunell, Miriam. "Sugar and Spite." In *Small Worlds: Children and Adolescents in America, 1850–1950*, edited by Elliott West and Paula Petrik, 107–24. Lawrence: University Press of Kansas, 1992.

Fox, John. "Students of the Game." *The Smithsonian*, April 2006, 110–17.

Geertz, Clifford. *The Interpretation of Cultures*. New York: Basic Books, 1973.

Geiger, Bob. "St. Paul's Metro Lofts Using Fun and Location to Market Condos." *Finance and Commerce*, February 10, 2005.

Ghartsang, Chodak Tashi. Interview, March 16, 2007.

Gill, Sam D. "Disenchantment: A Religious Abduction." In *Readings in Ritual Studies*, edited by Ronald L. Grimes, 230–39. Upper Saddle River, N.J.: Prentice Hall, 1996.

Gimbutas, Marija. *The Goddesses and Gods of Old Europe 6500–3500 BC: Myths and Cult Images*. 1974. Reprint, Berkeley: University of California Press, 1982.

———. *The Living Goddesses*. Berkeley: University of California Press, 1999.

Glickman, Lawrence B. *Consumer Society in American History: A Reader*. Ithaca: Cornell University Press, 1999.

Goffman, Erving. *The Presentation of Self in Everyday Life*. New York: Anchor Books, 1959.

Goldstein, Jeffrey. "Aggressive Toy Play." In *The Future of Play Theory*, edited by A. Pellegrini, 127–47. Albany: State University of New York Press, 1995.

Gomme, Alice. *The Traditional Games of England, Scotland and Ireland*. London: Thames & Hudson, 1984.

Goodison, Lucy, and Christine Morris, eds. *Ancient Goddesses: The Myths and the Evidence*. London: British Museum Press, 1998.

Goodman, Amy, and David Goodman. "Why Media Ownership Matters." *Seattle Times*, April 3, 2005. http://seattletimesnw source.com/cgi-bin/PrintStory.pl?document_id=2002228040& zsection_id=268883724&slub=sundaygoodman03&date= 20050403/.

Gordon, Gwen, and Sean Esbjörn-Hargens. "Are We Having Fun Yet? An Exploration of the Transformative Power of Play." *Journal of Humanistic Psychology* 47, no. 2 (2007): 198–222.

Greene, Richard Allen. "Christian Video Game Draws Anger." *BBC News*, December 14, 2006, http://news.bbc.co.uk/2/hi/technology/ 6178055.stm.

Grimes, Ronald L. *Beginnings in Ritual Studies, Revised Edition*. Columbia: University of South Carolina Press, 1995.

———, ed. *Readings in Ritual Studies*. Upper Saddle River, N.J.: Prentice Hall, 1996.

———. *Rite Out of Place: Ritual Media and the Arts*. Oxford: Oxford University Press, 2006.

Grover, Kathryn. *Hard at Play: Leisure in America, 1840–1940*. Amherst: University of Massachusetts Press, 1992.

Grubbs, Jason. "Updated: Does Doll Deliver Islamic Message?" *Scripps TV Station Group*, October 9, 2008, http://www.kjrh.com/

news/local/story/UPDATED-Does-doll-deliver-Islamic-message/
yjo4XNLDPUu0pVqBCLpJcQ.cspx.

Haberman, David L. *Journey through the Twelve Forests: An Encounter with Krishna.* Oxford: Oxford University Press, 1994.

Hallo, William. "The First Purim." *Biblical Archaeologist* 46, no. 1 (1983): 19–29.

Handelman, Don. "Play and Ritual: Complementary Frames of Meta-Communication." In *It's a Funny Thing, Humor,* edited by Antony J. Chapman and Hugh C. Foot, 185–92. Oxford: Pergamon, 1977.

Handler, Ruth, with Jacqueline Shannon. *Dream Doll: The Ruth Handler Story.* Stamford, Conn.: Longmeadow, 1994.

Hargrave, Catherine Perry. *A History of Playing Cards and a Bibliography of Cards and Gaming.* New York: Dover, 1966.

Hedges, Chris. *American Fascists: The Christian Right and the War on America.* New York: Free Press, 2006.

Hemsath, Dave, and Leslie Yerkes. *301 Ways to Have Fun at Work.* San Francisco: Berrett-Koehler Publishers, 1997.

Hendershot, Heather. *Shaking the World for Jesus: Media and Conservative Evangelical Culture.* Chicago: University of Chicago Press, 2004.

Henricks, Thomas. "Play as Ascending Meaning: Implications of a General Model of Play." In *Play Contexts Revisited,* edited by S. Reifel, 257–77. Play and Culture Studies 2. Stamford, Conn.: Ablex, 1999.

Herron, R. E., and Brian Sutton-Smith. *Child's Play.* New York: John Wiley & Sons, 1971.

Holmes, Robyn. "Kindergarten and College Students' Views of Play and Work at Home and at School." In *Play Contexts Revisited,* edited by Stuart Reifel, 59–72. Stamford, Conn.: Ablex, 1999.

Hoover, Stewart, and Lynn Schofield Clark, eds. *Practicing Religion in the Age of the Media: Explorations in Media, Religion & Culture.* New York: Columbia University Press, 2002.

Howell, Kay. "Games for Health Conference 2004: Issues, Trends, and Needs Unique to Games for Health." *CyberPsychology and Behavior* 8 (2005): 103–9.

Huizinga, Johan. *Homo Ludens: A Study of the Play Element in Culture.* Boston: Beacon Press, 1950.

Hutson, Jonathan. "The Purpose Driven Life Takers," part 1, *Talk2 Action,* May 29, 2006, http://www.talk2action.org/story/2006/5/29/195855/959.

Jackson, Kathy Merlock, ed. *Rituals and Patterns in Children's Lives.* Madison: University of Wisconsin Press, 2005.

Jackson, Kevin. "G.I. Joe Creator Launches Biblical Action Figures Line." *Christian Post,* May 13, 2007, http://www.christianpost .com/Entertainment/General/2007/05/g-i-joe-creator-launches-biblical-action-figures-line-13/index.html.

Jacoby, Susan. *The Age of American Unreason.* New York: Pantheon, 2008.

Johl, Janet Pagter. *The Fascinating Story of Dolls.* New York: H. L. Lindquist, 1941.

Jones, L. Gregory. "The Games We Play." *Christian Century* 121, no. 7 (2004): 32.

Jong, Erica. "Twelve Dancing Barbies." In *The Barbie Chronicles: A Living Doll Turns Forty,* edited by Y. Z. McDonough, 201–3. New York: Touchstone, 1999.

Jung, C. G. *The Archetypes and the Collective Unconscious.* Translated by R. F. C. Hull. Princeton: Princeton University Press, 1977.

King, Stephen. "The Role of the Amygdala in Aggression," http://www.wiu.edu/users/smk102/psy452.html.

Koster, Raph. *A Theory of Fun for Game Design.* Scottsdale, Ariz.: Paraglyph, 2005.

Kurke, Leslie. "Ancient Greek Board Games and How to Play Them." *Classical Philology* 94, no. 3 (1999): 247–67.

Labash, Matt. "Are We Having Fun Yet? The Infantilization of Corporate America." *Weekly Standard,* September 17, 2007.

Labib, Malak. "Veiled Fulla Is Arab Answer to Barbie: Sartorial Evolution of Little Muslim Girls' Toy Doll Mirrors Broader Phenomenon of Islamisation in Arab Society." *Middle East Online,* January 11, 2006, http://www.middle-east-online.com/english/?id=15449.

LaFleur, William. *Buddhism: A Cultural Perspective.* Englewood Cliffs, N.J.: Prentice Hall, 1988.

Leveritt, Mara. "School Prayer and Football Games: Don't Sideline the U.S. Constitution." *Church and State* 53, no. 1 (2000): 20.

Lo, Andrew. "The Game of Leaves: An Inquiry into the Origin of Chinese Playing Cards." *Bulletin of the School of Oriental and African Studies* 63, no. 3 (2000): 389–406.

Long, Diane, David Elkind, and Bernard Spilka. "The Child's Conception of Prayer." *Journal for the Scientific Study of Religion* 6, no. 1 (1967): 101–9.

Lord, M. G. *Forever Barbie.* New York: Walker, 2004.

Lyon, David. *Jesus in Disneyland: Religion in Postmodern Times.* Cambridge: Polity Press, 2000.

Lyons, Kendall. Interview with Chris Waters, *Animation Insider,* January 18, 2007, http://www.animationinsider.net/article.php? articleID=1253.

MacGregor, Robert. "The Eva and Topsy Dichotomy in Advertising." In *Images of the Child,* edited by Harry Eiss, 287–306. Bowling Green, Ohio: Bowling Green State University Popular Press, 1994.

MacKinnon, Mark. "Bye-Bye Barbie: Muslim Families Pick Modest Fulla Doll." *Chicago Sun-Times,* October 30, 2005.

Matorin, Abigail, and John McNamara. "Using Board Games in Therapy with Children." *International Journal of Play Therapy* 2 (1996): 3–16.

McClymond, Kathryn. "That Can't Be Religion—They're Having Fun!" American Academy of Religion panel response. Washington, D.C., November 19, 2006.

McDannell, Colleen. *Material Christianity: Religion and Popular Culture in America.* New Haven: Yale University Press, 1995.

———. Personal communication, November 1, 2008.

McDonough, Yona Zeldis, ed. *The Barbie Chronicles: A Living Doll Turns Forty.* New York: Touchstone, 1999.

McElvaine, Robert. *Grand Theft Jesus: The Hijacking of Religion in America.* New York: Crown, 2008.

McMahon, F. F., Donald E. Lytle, and Brian Sutton-Smith, eds. *Play: An Interdisciplinary Synthesis.* Play and Culture Studies 6. Lanham, Md.: University Press of America, 2005.

Meschiany, Alberto, and Krontal, Sharon. "Toys and Games in Play Therapy." *Israel Journal of Psychiatry and Related Sciences* 35, no. 1 (1998): 31–37.

Michlig, John. *G.I. Joe: The Complete Story of America's Favorite Man of Action.* San Francisco: Chronicle Books, 1998.

Miller, Vincent. *Consuming Religion: Christian Faith and Practice in a Consumer Culture.* London: Continuum, 2003.

Moore, R. Laurence. *Selling God: American Religion in the Marketplace of Culture.* Oxford: Oxford University Press, 1994.

Morgan, Ivor, and Jay Rao. "Making Routine Customer Experiences Fun." *MIT Sloan Management Review* 45, no. 1 (2003): 93–95.

Motz, Lotte. *Faces of the Goddess.* Oxford: Oxford University Press, 1997.

Murray, H. J. R. *A History of Board Games Other Than Chess*. Oxford: Clarendon, 1951.

Nelson, Craig. "Modest Fulla Doll Displaces Barbie in Mideast Toy Stores." *Cox News Service*, November 20, 2005.

Nickerson, Eileen, and Kay O'Laughlin. "It's Fun—But Will it Work? The Use of Games as a Therapeutic Medium for Children and Adolescents." *Journal of Clinical Child Psychology* 9, no. 1 (1980): 78–81.

Nicoloff, Philip L. *Sacred Kōyasan: A Pilgrimage to the Mountain Temple of Saint Kōbō Daishi and the Great Sun Buddha*. Albany: SUNY Press, 2008.

Niebuhr, H. Richard. *The Kingdom of God in America*. New York: Harper & Row, 1959.

Nisizawa, Tekiho. *Japanese Folk-Toys*. Translated by S. Sakabe. Tokyo: Board of Tourist Industry, Japanese Government, 1939.

Norris, Rebecca Sachs. "Examining the Structure and Role of Emotion: Contributions of Neurobiology to the Study of Embodied Religious Experience." *Zygon: Journal of Religion and Science* 40, no. 1 (2005): 181–99.

———. "The Paradox of Healing Pain." *Religion* 39, no. 1 (2009): 22–33.

Nygaard, Elizabeth Teresa. "Board Games." M.A. thesis, Iowa State University, 2001.

O'Flaherty, Wendy Doniger. *Dreams, Illusions, and Other Realities*. Chicago: University of Chicago Press, 1984.

O'Loughlin, Ed. "Fulla Has the Mid-East Doll Market Covered." *Sydney Morning Herald*, December 23, 2005.

Orsi, Robert. *Between Heaven and Earth: The Religious Worlds People Make and the Scholars Who Study Them*. Princeton: Princeton University Press, 2005.

Ostriker, Alicia. "Esther, or the World Turned Upside Down." *Kenyon Review* 13 (1991): 18–21.

Parlett, David. *The Oxford History of Board Games*. Oxford: Oxford University Press, 1999.

Parry, Tom. "Girls Burn Barbie in Hate Ritual." *Daily Mirror*, online edition, December 19, 2005, http://www.mirror.co.uk/news/top-stories/2005/12/19/girls-burn-barbie-in-hate-ritual-115875-16499826/.

Peck, Janice. *The Gods of Televangelism*. Cresskill, N.J.: Hampton Press, 1993.

Piaget, Jean. *Play, Dreams and Imitation in Childhood*. New York: Norton, 1962.

Plumb, J. H. "The Great Change in Children." *Horizon* 13, no. 1 (1971): 5–12.

Postman, Neil. *Amusing Ourselves to Death: Public Discourse in the Age of Show Business*. New York: Penguin Books, 2006.

———. *The Disappearance of Childhood*. New York: Vintage Books, 1994.

Primiano, Leonard. "Vernacular Religion and the Search for Method in Religious Folklife." In *Reflexivity and the Study of Belief*. edited by David Hufford. Special issue of *Western Folklore* 54, no. 1 (1995): 37–56.

Priyadarshi, Rajesh. "Harrods Apology over Hindu Bikinis." *BBC News*, April 22, 2009, http://news.bbc.co.uk/1/hi/world/south_asia/3790315.stm.

Prothero, Stephen. *American Jesus: How the Son of God Became a National Icon*. New York: Farrar, Straus & Giroux, 2003.

Rafter, Nicole. *Criminal Brain: Understanding Biological Theories of Crime*. New York: New York University Press, 2008.

Rappaport, Roy A. *Ritual and Religion in the Making of Humanity*. Cambridge: Cambridge University Press, 1999.

Rayson, Emily. "Capturing the Joy of Online Experiences." *Marketing Magazine*, March 1, 2004, 17.

Robertson, C. K., ed. *Religion as Entertainment*. New York: Peter Lang Publishing, 2002.

Rogers, Mary. *Barbie Culture*. London: Sage Publications, 1999.

Rollefson, Gary. "A Neolithic Game Board from 'Ain Ghazal, Jordan." *Bulletin of the American Schools of Oriental Research* 286 (1992): 1–5.

Romanowski, William. *Pop Culture Wars: Religion and the Role of Entertainment in American Life*. Downers Grove, Ill.: InterVarsity, 1996.

Rozik, Eli. "The Adoption of Theatre by Judaism Despite Ritual: A Study in the Purim-Shpil." *European Legacy* 4, no. 2 (1999): 77.

Salen, Katie, ed. *The Ecology of Games: Connecting Youth, Games, and Learning*. Cambridge, Mass.: MIT Press, 2008.

Schechner, Richard. *The Future of Ritual: Writings on Culture and Performance*. London: Routledge, 1993.

Schmidt, Leigh. *Consumer Rites: The Buying and Selling of American Holidays*. Princeton: Princeton University Press, 1995.

Schwartzman, Helen. *Transformations: The Anthropology of Children's Play*. New York: Plenum Press, 1978.

Scott, Linda M. *Fresh Lipstick: Redressing Fashion and Feminism*. New York: Palgrave Macmillan, 2005.

Seligman, Adam B., Robert P. Weller, Michael J. Puett, and Bennett Simon. *Ritual and Its Consequences*. Oxford: Oxford University Press, 2008.

Siegel, Allan. *The Neurobiology of Aggression and Rage*. Boca Raton, Fla.: CRC Press, 2005

Simmons, Terri. Guest Bio, "Don Levine: Noah, Moses and G.I. Joe." *The 700 Club*, http://www.cbn.com/700club/guests/bios/don_levine081808.aspx.

Smaller, Barbara. "Fun Is Work" cartoon. *The New Yorker*, January 8, 2007, 60.

Smith, Christian, and Melinda Lundquist Denton. *Soul Searching: The Religious and Spiritual Lives of American Teenagers*. Oxford: Oxford University Press, 2005.

Smith-Spark, Laura. "Faith-Based Toys to Hit US Stores." *BBC News*, July 30, 2007, http://news.bbc.co.uk/2/hi/americas/6916287.stm.

Spence, Lewis. *Myth and Ritual in Dance, Game and Rhyme*. London: Watts, 1947.

Sugarman, Sally. "Children on Board: Images from Candy Lands." In *Images of the Child*, edited by Harry Eiss, 323–34. Bowling Green, Ohio: Bowling Green State University Popular Press, 1994.

———. "Playing the Game: Rituals in Children's Games." In *Rituals and Patterns in Children's Lives*, edited by Kathy Merlock Jackson, 124–38. Madison: University of Wisconsin Press, 2005.

Sutton-Smith, Brian. *The Ambiguity of Play*. Cambridge, Mass.: Harvard University Press, 1997.

———. "Evolving a Consilience of Play Definitions: Playfully." In *Play Contexts Revisited*, edited by Stuart Reifel, 239–56. Stamford, Conn.: Ablex, 1999.

———. "Play as a Parody of Emotional Vulnerability." In *Play and Educational Theory and Practice*, edited by Donald Lytle, 3–17. Westport, Conn.: Praeger, 2003.

———. *Toys as Culture*. New York: Garden Press, 1986.

Tatz, Mark, and Jody Kent. *Rebirth: The Tibetan Game of Liberation*. Garden City, N.Y.: Anchor Books, 1977.

Thomas, Jeannie Banks. *Naked Barbies, Warrior Joes, and Other Forms of Visible Gender*. Urbana: University of Illinois Press, 2003.

Thomas, Sabrina. "The Ritual of Doll Play: Implications of Under-standing Children's Conceptualization of Race." In *Rituals and Patterns in Children's Lives*, edited by Kathy Merlock Jackson, 111–23. Madison: University of Wisconsin Press, 2005.

Tsering, Lisa. "Barbie Goes Indian with Diwali-themed Doll." *India West*, news feature, October 21, 2006.

Turner, Victor. "Body, Brain, and Culture," *Zygon* 18, no. 3 (1983): 221–45.

Twitchell, James. "Two Cheers for Materialism." In *The Consumer Society Reader*, edited by Juliet Schor and Douglas Holt, 281–90. New York: The New Press, 2000.

Vennum, Thomas, Jr. *American Indian Lacrosse: Little Brother of War*. Washington, D.C.: Smithsonian Institution Press, 1994.

Von Boehn, Max. *Dolls and Puppets*. Translated by Josephine Nicoll. New York: Cooper Square Publishers, 1966.

Walmsley, Andrew. "No One Wants to Shop in a Vacuum." *Marketing Magazine*, November 22, 2006, 13.

Weber, Max. *The Protestant Ethic and the Spirit of Capitalism*. Trans-lated by Stephen Kalberg. Los Angeles: Roxbury, 2002.

West, Elliott, and Paula Petrik, eds. *Small Worlds: Children and Ado-lescents in America, 1850–1950*. Lawrence: University Press of Kansas, 1992.

Wolfenstein, Martha. "The Emergence of Fun Morality." *Journal of Social Issues* 7, no. 4 (1951): 15–25.

Wuthnow, Robert. *God and Mammon in America*. New York: Free Press, 1994.

Xinhua News Agency. "Dispute over Sports Car for China's Most Famous Monk." *China View*, August 22, 2006, http://news3.xin huanet.com/english/2006-08/22/content_4993996.htm.

Yerkes, Leslie. "How to Create a Place Where People Love to Work." *The Journal for Quality and Participation* 26, no. 4 (2003): 47–50.

Zes, Rebekah. "A Special Word for Proverbs 31 Tomboys." Speech given at the Vision Forum Ministries 2003 Father and Daughter Retreat in San Antonio, Texas, October 21, 2003, http://www.visionforum ministries.org/issues/family/a_special_word_for_proverbs_31 .aspx.

Zirkel, Perry A. "The Games, They Are a-Changin'." *Phi Delta Kap-pan* 82, no. 2 (2000): 175–76.

Zoepf, Katherine. "Bestseller in the Mideast: Barbie with a Prayer Mat." *The New York Times*, September 22, 2005.

INDEX

Abrahamic religious traditions, 2, 137, 145, 170
Abrams, Douglas Carl, 73
action figures, 47–51
adults, 28–29, 33, 64, 131, 158–59, 167; *see also* children; parents
advertisements: advertising, 43, 50, 62, 64, 78, 88–90, 115, 117, 120–22, 149–50, 175; Macy's ad, 157
Allah: images forbidden, 123
Allman, Mark, 179
Almighty Heroes, 48–51
ambiguity, 151, 182; *see also* liminality
American culture, 12, 16, 18, 29, 113, 117, 119, 172
Amma doll, 40–41
amusement, 115, 124, 134, 178
Aphrodite doll, 40–41
Apples to Apples, 120
archetypes, 165–66
Armor of God, 2, 196n20
artifacts, 1, 14, 22, 32–33, 173
Asha, Game of, 23
ATMs, 100
attention, 106, 115, 122, 166; somatic modes of, 154
authority, 113–14, 155–56, 158,

166; exerting, 94; institutional, 155; limited, 157; religious, 113; ultimate, 156; undermine power of, 113
autonomy, 112, 129
Aztec ball game, 20

Baby Einstein, 131
Bado-Fralick, Nikki, 14, 144
Barbie, 38, 57–66; anti-Barbie clubs, 64; anti-Barbies, religious, 7, 38–39, 55–67, 173; Goddess Barbies, 36, 41–42; influences of, 47, 61–64; marketing of, 87–88; mutilated, 160–61; as ontologically empty, 59–61, 67; racial issues, 41–42; transgressive: Big Dyke, Drag Queen, Exorcist, Trailer Trash, Transgender, 64–65
Barthes, Roland, 146
Battle for the Toybox, 49–53, 171
belief bites, 117; *see also* superficiality
Believe in God Breath Spray, 9
Belk, Russell, 60
Bennett, Stith, 18
Best, Joel, 157
Bible Characters, 1